THE
SOUTHERN OCEANS
AND THE SECURITY
OF THE
FREE WORLD

Admiral T. H. Moorer, Patrick Wall MP
Brigadier W. F. K. Thompson, Admiral H. H. Biermann
Major-General D. H. V. Buckle, Sir Robert Thompson, William Schneider Jr
Representative Bob Wilson, Anthony Harrigan, General Jean Callet
Rear-Admiral Shoa Majidi, Robert O'Neill, Robert Moss
Rear-Admiral Mario Lanzarini

THE SOUTHERN OCEANS AND THE SECURITY OF THE FREE WORLD

NEW STUDIES IN
GLOBAL STRATEGY

edited by
Patrick Wall

STACEY INTERNATIONAL

ISBN 0 905743 06 7 hardback
ISBN 0 905743 07 5 paperback

First published by Stacey International 1977
© Stacey International, Admiral T. H. Moorer,
Patrick Wall MP, Brigadier W. F. K. Thompson,
Admiral H. H. Biermann, Major-General D. H. V. Buckle, Sir Robert Thompson,
William Schneider Jr, Representative Bob Wilson, Anthony Harrigan,
General Jean Callet, Rear-Admiral Shoa Majidi, Robert O'Neill,
Robert Moss, Rear-Admiral Mario Lanzarini

Stacey International
128 Kensington Church Street, London W8 4BH
Set in Times by Tradespools Limited, Frome, Somerset
Printed and bound in Great Britain by
R. J. Acford Limited, Chichester, Sussex
Design: Anthony Nelthorpe MSIAD

The publishers wish to thank the following
for providing the illustrations between pages 128 and 129:
the Argentine Embassy, the Australian High Commission, the Iranian Embassy,
the Ministry of Defence, London, the South African Embassy
and the United States of America Embassy.

CONTENTS

The Southern Oceans

U.S.A.

CUBA

TUNISIA

MOROCCO

ALGERIA

LIBYA

MAURITANIA

MALI

NIGER

CHAD

St. Louis
Dakar
SENEGAL
Ziquincher
Bissau
GUINEA
BISSAU
Conakry
GUINEA

IVORY
COAST

NIGERIA

CENTRAL
AFRICAN

Takoradi

LIBERIA
SIERRA
LEONE

GHANA

Accra
TOGO

DAHOMEY

CAMEROUN

GABON

CONGO
BRAZZAVILL

ZAIF

Dolise
Cabinda
Matardi
Luanda
Lobito

Brazzavil
Kinshasa

ANGOLA

SOUTH WEST
AFRICA

Walvis
Bay

BOT

SOU
AFRI

Cape Town
Simonstown

*SOUTH
PACIFIC
OCEAN*

ARGENTINA

*SOUTH
ATLANTIC
OCEAN*

**Comparative
Oil Traffic
1960**

NORTH
AMERICA

To Europe

EUROPE

U.S.S.R

JAPAN

To U.S.

AFRICA

MIDDLE
EAST

To Japan

To U.S.

FAR EAST &
AUSTRALASIA

SOUTH &
CENTRAL
AMERICA

To Europe

*SOUTH
PACIFIC
OCEAN*

To Europe &
North America

*SOUTH
ATLANTIC
OCEAN*

*INDIAN
OCEAN*

AUSTRALIA

Source: **Oil Statistics 1960–1975** published by OECD

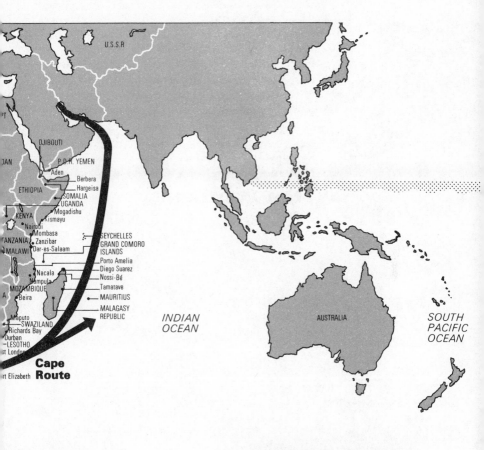

Cape Route

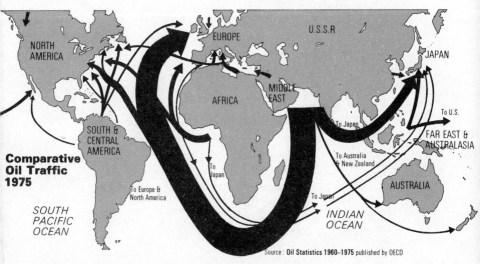

Comparative Oil Traffic 1975

Source : **Oil Statistics 1960–1975** published by OECD

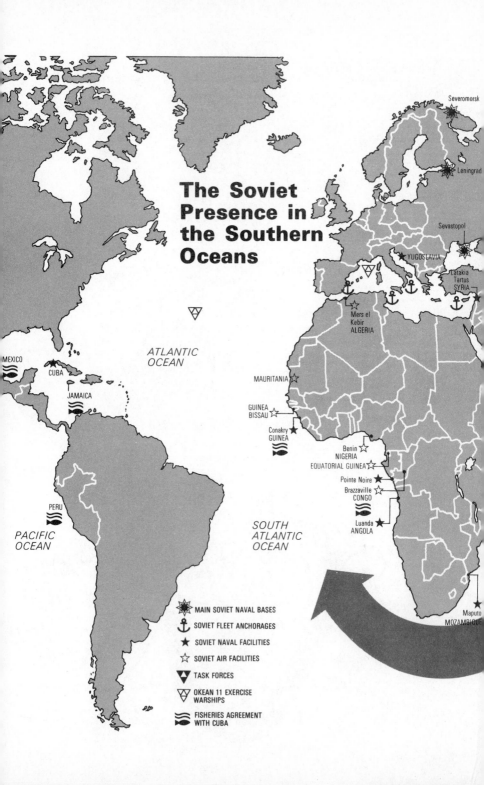

The Soviet Presence in the Southern Oceans

Severomorsk

Leningrad

Sevastopol

YUGOSLAVIA

Latakia
Tartus
SYRIA

ATLANTIC
OCEAN

Mers el
Kebir
ALGERIA

MEXICO

CUBA

JAMAICA

MAURITANIA

GUINEA
BISSAU

Conakry
GUINEA

Benin
NIGERIA

EQUATORIAL GUINEA

Pointe Noire

Brazzaville
CONGO

Luanda
ANGOLA

PERU

PACIFIC
OCEAN

SOUTH
ATLANTIC
OCEAN

Maputo
MOZAMBIQUE

MAIN SOVIET NAVAL BASES

SOVIET FLEET ANCHORAGES

SOVIET NAVAL FACILITIES

SOVIET AIR FACILITIES

TASK FORCES

OKEAN 11 EXERCISE
WARSHIPS

FISHERIES AGREEMENT
WITH CUBA

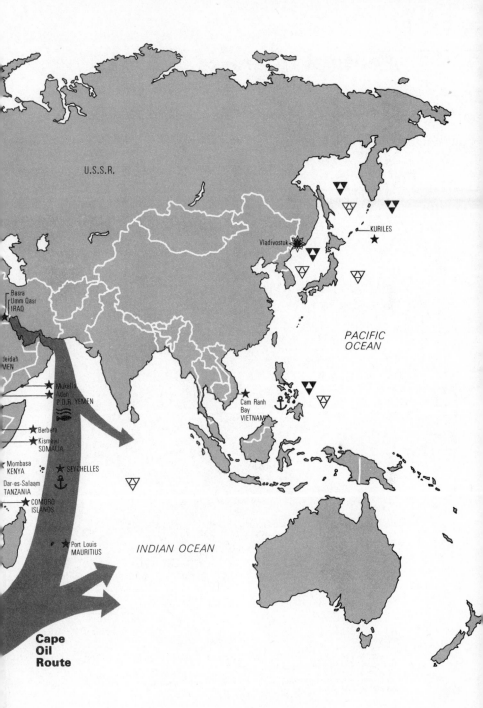

U.S.S.R.

Basra
Umm Qasr
IRAQ

Jeidah
MEN

Mukalla
Aden
P.D.R. YEMEN

Berbera

Kismayu
SOMALIA

Mombasa
KENYA

Dar-es-Salaam
TANZANIA

SEYCHELLES

COMORO
ISLANDS

Port Louis
MAURITIUS

Vladivostok

KURILES

PACIFIC
OCEAN

Cam Ranh
Bay
VIETNAM

INDIAN OCEAN

**Cape
Oil
Route**

Source : **The Institute for the Study of Conflict** 12A Golden Square, London

Political Interests in Africa

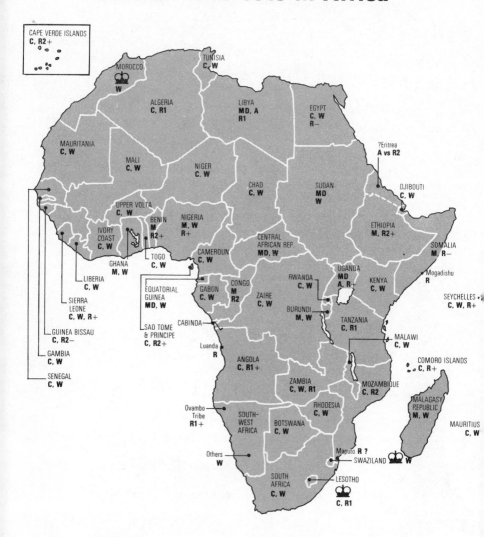

CAPE VERDE ISLANDS
C, R2+

MOROCCO
W

TUNISIA
C, W

ALGERIA
C, R1

LIBYA
MD, A
R1

EGYPT
C, W
R−

MAURITANIA
C, W

MALI
C, W

NIGER
C, W

CHAD
C, W

SUDAN
MD
W

?Eritrea
A vs R2

DJIBOUTI
C, W

UPPER VOLTA
C, W

BENIN
M
R2+

NIGERIA
M, W
R+

CENTRAL
AFRICAN REP
MD, W

ETHIOPIA
M, R2+

SOMALIA
M R−

IVORY
COAST
C, W

TOGO
C, W

CAMEROUN
C, W

UGANDA
MD
A, R+

Mogadishu
R

GHANA
M, W

LIBERIA
C, W

EQUATORIAL
GUINEA
MD, W

GABON
C, W

CONGO
M
R2

ZAIRE
C, W

RWANDA
C, W

KENYA
C, W

SEYCHELLES
C, W, R+

SIERRA
LEONE
C, W, R+

BURUNDI
M, W

TANZANIA
C, R1

GUINEA BISSAU
C, R2−

SAO TOME
& PRINCIPE
C, R2+

CABINDA

MALAWI
C, W

GAMBIA
C, W

Luanda
R

ANGOLA
C, R1+

ZAMBIA
C, W, R1

MOZAMBIQUE
C, R2

COMORO ISLANDS
C, R+

SENEGAL
C, W

MALAGASY
REPUBLIC
M, W

MAURITIUS
C, W

Ovambo
Tribe
R1+

SOUTH-
WEST
AFRICA
C, W

BOTSWANA
C, W

RHODESIA
C, W

Others
W

Maputo R ?

SWAZILAND W

SOUTH
AFRICA
C, W

LESOTHO
C, R1

MONARCHY
C CONSTITUTIONAL CIVILIAN
GOVERNMENT
MD MILITARY DICTATORSHIP
M MILITARY GOVERNMENT
W BROADLY FRIENDLY TO THE WEST
A STRONGLY PRO-ARAB

R1 EAST LEANING, PRO-RUSSIAN,
EVEN PRO-MAOIST
R2 STRONGLY PRO-RUSSIAN,
EVEN RUSSIAN CONTROLLED
R+ RUSSIAN INFLUENCE INCREASING
R− RUSSIAN INFLUENCE DECREASING
R RUSSIAN BASE, OR SPECIAL
DEFENCE ARRANGEMENTS

Two separate symbols mean divided political tendencies

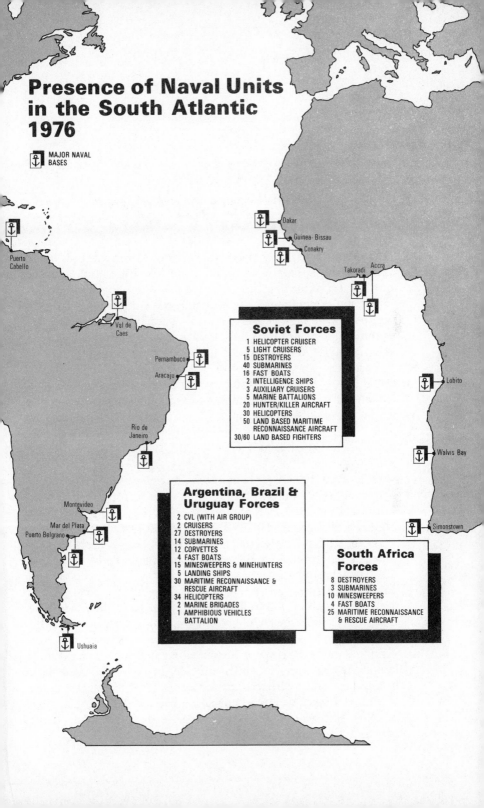

Presence of Naval Units in the South Atlantic 1976

⚓ MAJOR NAVAL BASES

Puerto Cabello

Dakar
Guinea- Bissau
Conakry
Takoradi   Accra

Val de Caes

Pernambuco
Aracaju

Lobito

Rio de Janeiro

Walvis Bay

Soviet Forces

1	HELICOPTER CRUISER
5	LIGHT CRUISERS
15	DESTROYERS
40	SUBMARINES
16	FAST BOATS
2	INTELLIGENCE SHIPS
3	AUXILIARY CRUISERS
5	MARINE BATTALIONS
20	HUNTER/KILLER AIRCRAFT
30	HELICOPTERS
50	LAND BASED MARITIME RECONNAISSANCE AIRCRAFT
30/60	LAND BASED FIGHTERS

Montevideo
Mar del Plata
Puerto Belgrano

Simonstown

Argentina, Brazil & Uruguay Forces

2	CVL (WITH AIR GROUP)
2	CRUISERS
27	DESTROYERS
14	SUBMARINES
12	CORVETTES
4	FAST BOATS
15	MINESWEEPERS & MINEHUNTERS
5	LANDING SHIPS
30	MARITIME RECONNAISSANCE & RESCUE AIRCRAFT
34	HELICOPTERS
2	MARINE BRIGADES
1	AMPHIBIOUS VEHICLES BATTALION

South Africa Forces

8	DESTROYERS
3	SUBMARINES
10	MINESWEEPERS
4	FAST BOATS
25	MARITIME RECONNAISSANCE & RESCUE AIRCRAFT

Ushuaia

FOREWORD

TODAY WE are witnessing a rapid change in the world at large. We are shifting from a world of surplus to a world of shortage with respect to the essential commodities which support the ever-expanding population. It is clear that the confrontations of the future between nations will stem from perceived national interest as these nations are forced to make maximum efforts to acquire and transport critical raw materials – oil, minerals, and food.

For many years transport of these critical materials was contested by the great seapowers of history: Portugal, Spain, Holland, France, and Britain. And for well over a century the Royal Navy's "Pax Britannica" kept the world at peace. This peace was shattered by two world wars, and the rise of the Super-powers, the United States and the USSR, who now compete for control.

Others are stirring, for example China and Japan, and possibly a re-born United Europe in the shape of the European Economic Community, but today we live in the era of the two Super-powers and their allies grouped in NATO and the Warsaw Pact.

At the end of the Second World War NATO was militarily supreme but gradually the Warsaw Pact caught up by exploiting the divisions and weaknesses of the West through subversion and political pressure backed by military power. The struggle has veered sometimes in one direction, sometimes in the other, e.g., Berlin, the Middle East, Cuba, Vietnam, Angola.

Today the Russians, who have a two to one advantage in conventional military power in Europe, are challenging NATO both in nuclear missile power and at sea. Her nuclear submarine fleet, fishing fleet and hydrographic survey fleet are the largest in the world. Her surface fleet contains some of the world's most modern and heavily armed warships and operates in all the oceans of the world.

The Soviets have had considerable success in Cuba, South-East Asia, and on the Indian sub-continent. They have now turned their attention to Africa, particularly southern Africa, where are to be found the largest reserves of many vital minerals as well as a great concentration of the world's shipping routes, which, even in these days of very large aircraft, carry over 90 per cent of the world's trade.

This book contains a linked series of independent appraisals by knowledgeable scholars and officials of the prospects and problems of the Southern Oceans in general and of southern Africa in particular. Although they began from different vantage points, interestingly enough, they arrive at similar conclusions.

Each writer sees a common danger and each in his own way attempts to serve warning on his countrymen and to suggest possible solutions. Their proposed solutions can succeed only if the West acts in time, but time may be running out.

As the Soviet official newspaper *Pravda* has said, "Peaceful co-existence does not spell an end to the struggle between the two world social systems. The struggle will continue between the proletariat and the bourgeoisie, between world socialism and imperialism, up to the complete and final victory of Communism on a world scale."

This symposium represents an international endeavour to inform the free world of the obvious importance the USSR attaches to the most critical regions of the world and of the Soviets' openly declared plans to expunge Western influence and presence from this vital region of the world and replace it by that of the Kremlin.

Thomas H. Moorer
ADMIRAL, US NAVY (RET)

Admiral Moorer has said that we live in a world of change, a world in which Western influence is on the decline, a decline that can perhaps be halted by greater unity of purpose and the courage to take long-term decisions. As nuclear stalemate continues in central Europe the flashpoints appear to be in the Middle East and southern Africa, but perhaps an even greater danger is that of erosion of Western industries through the control of the sources of essential raw materials and the manipulation of their prices. We have not yet seen the full effects of the rise in Middle Eastern oil prices on both the Western and the Third Worlds. If this were followed by similar rises in the price of key metals and other raw materials it could face Western Europe with the choice of surrender or nuclear war.

The struggle for control of southern Africa where many of the raw materials are found is described in these pages by men who are experts in this field. It is to be hoped that while there is still time to act their views and recommendations will be fully considered by the governments and the general public of all countries facing the threat of Soviet imperialism.

Patrick Wall
EDITOR

*To those great ships
of the Union Castle line which maintained
the links between Britain and South Africa
for over a century.*

THE SOUTHERN AFRICAN BACKGROUND

Patrick Wall MP

Patrick Wall is currently Chairman of the Southern Africa Group of the Conservative Foreign Affairs Committee, a Vice-Chairman of the Conservative Parliamentary Defence Committee, the General Rapporteur of the Military Committee of the North Atlantic Assembly and until recently was a member of the Defence Committee of the West European Union. As a British Member of Parliament he has specialised in defence and foreign affairs, and was Vice-Chairman of the Conservative Commonwealth Affairs Committee from 1960–68, and of the Overseas Bureau from 1963–73. He was a regular officer in the Royal Marines from 1935–50, serving with the Royal Navy, the US Navy and the Commandos. He was awarded the Military Cross and the US Legion of Merit. After the War he qualified at the Naval Staff College and the Joint Services Staff College and entered Parliament in 1954. He was recently elected Chairman of the Christian Democrat Conservative Group of the NATO Parliamentarians.

He is a frequent visitor to southern Africa and has written a number of books and pamphlets on defence and on African affairs.

THE DEVELOPMENT of the continent of Africa and indeed of the countries surrounding the Indian Ocean has been the story of seapower. From the days of the great Portuguese navigators the Dutch, the French and then the British discovered, traded and colonised, bringing with them their civilisation with all its virtues and vices. In the last century and a half, it was the British Navy that patrolled these seas, putting an end to piracy and to the slave trade and maintaining the "Pax Britannica" under which indigenous states were able to grow and gradually to develop their own political and economic systems.

Suddenly, after two world wars, a period of history ended as the European powers withdrew, not as the Romans or Spanish had done because of military defeat, but of their own free will hastened by political pressure from the USA and the United Nations. But largely, one must admit because, in the words of a British statesman, "they no longer had the will to rule".

Look at the map of Africa today and compare it with the map before or immediately after the Second World War. Then there were only four independent states on the continent: Egypt, Ethiopia, Liberia and South Africa. Today there are forty-nine members of the Organisation of African Unity. Rhodesia declared her disputed independence in 1965 and the last territory, South-West Africa (Namibia), is now negotiating its independence. Only Spain still holds the two towns of Ceuta and Melilla: otherwise European administrators and governors have withdrawn virtually without bloodshed.

Black blood has, however, been shed; every year since 1963 has seen at least one attempted or successful military revolution. Since they became independent from the colonial powers, twenty-three African states have had their governments overthrown at least once, eleven have experienced this fate more than once, and one, Dahomey, now Benin, has suffered this no less than five times.

In all, since 1952 there have been 107 coups or attempted coups in African states. Today, of the forty-nine member states of the OAU, only four can claim a form of democracy as we know it – Gambia, Botswana, Mauritius and the recently independent Djibouti: fifteen are today under direct military rule and thirty are one-party states (*see Appendix VIII*).

In spite of this background there is a world chorus of indignation, led by the USSR and echoed by the Third World, against colonialism, neo-colonialism and racism, all of which are

18

practised in the USSR, yet all are cleverly exploited against the West. But even in their wildest dreams Soviet planners never expected that they could persuade the West to become thoroughly ashamed of its colonial past.

H. J. Taylor, the American historian, once wrote: "Considering its scope, the British Commonwealth of Nations is the most remarkable political achievement in history. It has overcome more tyranny, supplied more safety, removed more fear, taught more justice, and given more freedom to more people than any other institution on earth."

Yet today the British are taught, by those who should know better, to be ashamed of their imperial past.

The story of White Southern Africa is the story of two tough peoples, the Dutch, who became the "Voortrekkers" and today's Afrikaners, and their former opponents, who have been rightly called the "Seatrekkers" – the British.

Historical Development of South Africa

The roots of the present conflict of ideas, which could well develop into a Third World War, lie deep in the history of southern Africa and can be traced back to 1652, when White settlement was begun by the Dutch East India Company as a halfway house to their settlements in Java. Later, slave labour was imported from East and West Africa and from the East Indies, one outcome of which was the banning of the marriage of Whites with freed slaves of full colour.

The British occupied the Cape in 1795 and again in 1806. With them came administrators and clergymen. The Boers believed that it was ordained that the Africans should serve the Europeans and that the relationship between them should be that of servant and master. This belief, together with the desire to be free from the restraints of British administration, led to a long struggle between Boer and Briton – a period which saw the abolition of slavery; the 1820 wave of British settlers; the growth of the missions; and the Great Trek of 1838, which resulted in the formation of the Boer Republics of the Orange Free State and Transvaal. The constitution of the old South African Republic stated categorically, that "the people desire to permit no equality between Coloured people and the White inhabitants of the country either in Church or State."

The Boer Republics were annexed by Britain under the Treaty of Vereeniging, which ended the Anglo-Boer War of 1899–1902.

19

A clause in that Treaty stated that the question of granting franchise to the natives would not be decided until after the introduction of self-government. This meant that the non-Whites continued to hold a more favourable position in the Cape than they did in the northern provinces. This difference applied (and was understood by the Colonial Office to apply) to the occupation and ownership of land and above all to electoral rights.

In 1909 the old Boer Republics joined with the Cape and Natal to form the Union of South Africa, and the delayed franchise doctrine referred to above was incorporated in the South Africa Act, which excluded non-Whites from both Houses of Parliament. However, the Cape native franchise was one of the entrenched provisions of the constitution which could be changed only by a two-thirds majority of both Houses sitting together. In fact it remained until the introduction of legislation by the Nationalist Government in 1951 which enlarged the Senate so as to create an artificial two-thirds majority, after which the Coloured (mixed race) voters were removed from the Cape Voters' Roll.

"Apartheid" was defined and proclaimed by Dr D. F. Malan, in 1948. His successor, J. G. Strijdon, determined to carry this policy to its ultimate conclusion, stated in 1955 in Parliament that the only way in which the White man could maintain his leadership was by domination. "Call it paramountcy, *baaskap*, or whatever you will, it is still domination." This was the apogee of Afrikaner belief and an attitude which appeared to be sealed in 1961 when, under the premiership of Dr H. F. Verwoerd, South Africa became a Republic and left the Commonwealth.

Since then, there has been a gradual shift of emphasis away from the domination factor, inherent in the original concept of apartheid, towards a more modern policy of separate development. Both the late Dr Verwoerd and the present Premier, Mr Vorster, have repeatedly indicated that the long-term aim of separate development is to create separate, but equal, freedoms for the various population groups and have expressly stated that the perpetuation of domination of one group by another could end only in chaos for all concerned. Although the merits of this policy of separate development and the Government's ability to face up to its inevitable consequences may be questioned, the movement away from a policy of domination as a cornerstone of Afrikaner belief represents a fundamental change, which the rest of the world has largely failed to appreciate. This lack of perception has been reflected subsequently in the reactions of most of South Africa's enemies and critics alike, and is one of the reasons why their comments and arguments have had so little impact on political opinion within that country.

South Africa's racial problem is particularly intricate for two reasons: first, because of the high proportion of Whites – 1 : 3.25, compared with Blacks, who are grouped in eight main nations, or 1 : 2.25 if Coloured (mixed race) are included among the Whites. Secondly, because South Africa is a modern industrial society, in which the technical knowledge and skill of the White man and his power to attract capital are at present as important as, or even more important than, the labour and growing skill of the Black man, which, as he progresses, will gain him increasing economic, and therefore political power.

What of the future? Can a multi-racial society be created out of the two White groups (Afrikaans- and English-speaking), the Coloureds, the Indian, and the several Bantu nations with their ten different languages? Dr Hilgard Muller, until recently South Africa's Foreign Minister, thinks not, and concludes: "all the evidence so far clearly suggests that where both Black and White communities are substantial and permanent in Africa there is essentially only a struggle for power – for supremacy – between them."

Is there, therefore, inevitably to be a continual and growing struggle? Many in Europe and the USA would answer yes, but most South Africans believe there is an alternative in separate development, with its aim of creating viable and autonomous Black nations alongside and in association with the White nation, the Indian community and the Coloureds – namely a South African Commonwealth of Peoples.

The first "homeland" to achieve independence was the Xhosa territory of the Transkei in October 1976. It is as independent as Lesotho or Swaziland, but its independence has not been accepted by the African states or the United Nations. Its future will prove a test case as the independence of the Transkei will soon be followed by other so-called Bantustans. Nowhere has a comparable problem been solved. It is, however, a matter which will have to be faced and settled by the people of southern Africa, not by outside intervention. Some prophesy revolution; but until recently evolution seemed far more probable – and only evolution can bring peace and prosperity to the people of all races on that continent.

The Importance of South Africa

MINERAL RESOURCES

South Africa is the world's largest supplier of the world's most precious metal, gold, and its most precious stone, the diamond. For centuries men have fought over these exotic minerals. Today, modern technology has given enhanced importance to other minerals such as uranium, chrome, and vanadium, all of which are found in large quantities in the Republic of South Africa. Export of these minerals to the West is of great economic and strategic importance.

In fact South Africa produces 99 per cent of the Western world's platinum, 84 per cent of its chrome and manganese, 61 per cent of its gold, 50 per cent of its fluorspar, and 40 per cent of its titanium. It is the world's largest producer of gold, platinum, vanadium and antimony, its second largest producer of chrome and manganese and its third largest producer of industrial diamonds and asbestos. It also contains the world's greatest reserves of platinum, chrome, vanadium, gold, manganese, and fluorspar (*see Appendix I*).

The USSR has, of course, little need of South Africa's minerals for its own use as it is largely self-sufficient. However, should the Soviets secure even temporary control over South Africa's supplies the USSR would then possess 94 per cent of the world's platinum production and 99 per cent of its reserves; 67 per cent of its chrome and 84 per cent of its reserves; 62 per cent of its manganese and 93 per cent of its reserves; 72 per cent of its gold and 68 per cent of its reserves; 70 per cent of its vanadium and 97 per cent of its reserves; 26 per cent of its fluorspar and 50 per cent of its reserves; 35 per cent of its iron ore and 46 per cent of its reserves; 47 per cent of its asbestos and 35 per cent of its reserves; 43 per cent of its uranium production and at least 17 per cent of its reserves. With Zambia and South-West Africa added to these figures it would then control a very large proportion of the world's key minerals. Should the USSR ever be in a position to control their cost or to deny their production to the West they would have succeeded in striking a blow that could well cripple Europe's industrial economy as well as gravely damaging that of the USA. In the short term such a blow could well prove fatal in undermining Europe's will to resist Soviet domination.

At a recent conference of mining experts held in Swaziland in June, 1976, Dr John E. Tilton of the Department of Mineral Economics of Pennsylvania State University pointed out that

22

"the industrialised nations of Western Europe, Japan and the USA are the major consumers of mineral products outside the Communist *bloc.* Although mining and mineral processing account for only a small part of the national income of these countries, their economies would soon collapse if their access to minerals were cut off."

At the conference referred to above, Dr Kilmarx of Georgetown University, commented that "the development and implementation of a coherent minerals policy in the case of the United States requires the maintenance of an adequate naval capability to meet the Soviet threat to the sea-lanes." He added that "to defend them calls for secure and dependable port access. With the loss of facilities in Angola and Mozambique, only the Republic of South Africa, with its strategic position at the Cape and its excellent facilities, can provide such support. In short, the importance of these ports to the Free World must be given more recognition. In time this will occur."

Dr Janke of the Institute for the Study of Conflict in London added: "The non-Communist world in its present non-totalitarian form is faced with a threat to its existence which is greater than that presented by the rise of fascism in the 1930s, the more so because it is not so clearly perceived."

As long ago as 1957 in his book *Strategy and Economics*, Major General Lagovskiy of the USSR drew attention to the fact that the United States has almost no chrome of its own and that this mineral is essential for the production of alloys for jet engines, gas turbines and armour-piercing projectiles. This, he said, was the weak link of the United States and one which the USSR should exploit.

So far as food is concerned South Africa is virtually self-supporting and exports maize, sugar, tobacco and fruit as well as wood, karakul, mohair and hides. In fact, South Africa has everything she needs, except oil, for which widespread prospecting, both on-shore and off-shore, has been carried out for some years. At the time of the crisis with the United Nations over South-West Africa in 1966, the Government is said to have stockpiled two to three years' oil supplies in disused mines.

TRADE

South Africa is one of the world's leading trading nations. Its 1976 exports, excluding gold, were valued at R (Rand) 4,841 million, and its total imports at R7,433 million, the balance being

23

more than made up by gold exports. The value of exports by continents in 1976 were as follows:-

	Rand
Europe	2291.3 million
America	648.3 million
Africa	417.6 million
Asia	683.7 million
Oceania	44.4 million

(£1 = 1.6 Rand.1 US dollar = 1 Rand—*Jan. 1977*)

Total foreign liabilities in 1975 were   R 16,450 million
Gross domestic investment in 1976 was R   8,736 million

Imports in the same year were:	Rand
Europe	2995.4 million
America	1305.7 million
Africa	285 million
Asia	785.2 million
Oceania	88.8 million

As far as Great Britain and the USA were concerned, the figures were as follows:

Great Britain	Exports to,	R 997.1 million
	Imports from,	R 1030.7 million
USA	Exports to,	R 456.6 million
	Imports from,	R 1,266.8 million

All these figures emphasise the Republic's economic attachment to the West; over half her exports and imports being with Europe, and some 7 per cent of her exports and over 30 per cent of her imports with the USA. The figures also explain why overseas investment in South Africa has continued for so many years and has brought such a good return, the average being 14 per cent, one of the highest in the world. Total investments in 1972 were R7,796 million and net inflow was R415 million. The sterling area had the major share, some R4,343 million or about 58 per cent and the dollar area about 18 per cent.

It is sometimes argued that, for political reasons, Britain would do better to increase her investments in Black Africa and decrease her stake in South Africa. A comparison of the latest figures available are shown opposite.

Investments, therefore, are heavily in favour of the South, while trade increasingly favours the North. However, this must be

	In Black Africa	In Southern Africa
Book value of investment less oil, banking and insurance	£413,000,000	£817,000,000
Oil investment	£300,000,000+	Nil
Holding of securities	Nil	£1,500,000,000

Note: These figures are all approximations given in answer to Questions in the House of Commons or in various trade publications.

1975 imports: from Black Africa	£845 million including oil (1972: £457 million)
from Southern Africa	£623 million (1972: £452 million)
1975 exports: to Black Africa	£985 million (1972: £405 million)
to Southern Africa	£723 million (1972: £342 million)

balanced against the security of British trade investment in the South compared with the growing practice of nationalisation and expropriation in the North.

South Africa is fortunate in having no acute balance of payments problem. This is attributable to the fact that she is not dependent on oil to the same extent as are other countries. In fact, she depends upon oil for only just over 20 per cent for her energy. Gold also earns valuable foreign exchange for the Republic and, as has been shown, she exports many raw materials and commodities.

While countries such as the United States and West Germany have suffered severe slumps in the past years, South Africa has achieved a growth of 7 per cent (in 1974) and has maintained an average of 5 per cent real growth per year over the past 25 years. However, in the world trade recession of 1975–76 this was reduced to 3 per cent.

Inflation is one of the world's greatest headaches at the moment. South Africa has not escaped – indeed her rate has been high – but few countries have done better. Most comparable countries in fact, have had a much higher rate of inflation. At least, in South Africa the growth rate has risen simultaneously with inflation. Until recently the Republic had no real unemployment; on the contrary there is a shortage of skilled workers. Even among unskilled workers there has been very little shortage of work. In view of South Africa's plans to proceed with the impressive list of undertakings initiated by the State or State-owned corporations – the construction of railways, telecommunications and harbours, new mines, television broadcasting stations, the new SASOL plant now being planned, and numerous other works – it is quite clear that a large volume of manpower will be required.

The economic development of the Homelands is also receiving top priority from the South African Government. Over the past four years the Bantu Mining Corporation has carried out 315 prospecting surveys and has completed 37 mine leases.

In 1970 the income of Blacks in South Africa, excluding foreign black workers, amounted to a total of R1,804 million. In 1973 this figure rose to R3,688 million. The per capita income of all South African Blacks rose from R75 in 1960 to an estimated R166 in 1973. The per capita income of the Blacks in the Homelands rose from R54.1 per head to an estimated R132.7 for the same period. Among the peoples of the eight Homelands, as well as the Swazis (who do not yet have a politically declared Homeland), the amount earned by Blacks rose from R173.3 million in 1970 to R282.5 million in 1973. Naturally, not all the money earned by Black South African migrant labourers is returned to the Homelands, but it is estimated that 20 per cent of the earnings find their way back. In 1970 the migrant workers earned approximately R345.7 million as opposed to R547.7 million in 1973.

South Africa is, therefore, the most industrialised and economically strong area not only in the African continent but also in the whole of the Southern Hemisphere. Hence the growing importance of her links with such countries as Argentina and Brazil and also with Australia and New Zealand. The Cape of Good Hope is one of the world's major communication centres, lying as it does at a strategic point between the Southern Oceans. The reopening of the Suez Canal has not greatly reduced the importance of the Cape Route. The larger tankers cannot pass through the Canal and, in any case, it would be closed in wartime or, more probably, at the threat of war. Additionally, the passenger liners, which once formed a considerable part of the traffic through the Suez Canal, have now virtually disappeared and with them has gone much of the revenue for the Canal Authorities.

The Cape Route
For many years military experts have been stressing the

importance of the Cape Route to the Western world. However, it has taken a world oil crisis to bring this home to the man in the street, who now appreciates how much his future, for at least the next decade, depends upon Middle East oil which has to be conveyed round the Cape of Good Hope. The concern of the West is not wholly focused on oil but also on food-stuffs and the important mineral supplies we import via the Cape Route. We must also bear in mind that South Africa provides the gold backing for most of the Free World's monetary systems.

In the Cuba crisis of 1962 the Soviets were forced to turn back by the presence of American seapower, to which at that time they had no adequate answer. This was a lesson they could not forget and it provided the lever for which Admiral Gorshkov, appointed Commander-in-Chief of the Soviet Navy in 1955 at the early age of 45, had been looking. He was now able to persuade the Kremlin that the Soviet Navy should no longer be a mere adjunct to the Army, but should function in its own right and carry Soviet political influence to the far corners of the seven seas. The Soviet fleet has now become second in strength only to that of the United States, and it already has considerable advantages over the United States Navy, as 25 per cent of the Russian ships are less than ten years old. The Soviet Union also possesses more nuclear-powered submarines than do the combined NATO fleets and is building at the rate of at least sixteen a year, which is considerably in excess of the building rate of the NATO navies.

The Soviet surface fleet consists of modern vessels, including three aircraft carriers (one of which has just been completed), in addition to two rather slightly smaller helicopter carriers and the world's heaviest armed cruisers – the *Kara* class – carrying both surface-to-surface and surface-to-air missiles. She has a powerful naval air arm of over 1,000 aircraft together with an amphibious force of over 200 vessels and a large number of coastal escorts, fleet auxiliaries and replenishment ships which would enable the Soviet Navy to operate without foreign bases. This, however, is but a single aspect of Soviet seapower. In 1930 some 400 merchant ships of 2 million tons flew the "Hammer and Sickle"; by 1970 this number had increased to 6,000 of 15 million tons, which gives the Soviet merchant fleet the sixth place among comparable fleets of the world. She intends to increase this tonnage to 27 million tons by 1980. Her 4,500-vessel fishing fleet is the largest in the world, as is her fleet of hydrographic survey ships, both of which supply her with detailed intelligence. What is more, unlike the West, *all* her maritime power is controlled from a single source, Moscow, for maximum flexibility (*see Appendix VI*).

The USSR established a permanent fleet in the Mediterranean in 1967. It is now second only to the American Sixth Fleet and has considerably altered the balance in that inland sea. In 1968, having learned from her successes in the Mediterranean she began to deploy warships in the Indian Ocean. The number of Soviet naval surface and auxiliary vessels in that area doubled in 1972 and again in 1973. The USSR now has important base and supply facilities in the Indian Ocean at such places as Hodeidah in the Yemen, Aden, Berbera in the Somali Republic, and Umm Qasr in Iraq, together with facilities in certain ports in India and Bangladesh, Port Louis in Mauritius, Kismayu and Mogadishu, as well as mooring facilities off the Seychelles, Mauritius and Madagascar and off the East African coast. All this is of concern to the Western nations and to South Africa. The main reason is that the Cape Route is now one of the most crowded shipping lanes in the world. Over half of Britain's oil supplies and a quarter of its food comes round the Cape of Good Hope and through the South Atlantic. Different sources estimate that in 1977 between 40 and 60 per cent of the USA's oil imports will also be supplied by this route.

The number of ships calling at South African ports each year has been as follows:-

1957/58	6,300	1963/64	6,970	1969/70	12,315
1958/59	6,360	1964/65	7,468	1970/71	12,528
1959/60	6,051	1965/66	7,941	1971/72	12,021
1960/61	6,256	1966/67	8,101	1972/73	11,469
1961/62	6,352	1967/68	12,701	1973/74	16,823
1962/63	6,546	1968/69	12,275	1974/75	16,395

The problem of defending this vital shipping route in time of war would be immense. Recent events have at least brought to the notice of the general public the West's present dependence on Middle Eastern oil and Southern Africa's minerals.

In October 1975, 818 ocean-going ships called at South African ports, 279 at Durban, 244 at Cape Town and 145 at Port Elizabeth. In the same period thirteen Eastern *bloc* ships called at South African ports and seven more rounded the Cape, while thirty-one fishing trawlers were fishing off the South or South-

West African coast. The slump in world shipping due to the energy crisis can be seen by comparing these figures with the equivalent numbers in June 1972: 1,030 ocean-going ships which called at South African ports, 184 Eastern *bloc* ships which passed the Cape and 58 Soviet fishing vessels and support ships which were in the area. It was then estimated that some 24,000 ships passed the Cape each year. Because of the oil crisis and the subsequent trade recession, this figure is now down to about 10,000. Clearly, these ships, carrying oil, food and other raw materials or minerals, are vital to the Western nations, but there are no collective NATO plans for their protection until they cross the Tropic of Cancer in the Northern Atlantic which is the southern boundary of the NATO area.

In one month, January 1976, the following ships passed the Cape of Good Hope:

	Freighters	Tankers	Total	% of total
Liberian (flag of convenience mostly US)	47	98	145	21.97
British	56	43	99	14.97
Norwegian	18	19	37	5.60
Greek	42	13	55	8.32
Warsaw Pact	20	—	20	3.03
Netherlands	25	5	32	4.84
French	10	32	42	6.35
West German	21	16	37	5.60
Italian	12	9	21	3.18
United States	8	3	11	1.66
South African	33	4	37	5.60
Japanese	18	5	23	3.48
Indian	8	—	8	1.21
Spanish	2	3	5	76
Portuguese	3	4	7	1.06
Panamanian	13	8	20	3.03
Danish	10	7	17	2.57
Swedish	4	2	6	91
Miscellaneous	33	6	39	5.90
Total NATO Nations	253	250	503	76
Grand Total	383	278	651	100.00
Daily average	12.35	8.97	21.32	

In 1972 the North Atlantic Assembly passed a resolution in the following terms:

The Assembly recommends the North Atlantic Council:

(a) to study the recommendations set out in paragraphs 147 to 148 of the Report of the Military Committee's Sub-Committee on the Soviet Maritime Threat.

(b) to give SACLANT authority to plan for the protection of NATO- Europe's vital shipping lanes in the Indian Ocean and the South Atlantic including surveillance and communications.

(c) to complete a detailed survey of the present oil requirements of North America and NATO- Europe together with a ten-year forecast in the light of present and prospective sources of supply, to reconsider the question of strategic stocks in NATO- Europe, and to examine ways and means of increasing present stocks.

The recommendations referred to in (a) above included: increased British naval support of Norway; the basic need for more anti-submarine vessels and aircraft; methods of holding the Baltic, Dardanelles and the Straits of Gibraltar; the need for a NATO Standing Naval Force in the Mediterranean; the need to protect thirty-two convoys a month that would pass the Cape in war, bound for Europe; the need for a permanent NATO naval presence in the Indian Ocean; the danger of NATO dependence on Middle East oil supplies; the need for ship-borne anti-missile missiles; the use of container ships and tankers to carry helicopters and VSTOL aircraft in war; the need for improved surveillance in the Southern Hemisphere and so on. The NATO Council referred these resolutions to SACLANT, whose report and conclusions are now being considered by the various NATO governments.

Meanwhile the British Labour Government denounced the only defence agreement between a NATO member and South Africa − the Anglo-South African Simonstown Agreement, signed in 1955 when South Africa was still a member of the Commonwealth. Under this agreement Britain not only secured facilities at the Simonstown base but, more important in time of war, the Royal Navy had the right to use *all* South African ports, even if South Africa was not a belligerent. The close wartime cooperation between the Royal Navy and the South African Navy was to continue, and the Agreement provided for specialised training, the exchange of intelligence, and particularly for the surveillance of Soviet surface ships and submarines, a matter which is of particular importance to NATO today. In spite of the fact that only 5.6 per cent of the ships using the Cape Route were South African, the Government of the Republic regarded itself as trustee for the Western nations for the adequate protection of the Cape Route. An ultra-modern maritime headquarters was completed at Muizenberg with two subsidiary headquarters, one in each ocean at Durban and Walvis Bay.

While this work was proceeding, the Labour Government declined to replace South African surface warships and reconnaissance aircraft. Under pressure from the United Nations, successive British Labour Governments have refused to supply South Africa with modern warships and equipment, so she has been forced to switch her procurement to France. Her three submarines are French-built, and two more of a larger type are now under construction. She has just announced that she is planning to build French-type fast missile boats in Durban and may well follow up with Corvettes, some of which may also be built in South Africa. Her most urgent need is to replace her maritime reconnaissance Shackleton aircraft, which were British built but are now virtually obsolete. Both the French and the Americans are pushing their own aircraft, the Atlantique and the Orion respectively. South Africa has, however, been greatly impressed by British Nimrod anti-submarine aircraft, but the disadvantage of these planes is their cost, which is over £3,000,000 each now increased by inflation. She would like to buy a few and operate a squadron on a joint-user basis with the Royal Air Force but this idea has been turned down by the present British Government. The South African Air Force is equipped also with British-built Buccaneers, the maritime strike aircraft in use by the Royal Navy. Completion of the order for sixteen of these aircraft was authorised by a previous Labour Government, which said that no more would be supplied. Since then, a number of aircraft have been lost, some on exercises with the Royal Navy. Two Buccaneers crashed during joint RN-SAN exercises at the end of 1974; replacements were requested but were refused.

There is now a school of thought, current in the South African Defence Forces, which holds that the West, if it is really interested in tracking the movements of Soviet surface vessels and submarines, should carry out this work for itself, and not expect South Africa to perform it with obsolete equipment, while at the same time taking every possible opportunity to insult her by refusing to supply her with modern aircraft or other anti-submarine equipment. There is also an understandable view within the South African Defence Forces, particularly the Army, that a much higher priority should be put on land defence in the north and less money spent on the defence of the Cape Route – a route which is not vital to South Africa, with her abundance of foodstuffs and minerals (except for oil) within her own borders.

Because of the obvious strategic importance to Britain of the Cape Route, the behaviour of the present British Labour Government is surprising. It has been reported, for example, that there was a governmental reluctance to allow a South African frigate to call at Portsmouth and that this reluctance continued until the British Government was informed that the next frigate outbound to maintain the then Beira patrol would not be allowed to enter Simonstown.

The basis of this British Labour policy is, of course, dislike of apartheid. It is to be hoped that if the policy of détente succeeds in southern Africa, the political obstacles to good relations between South Africa and certain powers in the West, particularly the present Socialist Governments of Britain, the Netherlands, Norway and Denmark will be removed. If this does happen, it will greatly strengthen Western maritime defence and would partially offset recent NATO setbacks in the Eastern Mediterranean. It is well known that military authorities in the Western world are becoming increasingly alarmed at the growth of Soviet influence in the Indian Ocean. The success of the détente policy would not only affect relations within southern Africa but might well cause considerable change in the official relations between the southern African governments and a number of Western and American governments. Hopefully, this might lead, in due course, to some form of Southern Hemisphere Maritime Defence Pact embracing not only South Africa but Australia and New Zealand, Brazil and Argentina, assisted by other maritime powers such as the United States, Great Britain and France. This, unfortunately, lies in the future but today we must remember that neither the Royal Navy nor the US Navy rules the waves.

The strength and mobility of the centrally-controlled Soviet naval and merchant fleets, and their potential threat, in particular through their nuclear-powered submarine fleet to the West's long and vulnerable route round the Cape has already been commented upon. The danger lies not so much in the possibility of an outbreak of war, but in the power of the USSR to blackmail the

West into accepting Soviet influence and interference in the Indian Ocean and in the countries bordering it.

The Oil Crisis

For generations we have taken cheap oil for granted. Our energy policy has been based upon industrial manufacture. Hence the traumatic shock felt by the Western world and Japan when faced with the sudden and unilateral action by the Arab States in not only restricting supplies of their oil but demanding higher and still higher prices for it. This is not a matter affecting the Western world only. The effect of higher oil prices on the economies of the countries of the Third World could become catastrophic. Estimates show that the developing countries, as a whole, would have to face up to an eight-fold increase in their total oil import bill. This, in turn, would have repercussions on their economies, which could be further affected, should some primary producers attempt to emulate the Arabs by withholding their minerals or raw materials in order to force up world prices. The Western world's appetite for oil is enormous. The world's requirements escalated from 539,000,000 tons in 1950 to 1,061,000,000 in 1960; to 2,276 million tons in 1970. It is estimated that the figure will be 4,221 million tons by 1980. The US has its own supply of crude oil, amounting to about 75.5 per cent of its requirements, but its reserves are becoming exhausted and imports are rising. In 1973, 8.5 per cent of America's oil came from Canada, 6.5 per cent from the Middle East, 3.7 per cent from Black Africa, 2.6 per cent from South America, 1 per cent from Iran and lesser quantities from Indonesia and other suppliers. The American position is, therefore, worrying though not desperate. Europe, however, is in a much more vulnerable position. Western Europe imports most of its oil from the Middle East. Gulf oil amounts to some 57 per cent of Europe's imports or about half the total Middle East production, an additional 25 per cent going to Japan, which is almost wholly dependent on the Middle East.

Until recently it was thought that while America's imports from the Gulf would greatly increase, those of Europe would remain almost static, since the new North Sea oilfields would supply the additional European requirements for the foreseeable future. It was also thought that Arctic oil and the new off-shore oilfields would probably make the US less dependent upon the Middle East, although a twenty-year energy gap was envisaged, during which both Europe and the US would rely upon Middle

East oil, most of which would be shipped round the Cape of Good Hope. Recent events in the Middle East have changed this picture. The Arab nations have made it clear they will not only use oil as a weapon in war against Israel, but will cut off supplies to some nations for political reasons unconnected with Arab-Israeli hostilities. One example is the boycott of South Africa and Rhodesia, countries which played no part in the Yom Kippur war of 1973. This, and possible parallel actions, together with the nationalisation of oilfields and the erratic and escalating price of oil, means that the whole of the industrialised West will now turn its efforts to finding alternative sources of supply. It is probable that the intensity of this search will reduce the "Oil Gap" – during which the West is bound to Middle East oil supplies – from some twenty to ten years.

Despite all this, one fact remains clear: until the mid-1980s Middle East oil and its supply routes will continue to be of prime importance to the West. At present, North America needs to import 6 million barrels a day; Europe, 12.4 million and Japan, 5 million; the estimated corresponding figures for 1985 are: North America, 8 to 12 million; Europe, 12 to 14 million and Japan, 7 to 8 million barrels a day. This raises two major problems. Can this oil be denied to the West by the producing nations or by other powers (e.g. the USSR and her allies) either at the source or by the cutting of supply routes? The Arab nations have shown us how far they are prepared to go in cutting their oil supplies for political purposes, but their solidarity has already been breached and individual States are making bilateral supply agreements with some European nations.Moreover, the Arab nations would suffer too much themselves, as they are dependent on the West for manufactured goods. A serious long-term cutback in supplies is therefore unlikely and price-manipulation is likely to continue to be their major political weapon. The enormous and inflated oil royalties they will receive and invest in the world's money market will make this a very powerful weapon indeed. Taking Saudi Arabia alone, earnings from foreign oil sales were $22.6 billion in 1974 and $25.7 billion in 1975, despite a 15 per cent cut-back. Reserves which in 1970 were worth $662 million reached $27.7 billion by 1976.

What, then, is the danger of intervention by a third power (namely the USSR) in the Gulf area, in the immediate future? The division of Gulf oil production between a number of States prone to dynastic rivalry provides the Soviet Union, as the nearest major military power, with an opportunity to fill the political and military vacuum which has existed in the Gulf since the British withdrew from that area – despite the steps which have been taken to build up Iranian forces, which are now the most powerful in the Gulf. In present conditions, the possibility of Soviet intervention in any new dynastic dispute between Gulf States, in order to obtain oil or to deny it to others, must be a matter of anxiety to the West – in particular, the possibility that the Persian Gulf might be closed, by, for example, the mining of the Straits of Hormuz, so preventing the exit of oil tankers bound for the United States or Europe.

There is, of course, no need for the Soviet Union to take special political or military action to obtain oil supplies for herself from the Persian Gulf. All the Governments concerned have access to "royalty oil" which they are free to sell to the Soviet Union or to Eastern Europe, at any time.

As far back as 1921 the Soviet Union restated her oil claims in northern Iran. In 1947, she made them a condition of withdrawing her troops from Azerbaijan. Today, her need for oil from the Middle East is greater than in either 1921 or 1947. Although the USSR is the world's largest oil producer (372 million tons in 1971, with production growing at the rate of some 7 per cent a year) she now seems to be close to the point of being unable to satisfy all her own needs from her indigenous resources, let alone supplying the needs of Eastern Europe.

World Production and Consumption of Oil, 1974
(million barrels daily)

	Production	Consumption
USSR, E. Europe and China	11.03	9.48
W. Hemisphere excluding US	6.95	5.56
US	10.48	16.22
W. Europe excluding UK	0.45	12.02
UK	—	2.15
Middle East	21.72	1.35
Africa, S.E. Asia excluding Japan*	7.34	3.90
Japan	—	5.31
World	57.97	555.99

*Including Australasia and S. Asia.

(Source: BP Statistical Review of the World Oil Industry, 1974).

It is expected that the USSR will become an importer of high-grade oils during the coming decade (unless she discovers more oil in the Arctic), as she is unable to meet the needs of her own industries which function inefficiently on low-grade oils, and must retain control over the major deliveries of oil resources to Eastern Europe, where her satellites are becoming restless. In 1969, she exported 25 million tons of oil to Eastern Europe (some 55 per cent of its requirements); by 1980, this may well grow to 140 million tons a year.

The Soviet Union has, therefore, a direct interest in the Gulf for her own, as yet comparatively small, needs. This can provide a valid excuse for pursuing her longer-term plans to fill the military vacuum left by the British; to step up her influence in such Socialist states as Iraq and Syria; to reduce present US interests in Saudi Arabia; and, through client governments, to gain direct control of the main source of European and Japanese energy supplies.

Such methods are more likely than a military intervention, even if this latter were required by one of the smaller Arab states, since any intervention in a key area such as the Gulf would run the risk of precipitating a Third World War. There are, of course, other options, such as the interruption of oil supply routes round the Cape, which would seem to offer more vulnerable and less risky targets.

The Cold War in Africa
A great change has been caused by the rapid withdrawal of the European Colonial powers, who introduced modern technology to Africa but left before creating a large enough cadre of those required to govern, administer and control a modern state.

The result has been a revival of tensions and rivalries, which have been more tribal and internal than external disputes between nations. The clashes which have taken place in recent years include civil wars in Nigeria, the Sudan and the Central African Republic; protracted revolts and assaults on the Tutsi by the Hutu in Rwanda, and vice versa in Burundi; the struggle between the Eritreans and the Amhara in Ethiopia. These are paralleled by the local national rivalries in Africa today – for example, between Somalia and Ethiopia.

As, seemingly, the Arabs can unite only in one cause (against Israel), so Africans appear to be capable of unity only in the single objective of "freeing" the South. They can come together in conferences and join in propaganda, but they still find it difficult to achieve any cohesive or purposeful unity of action.

This desire for liberation, coupled with the strategic importance of southern Africa, gives the Communist powers – the USSR and China – the opportunity to strike a blow not only at the West, but at each other. It is significant that every national liberation movement in southern or central Africa has two organisations – one backed and armed by the USSR, the other by China. The activities of these liberation movements rose to a peak between 1962 and 1969 and then declined. A fresh initiative took place in 1973, which, assisted by the revolution in Portugal, gained the "liberation" of Angola and Mozambique and is at present concentrated on Rhodesia and South-West Africa. Each of the African Nationalist organisations has been backed with arms and military training from either the Soviet Union or China. Training has taken place in the USSR and in China – also in Tanzania and Algeria, under the auspices of one or more of the Communist powers. As a rule, Russian or Chinese influences have been represented in rivalries between the organisations competing for support in each of the territories. Now, because the USSR have won control of the Indian Ocean by their maritime power, Chinese influence in Africa is everywhere decreasing.

Guerrilla Warfare
SOUTH AFRICA
The ANC (African National Congress) was founded in 1912, but became actively involved in direct defiance of the Government only from 1952 until it was banned in 1960 after Sharpeville.

The PAC (Pan African Congress) broke away from the ANC in 1958 and was also banned in 1960. In the same year both organisations went underground and formed activist wings – the Spear of the Nation (ANC) and Poqo (PAC). Guerrilla fighters were trained abroad from about 1972. Poqo's "great revolution" failed in 1963 and many underground leaders were rounded up at Rivonia in the same year. Since then, little has been heard of either organisation in South Africa, but both have been active abroad. In 1967 ANC combined with ZAPU (Zimbabwe African Peoples' Union) to invade Rhodesia from Zambia, in order, in the words of their communiqué, "to fight their way to strike at the Boers themselves in South Africa". The invasion ended in the Wankie game reserve, near the Zambian border, where the guerrilla forces were killed or captured, except for a few who

37

crossed the frontier into Botswana where they were, to their great surprise, imprisoned. The ANC remained quiescent until 1976 when there is considerable evidence that they were behind the unrest in Soweto and the African townships in the Cape. In this they were assisted by the underground Communist Party.

SOUTH-WEST AFRICA (NAMIBIA)
SWANU (South-West African National Union), consisting mainly of the Herero tribe, was founded in 1960, after the Windhoek riots. SWAPO (South-West African Peoples' Union) was organised in the following year, mainly from among the Ovambo tribe, which is by far the largest tribe in the country. In 1964 SWAPO sent guerrillas to be trained abroad; they returned in 1966 and engaged in minor clashes with the South African Police. There have been no large-scale guerrilla activities since, except for minor raids from Zambia into the Caprivi strip together with quite frequent laying of anti-personnel mines. The victory of the MPLA forces in Angola clearly indicates that in due course they will give SWAPO considerable support. By mid-1976 minor actions between SWAPO guerrillas, assisted by the MPLA, and the South African security forces were reported inside South-West Africa itself.

Constitutional Progress
Over 150 delegates from Namibia's eleven different population groups first met on the 1st September 1975 in the Turnhalle at Windhoek, to discuss the constitutional future of South-West Africa – Namibia. The conference's first action was to adopt a declaration of intent which read:

1 We, the true and authentic Representatives of the inhabitants of South-West Africa, hereby solemnly declare:
2 That in the exercise of our right to self-determination and independence we are voluntarily gathered in this Conference in order to discuss the Constitutional future of South-West Africa;
3 That we most strongly condemn and reject the use of force or any improper interference in order to overthrow the existing order or to enforce a new dispensation;
4 That we are firmly resolved to determine our future ourselves by peaceful negotiations and cooperation;
5 That mindful of the particular circumstances of each of the

population groups it is our firm resolve, in the execution of our task, to serve and respect their wishes and interests;

6 That mindful of the interdependence of the various population groups and the interests of South-West Africa in its entirety to create a form of government which will guarantee to every population group the greatest possible say in its own and national affairs which will fully protect the rights of minorities and will do right and justice to all.

And we further declare:

That we are resolved to devote continuous attention to social and economic conditions which will best promote the welfare, interests and peaceful co-existence of all the inhabitants of South-West Africa and their prosperity;

That we are resolved to exert ourselves towards the promotion of and deference towards human rights and fundamental freedoms of all without discrimination merely on the basis of race, colour or creed.

We therefore resolve:

a) to draft a Constitution for South-West Africa as soon as appropriate and if possible within a period of three years.

b) to devote continuous attention to measures implementing all the aims specified in this declaration.

The Conference then set up five committees with the following responsibilities:

The first Committee, under the Chairmanship of Dr B. J. Africa (Rehoboth Baster), had the task of finding a solution for practices of discrimination on the grounds of race or colour, with specific references to salaries, equal pay for equal work, equal pension schemes, general conditions of service, minimum wage scales, equal opportunities, work reservation and labour legislation, and the abolition of pass laws.

The second Committee, under the chairmanship of Mr D. F. Mudge (White), was responsible for investigating the economic elevation of all inhabitants of the territory with special reference to the owners, entrepreneurs and professional groups, with reference to, among other things, rights to property in respect of house ownership in urban areas, the infrastructure and finance.

The third Committee, under the chairmanship of Mr L. J. Barnes (Coloured), investigated the social advancement of all inhabitants of Namibia with special reference to housing, public amenities and services, national social pensions and welfare, elimination of discrimination in the police force and the elimination of inequality in medical services.

The fourth Committee, under the chairmanship of Mr E. T. Meyer (White), investigated teacher facilities and education.

A financial committee and a constitutional committee were later set up to investigate finance and to make proposals about the future financing of the territory and constitutional proposals including an interim government.

Of those who attended the Conference, six – the Whites, Coloureds, Rehoboth Basters, Kavangos, East Caprivians and Ovambos – (representing 74 per cent of the population) had elected representative bodies and sent elected members to the Turnhalle. Of the remainder, the Herero sent a delegation of forty-four under the leadership of Mr Clemens Kapuuo, the leader of the National Union Democratic Organisation and of the Herero Chiefs Council. The Nama sent six of its nine headmen and ten additional delegates, eight of whom were teachers. The Damara sent representatives from each of its four different political groups. The Tswana were represented by one chief and five others who were appointed as delegates after a series of tribal meetings. The Bushmen's representatives were appointed at a people's meeting held at Tsunkwe.

Conference Resolutions
In August 1976 the conference members were in a position to announce their unanimous decision to establish a multi-racial interim government for Namibia and to set 31st December 1978 as the date for the territory's independence. The resolution stated that 'the Committee is in agreement that the date for independence for South-West Africa can with a reasonable measure of safety be stated as 31st December 1978. Meanwhile negotiations will have to be entered into with South Africa regarding a number of matters – for example, Walvis Bay, the South African railways, water and electricity supply, monetary and financial matters, security, etc. As soon as a Constitutional basis has been agreed upon and negotiations mentioned above completed, we intend to establish an interim government in terms of such a constitutional basis to attend to the transfer of functions and the establishment of a permanent government based on a Constitution to be finalised in the interim period."

The Conference reaffirmed its desire to retain Namibia as a unitary state and to recognise the interdependence of the different population groups and it announced that it envisaged a system of government in which sufficient provision would be made for the protection of minority groups at all levels.

It was hoped that the creation of an interim government might be the first step towards including SWAPO in the country's future constitutional order. The leader of the Ovambo delegation, Pastor Njoba said, however, that there was one single condition that SWAPO must meet before it could join the Conference and that was that they must unequivocally and openly state their acceptance of peaceful negotiation and settlement.

The Future Constitution

The Conference accepted in principle a three-level structure of government on the following lines:

1 A first level in which all the population groups in Namibia would be represented and would be responsible for matters of national and state concern.
2 A second level government elected by members of the various population groups, which would be responsible for matters which are regarded as inherent in each group.
3 A third level of local authorities for the different towns, elected by the inhabitants of the respective towns.

Discussions took place between the members of the Constitutional Committee and the South African Prime Minister in Pretoria in November 1976. In January and February 1977 it was decided that the central government of Namibia would consist of a President, an executive body called the Council of Ministers, a legislative body called the National Assembly and a judiciary. The Prime Minister would be appointed by an absolute majority of the National Assembly. The Council of Ministers would consist of a chairman and eleven members, each of the eleven population groups electing one member to the Council of Ministers in consultation with their electoral colleges. (Because of their numerical superiority the Ovambos were demanding an additional minister). The National Assembly would be the legislative body for the Republic of Namibia and among its functions would be immigration and passport control, water affairs and energy, information, trade and industry, labour and unemployment, national health, fisheries, justice, nature conservation, agriculture, technical services, and marketing.

During the period of the interim government, the South African

Government would retain legislative and executive powers over defence, and posts and telecommunications.

The second tier authorities would consist of the existing elected authorities of the various population groups. In the case of the population groups that as yet had no such elected bodies, i.e. the Damaras, the Tswanas and the Hereros, the present Turnhalle delegations would be regarded as an electoral college for the elections of the Ministers' Council of the National Assembly. The second tier authorities would act as electoral colleges for the election of members of the National Assembly; they would advise the Assembly on matters referred to them by that body, or matters pertaining specifically to their population group.

A Bill of Rights was also agreed.

These plans however omitted SWAPO which was formed in 1961 and has led the campaign of guerrilla warfare against South Africa. It is split into an external wing under its President Sam Nujoma and an internal wing, at present under Mr Tjongarero.

SWAPO has the backing of the UN, the OAU etc, in its attempt to be recognised as the government of Namibia. It is an Ovambo organisation and as such is not popular among the other groups. It is however feared, more because of its international backing than because of its guerrilla activities. In fact the latter has now, because of its excesses, become counter-productive in Ovamboland. Its external wing, however, appears to be irreconcilable and determined, with the help of the MPLA and the Cubans, to obtain its aims by force. However, its internal wing received a shock when the date for independence was announced and has since dropped some of its pre-conditions for joint talks.

The Western Governments are insisting on the inclusion of SWAPO in the negotiations for an interim government and for an internationally supervised general election before independence. They are also reputed to be demanding the withdrawal of the South African administration, which would cause an economic collapse, and of the South African Army, which would leave the country open to a Cuban/MPLA/SWAPO invasion. The South African Government has had to bend to this pressure and has agreed to appoint an Administrator General for the territory until elections can be held for a constitutional assembly. It has also been agreed that a representative of the UN Secretary General would observe the elections. It is expected that the Turnhalle conference will form a non-racial political party to fight SWAPO in the elections.

It is difficult to estimate SWAPO's influence inside South-West Africa. In 1973 it demanded that the Ovambos boycott their election for a representative council and only 2.8 per cent voted. However in 1975 when this tactic was repeated, 75 per cent voted in Ovamboland and 56 per cent throughout the country.

One-third of the Ovambo tribe live across the border in Angola and are pro-UNITA. The South African withdrawal from Angola in March 1976 lowered confidence and increased SWAPO's support on both sides of the border. Now that it is clear that the South African troops are staying to defend the frontier and have been considerably reinforced, confidence has been restored. But, as one Afrikaner put it, 80 per cent of the Ovambo are uncommitted and are waiting to see who will win!

ANGOLA

The MPLA (Popular Movement for the Liberation of Angola) was formed in 1956, mainly from the more intellectual section of the population of that country. The FNLA was preceded, in 1951, by the UPA (Union of the People of Angola), which later became known as the FNLA (The National Front for the Liberation of Angola), based on the Bakongo tribe.

In 1961 the MPLA created trouble in Luanda, the capital, and in March of that year the UPA raised the Bakongo tribe in the north and invaded Angola from the Congo (now Zaire). For a few weeks it was touch-and-go but, in spite of appalling atrocities when people were fed live into sawmills, the Portuguese peasant farmers stayed firm, and when the army arrived from Portugal, a few months later, the north was gradually pacified. In 1965 both organisations attacked Cabinda, a Portuguese enclave to the north of the Congo river, but failed in this comparatively easy task.

In 1966 a third organisation, UNITA (Union for the Total Independence of Angola), based on the Ovimbindu tribe, initiated attacks from Zambia against the Benguela railway in Eastern Angola. In 1968 they were joined by the MPLA and in 1969 by the FNLA, but this important railway system continued to operate owing to pressure from Zambia and Zaire, for both of which it formed an essential outlet for the export of copper.

By the end of 1973 the Portuguese had virtually won the war in Angola, but in April 1974 came the Portuguese revolution under General Spinola, and, later, the decision of the left-wing Portuguese Government to effect a cease-fire in both Angola and

Mozambique and to negotiate the independence of those two countries. In 1975 a power-sharing executive was set up in Angola, between the Portuguese and the three independence movements. However, in spite of attempted cooperation, the MPLA's hostility to the FNLA and UNITA continued and broke out into a civil war. In March 1975 Luanda was threatened by the FNLA, assisted by American arms delivered through Zaire, but in the following months airborne supplies of Soviet arms were flown into Luanda and saved the capital. The FNLA then fell back towards the Zaire border.

Meanwhile in the south, UNITA, assisted by South African armoured cars, advanced almost to the line of the Benguela railway. In November the Portuguese, being unable to hand over power to any of the three movements, withdrew from Angola, leaving the civil war to proceed. About the same time Cuban troops arrived to assist the MPLA, and, by March of the following year, these troops defeated first the FNLA and then UNITA, the South African forces having withdrawn into South-West Africa. In February 1976 the MPLA Government was recognised by most of the world as the Government of Angola. UNITA, however, continued to fight and apparently had considerable success against both Cubans and the MPLA.

MOZAMBIQUE

The Portuguese were taken by surprise in Angola in 1961, but they were ready for the rising of the Maconde tribe in Northern Mozambique in 1964. MANU (Mozambique African National Union) initiated the first attack at Nagololo, but FRELIMO (Front for the Liberation of Mozambique), formed in 1962, was better organised, strongly supported by Tanzania and had considerable success. Its maximum penetration was achieved in the Northern Cabo Delgardo district in 1966, and in the adjacent Nyassa district along Lake Malawi in the same year. Despite this, the Portuguese continued to hold the towns and villages, even those on the frontier, and a counter-offensive virtually cleared the Nyassa district in 1969 and Cabo Delgardo in 1970.

Meanwhile the FRELIMO leader, Dr Mondlane, was killed in Dar-es-Salaam by a bomb planted by rival African Nationalists. Following his death, there were a large number of desertions and increasing dissension over the leadership. African Nationalists' attention then turned to the Tete district, where the Cabora Bassa dam was under construction. The year 1973 saw a major effort by both FRELIMO and COREMO (the successor organisation of MANU) in Tete. They were helped by the fact that many Africans had to be moved from the lakeside and re-housed in the protective villages, causing considerable disruption to their lives. Nationalist groups penetrated beyond Tete, over the Zambesi into the centre of Mozambique, in an attempt to spread subversion among the local Africans. Traffic on the Umtali-Beira road and railway was frequently interrupted, and small bands of guerrillas reached within thirty miles of Beira.

In 1974 came the collapse of the Caetano Government in Lisbon and the *volte face* in Africa, bringing a FRELIMO government into power in November 1975 in Lourenço Marques, now called Maputo.

Independence brought many political and economic difficulties to Mozambique, including increased tension between the FRELIMO-backed Maconde and the largest tribe, the Macua – a tension which could well lead to the outbreak of civil war similar to that in Angola. Meanwhile Mozambique continues to provide bases for anti-Rhodesian guerrillas. These bases have been the scenes of battles between rival factions of the ANC. A new, younger, guerrilla leadership appears to be emerging, trained and equipped by the Soviet Union. These men will present a serious threat to Rhodesia.

RHODESIA

ZAPU (Zimbabwe African People's Union) was formed from the National Democratic Party when this was banned in 1961. ZANU (Zimbabwe African National Union) broke away in 1963. Both established their headquarters in Lusaka, guerrillas being trained in China or the USSR and then held in training camps in Zambia. After Rhodesian UDI was declared (1965), ZANU infiltrated three groups across the Zambesi in 1966. The first major operation, however, took place under ZAPU, working in conjunction with the South African ANC in 1967, after the ending of the British and Rhodesian Governments' talks in HMS Tiger. By the end of that year five base camps were established inside Rhodesia. These were discovered early in 1968, when a major action took place, in which ZAPU was defeated.

In view of the cooperation of ANC with ZAPU, South African armed police moved north to assist the Rhodesian Security Forces in patrolling the Zambesi. After the governmental talks in HMS *Fearless*, two further incursions took place in 1968, one involving the South African police in military action. In 1969 the Rhodesian Government held a referendum and in 1970 declared the country a republic.

It was then claimed that 600 trained guerrillas were waiting to cross the Zambesi, but quarrels between ZAPU and ZANU continued and nothing happened except for two minor incursions in 1970. In view of these defeats, tactics changed and single men were infiltrated to create "cells" in the townships. These were of great assistance to Bishop Muzorewa's African National Committee in resisting the Pearce Commission's proposals for a settlement. In 1972 the Pearce Commission declared that the Home/Smith Agreement had failed to satisfy the African people in Rhodesia, and the British Government decided that, as the fifth principle had not been fulfilled, they would take no further action, but would leave the proposals on the table, in the hope of some future agreement.

The lull in guerrilla warfare between 1970 and 1972 ended at Christmas 1972 when guerrillas attacked Altena Farm, in the Centenary area of north-east Rhodesia. Other farms were subsequently attacked and two European land inspectors were murdered. The security forces discovered that, for the first time, subversion of the African people had been successful and had in fact been going on for several months. ZANU had been acting in cooperation with FRELIMO and had established base camps over the frontier, in Mozambique. As a result, Operation Hurricane was started, based on a number of independent companies of the Rhodesian Light Infantry and the African Rifles, supporting the Police, Security Branch and Internal Affairs Department. A Joint Operational Centre was established at Bindura with sub-centres at Mount Darwin and Mtoko. Each of these sub-centres was based on an airfield, from which operated the quick reaction forces of helicopters and gunships.

The year 1974 saw an increase of guerrilla activity in this area, and the Rhodesian Government started a policy of villagisation similar to that which had been carried out by British forces in Malaysia.

The whole of the strategic situation in southern Africa was then altered by the Portuguese revolution, which took place in April 1974. This led to the collapse of the Portuguese Empire and to the independence of Mozambique and Angola, and increased the pressure on Rhodesia, South-West Africa and South Africa itself. Later that year came Mr Vorster's major effort to achieve his policy of détente, which was supported by President Kaunda and led to the so-called Lusaka Agreement. As a result of this Agreement, a cease-fire was supposed to take place. This, however, was never effective and allowed the guerrilla forces to reorganise and retrain; thus the Rhodesian Security Forces lost the initiative that they had so dearly gained.

In 1975 considerable progress was made towards détente, and the South African police were gradually withdrawn from Rhodesia.

A Rhodesian Constitutional Conference eventually took place at the Victoria Falls, but it proved unsuccessful.

Meanwhile events in Angola and Mozambique had deteriorated. The Portuguese handed over control of the latter country to FRELIMO in June 1975, and at the end of that year a civil war raged in Angola, which finally became independent under the MPLA Government in November 1975. These events increased the pressure on Rhodesia and gravely damaged the concept of détente.

By the end of 1975, only three groups of ten guerrillas each were left in the Hurricane area and these later retired over the Mozambique border. However, by 1976 12,000 men had left Rhodesia for training, mostly in Mozambique. Zambia had kept ZAPU in check and there were therefore few Matabele recruits. Robert Mugabe was pushed by Samora Machel for the leadership of the Third Force, which was formed after a meeting of all parties in Tete in August 1975. A central committee of eighteen was set up, nine ZAPU and nine ZANU/ANC. The nine ZAPU were first relegated to inferior positions and later ousted, leaving the Third Force indistinguishable from ZANU. The Secretary General of the OAU Liberation Committee, Lt. Col. Mabika, then took over the command, assisted by Tanzania and Zambia. Rex Nhongo became field commander.

As far as Mozambique was concerned, Samora Machel had been at war with Rhodesia since mid-1975 but was preserving reasonable relations with South Africa, on which he depended for economic assistance and for running his ports and railways. The Mozambique army, the FPLM, works with the ZANU army, ZANLA. They are helped by regular units of the Tanzanian army in Manika province – 700 or more were involved in the attack on Umtali. Zambian troops are also present in the border area. Civilians have been cleared out of the frontier and a large airfield is being built at Villa Perry near Umtali.

The FPLM is organised and equipped by the USSR; Cubans and Chinese are present as advisers and instructors. There is dissension in the FPLM, because of lack of food and clothing. There is also a widespread breakdown of administration and technical services throughout the country, particularly in the tribal areas. President Machel is however in a strong position as he is supported by the USSR and by the youth movements. Village committees have been set up to encourage the inhabitants to work harder. The Maconde are turning against FRELIMO because they did the main fighting against the Portuguese but are not included in the Government. The Macua have always been hostile.

There are six terrorist schools run by the USSR in Mozambique. These, and guerrilla base camps, have been the objectives of a number of successful raids by Rhodesian forces.

Operation Thrasher, centred on Umtali with sub-JOCs at Inyanga and Chipinga, was set up in June 1976 when the first major incursion occurred both north and south of Umtali. This was followed by two further waves of guerrillas in April/May and in August/September, the object being to infiltrate as many as possible before the start of the rains. Of the 1,000 who crossed the frontier during these operations, some 200 have been killed and 250 wounded. The Rhodesians responded by raiding the Pungwe guerrilla training camp in Mozambique, in which over 300 guerrillas were killed. Umtali was then subject to a mortar attack, but no one was hurt. The guerrillas were assisted up to the Mozambique border by regular units of the Mozambique army and of the Tanzanian and Zambian armies.

As penetration increased, a new operational area was opened in July 1976. Operation Repulse was based on Fort Victoria, with sub JOCs and airfields at Chiredzi and Rutenga, and was designed to protect the road and rail communications with South Africa, and also to safeguard the local tribal trust lands, from which the majority of the security forces were recruited and where their families lived. Villagisation is now taking place in all three operational areas. In 1977 Mr Nkomo saw the importance of creating a guerrilla army of his own in order to counterbalance the power of Mr Mugabe. He therefore recruited throughout Matabeleland, and press-ganged schoolchildren, who were taken over the Botswana frontier to be trained in Zambia and the USSR. This led the Rhodesian Security Forces to open up yet another operational area in Western Rhodesia. It has now been stated that some 2,500 guerrillas of ZANU and ZAPU are operating inside Rhodesia, ZANU being based on Mozambique and ZAPU on Zambia. The frailty of the Patriotic Trust alliance is shown by these events. Should they eventually win, a bloody civil war between the Mashona (ZANU) and the Matabele (ZAPU) would appear inevitable. Bishop Muzorewa's (ANC) misfortune is that, although he may have the majority support among Rhodesia's Blacks, he has no guerrilla army.

Détente, and its Aftermath

The policy of détente was first proposed by Dr Verwoerd in 1965 to become government policy in 1969, when relations were established with Dr Busia of Ghana. These were short-lived since Busia was overthrown by the military in 1970. A dialogue with the Francophone states led by President Houphouët-Boigny of the Ivory Coast was more successful; these states included Madagascar, Gabon, Senegal and the Central African Republic. Predictably, the Organisation of African Unity expressed their opposition to this policy.

By 1972 the Prime Minister of South Africa, Mr Vorster, had switched the main emphasis of his foreign policy to Africa. Speaking in the South African Senate on 23rd October 1974, Mr Vorster said that it was his belief that South Africa had come to the crossroads. "I think that southern Africa has to make a choice," he said. "I think that the choice lies between peace on the one hand and an escalation of strife on the other. The consequences of an escalation are easily foreseeable. The toll of major confrontation will be high. I would go as far as to say that it would be too high for southern Africa to pay. If one adds to the threatening economic problems which could assume major proportions, then Africa and southern Africa should guard against heading for chaos. However, this is not necessary, for there is an alternative, there is a way. That is the way of peace, the way of normalising relations, the way of sound understanding and normal association."

But 1974 saw the violent political changes in Portugal, and the beginning of the abandonment of its overseas provinces. Soon after that development, it became clear that an escalation of guerrilla warfare was inevitable and that this would affect not only Rhodesia and South-West Africa but probably the Republic of South Africa itself. That country found a changing mood in the international community over her refusal to "ditch" Rhodesia or to hand over the administration of South-West Africa to the United Nations. There were clear indications that, because of these issues, South Africa's friends among the Western nations were finding it increasingly difficult to ward off attacks on her.

The South African Government was quick to realise that something had to be done and that the lack of political action which was already being strongly criticised in some of the areas of friction in southern Africa was likely to evoke a similar reaction in others. Mr Vorster himself declared that the alternatives to a peaceful solution "were too terrible to contemplate". The Government decided to move – and move quickly – to avert the polarisation of the political hostility which had been germinated against the Republic over the past years and which reached new expression during the course of 1974. A fresh shadow began to cloud the southern African political scene, as a result of the Portuguese coup d'état, the presence of China and the Soviet Union was suddenly felt to have become much closer to southern Africa than ever before.

Formal Sino-Soviet presence in southern Africa had been confined to diplomatic and trade links and to programmes of aid to countries such as Zambia and Botswana, although Rhodesia and South Africa always felt an uneasiness over the Tanzam railway which linked Dar-es-Salaam with Lusaka. This was considered to be an important channel for conveying military hardware and guerrilla fighters to the frontiers dividing the White South from the rest of Africa. Meanwhile political agreement was reached between the Rhodesian Government and Bishop Muzorewa but this was rejected by the ANC Executive and was followed by a general election in Rhodesia which again returned a Rhodesia Front Government.

Mr Vorster's Senate speech in October 1974 led to a favourable response from President Kaunda of Zambia. This in turn led to talks between the Presidents of Zambia, Tanzania, Botswana and the President-elect of Mozambique. In December came the so-called Lusaka Agreement, after which Mr Smith released Joshua Nkomo, the leader of ZAPU, and the Rev Ndabaningi Sithole of ZANU, who flew from detention to meet the three African Presidents in Lusaka. It was then decided that the reconstituted ANC should embrace ZANU, ZAPU and FROLIZI and come under the leadership of Bishop Muzorewa. A cease-fire was declared in Rhodesia and Mr Vorster said that the

South African Police would start withdrawal from that country, an operation completed some six months later.

The year 1975 saw considerable progress towards détente. "Talks about talks" began in Rhodesia, between the ANC and the Rhodesian Government. These continued for some months. In January, Mr Callaghan, then British Foreign Secretary, met Mr Vorster in Port Elizabeth, and the Portuguese set up a power-sharing executive including the three "liberation" movements in Angola. In February Mr Smith met Mr Vorster; but in March, the Rev Ndabaningi Sithole was arrested in Rhodesia. He was, however, released in the following month in order to attend an OAU conference. At this time civil war broke out in Angola; Luanda, the capital, was seriously threatened.

International cooperation continued in the months following. In May, Mr Vorster visited the Liberian Prime Minister and Mr Ennals, the Minister of State for the British Foreign Office, visited Rhodesia in June. It was then announced that the Rhodesian Government and the ANC had agreed to hold a Constitutional Conference but they failed to agree where this should take place. The Conference was eventually held at the Victoria Falls in July 1975, but broke down owing to the demand of the ANC that its members should be allowed to move about freely in Rhodesia, even if they had been convicted of terrorism. In a subsequent statement the Rhodesian Government maintained also that the ANC had demanded that the Rhodesian Government should hand over its authority to an interim council composed of equal numbers of Government and ANC Ministers with a chairman appointed by the British Government, who could exercise a casting vote. It was further alleged that the ANC had insisted upon a parliamentary structure and franchise qualifications which together would ensure a substantial African majority in Parliament at the first election. During this conference Mr Vorster met President Kaunda at the Victoria Falls, and they were reported to have made considerable headway in spite of the failure of the Rhodesians to agree among themselves.

For the rest of 1975 there was a cessation of diplomatic activity. Public attention was transferred to Angola, where the civil war between the Communist-backed MPLA, the Zaire-backed FNLA and the pro-Western UNITA became a dominant factor. Luanda had been saved for the MPLA by Soviet arms, and gradually the FNLA were forced back in the north. Meanwhile UNITA consolidated their hold roughly along the lines of the

Benguela railway. At this stage they received considerable South African support, probably about 1,500 to 2,000 troops, as well as armoured cars. It was reported that the South Africans had been asked to intervene in Angola by Zaire and Zambia and that America had promised to supply both money and arms. In November the Portuguese formally withdrew from Angola, leaving behind not a Council of National Unity as they had hoped, but three warring factions. Cuban soldiers then arrived upon the scene and this finally turned the balance of the war in Angola. On the other side of the continent, Mozambique became independent under President Machel, the leader of FRELIMO, in June 1975.

In 1976 came the turning of the tide against the West and against the policy of "détente". In January the US Congress banned any further military supplies to FNLA and UNITA. This led to the final defeat of the FNLA by Cuban soldiers and Russian armour, who then turned on UNITA in the south and gradually forced it back from the Benguela railway, capturing Lobito and Nova Lisboa (the UNITA capital) and finally defeating the UNITA forces. In February, most Western powers recognised the MPLA as the government of Angola. South African troops were withdrawn to protect the Ruacana Dam on the Cunene River on the borders of Ovamboland, and finally, after United Nations intervention and guarantees that the dam and irrigation works would be safeguarded and completed, the South African army withdrew into South-West Africa.

In Mozambique, supplies of Russian arms were delivered to FRELIMO and there were reports of Cuban advisers arriving in the country. All private property was seized, together with all the assets of any of the White Portuguese who had left the country. Mozambique closed its border with Rhodesia in February 1976, in return for promises of compensation from the United Nations and Western countries including Britain.

Meanwhile in Rhodesia, talks continued between the Rhodesian Government and Mr Joshua Nkomo, representing his wing of the ANC. These were concluded in March 1976, but failed because of the insistence of Mr Nkomo (backed by the British Government) upon a transfer of power within eighteen months to two years, a proposition that was unacceptable to the Rhodesian Government. They were reported to have offered a Parliament of one-third Black, one-third White and one-third elected by the common vote. Following this failure, Mr Smith appointed four African Senators to be Ministers in his Cabinet and three African Members of Parliament to be Junior Ministers. For the first time in Rhodesian history there were a number of Black Cabinet Ministers in that country's Government. Later two of the three Ministers resigned from the Government in order to start a new political party, the Zimbabwe United People's Organisation (ZUPO).

In the British House of Commons in the same month, Mr Callaghan, then the Foreign Secretary, made it clear that, if there were to be a peaceful settlement in Rhodesia, certain conditions would have to be fulfilled. These were: first, an acceptance of the principle of majority rule; secondly, elections for majority rule to take place in eighteen months to two years; thirdly, agreement that there would be no independence before majority rule; and fourthly, that negotiations should not be long-drawn-out. These conditions were unacceptable to the Rhodesian Government, as they would have meant a transfer of power to an African majority within two years, with probable consequences of inter-tribal warfare similar to that which had taken place in Angola. The Rhodesians then called up their territorial army and prepared for a widespread guerrilla war.

In April 1976, Dr Kissinger visited Africa and announced that the US would support majority rule for all the peoples of southern Africa. In June, Dr Kissinger and Mr Vorster met in West Germany, and in September Dr Kissinger visited Pretoria where the future of Rhodesia was ostensibly settled.

What happened at the Pretoria talks is now, in outline, clear. South Africa was in grave economic difficulties, mainly through the fall in gold prices caused partly by the International Monetary Fund sales of gold. The Americans are said to have promised their assistance in this matter and also in regard to the possible use of the veto in the UN over Namibia, provided that Mr Vorster put pressure on Mr Smith to come to terms with the African Nationalists. This Mr Vorster was easily able to do, as he controlled Rhodesia's communications with the outside world. In any case the South African Government had given Rhodesia up in the long term, on the grounds that her manpower was insufficient to beat the growing guerrilla threat.

It was understood that a package deal took place in Pretoria and that Mr Smith agreed to majority rule within two years on the following terms: that an interim government be set up, consisting half of Black and half of White members, with a White chairman without a special vote, together with a Council of Ministers with a majority of Africans and an African First Minister. The Minister of Defence and of Law and Order would be White. Decisions of the Council of Ministers would be taken by a two-thirds majority. The functions of the Council of State would include legislation, general supervisory responsibilities, and supervision of the process of drafting the constitution. The functions of the Council of Ministers would include delegated legislation and executive responsibility.

Once the interim government had been established, sanctions would be lifted and guerrilla warfare ended. Substantial economic support would then become available; pension rights, the investment of the individual in his own home and/or farm and the remittance overseas of an individual's liquid resources, within levels to be stipulated, would be guaranteed by the interim and subsequent governments.

As Dr Kissinger's immediate subordinate had met the "Front Line Presidents" it was assumed that they had agreed on behalf of their protegées in the Nationalist movements. This, however, was denied a few days later, after a meeting of the Presidents of Zambia, Botswana, Tanzania, Angola and Mozambique in Lusaka, who called on Britain to convene a constitutional conference outside Rhodesia and added that the proposals contained in the package deal were "tantamount to legalising the colonialist and racist structure of power".

This intervention of the Front Line Presidents (two Marxists, two non-Marxists and one, Julius Nyerere, balancing on a tight rope) was greatly resented by Rhodesian Blacks who were not supporters of the Patriotic Front and who appeared to condemn them to an immediate transfer of power to Marxist guerrilla bands. Having seen what had happened in neighbouring Mozambique they were decidedly unenthusiastic.

The British Government refused to confirm or deny that there had been a package and behaved in a thoroughly irresponsible manner, ending up by calling a conference at Geneva without any clear terms of reference. They appointed Mr Ivor Richard, the British Ambassador to the United Nations, as chairman – Mr Richard having been known, when in the House of Commons, for his brusqueness, and partiality for the Third World. He was soon seen to be bending over backwards to appease the two Marxist and one non-Marxist (ANC's Bishop Muzorewa) Black delegates while being as unsympathetic as possible to the White delegation.

The positions of the three delegations (assuming Mr Nkomo's Patriotic Front to be one delegation – at least temporarily!) soon became clear and were incompatible with each other. The Patriotic Front (ZANU and ZAPU) wanted a transfer of power to the Marxist militants led by the guerrilla army and sponsored by President Samora Machel of Mozambique. The ANC wanted an election and the formation of a non-Marxist Black government from which the Rhodesian Front Whites (who still represent the large majority of Whites) would be excluded and which the ANC would control. The Rhodesian Government stuck, and continued to stick, to the Kissinger package.

This impasse led the British Government very reluctantly to offer some form of direct participation in the interim government, an idea which Mr Richard proceeded to hawk unsuccessfully around Africa. On his return the idea of re-convening the Geneva Conference was dropped.

With Mr Carter's assumption of full Presidential duties in the USA, the Kissinger package was superseded by a fresh Anglo-American initiative. This involved visits of senior civil servants to all the African countries directly concerned, together with visits in May of the new American Vice-President Mr Mondale (who had been given responsibility for African affairs by the President) and their ambassador to the United Nations, Mr Young, to South Africa. Following the death of Mr Crosland, a rather more realistic line was adopted by the new British Foreign Secretary, Dr David Owen, who personally visited both Rhodesia and South Africa.

However the whole passage of events in southern Africa has been given a new direction by President Carter's attack on apartheid and his evident determination to see major changes in South Africa as well as majority rule by the end of 1979 in both Rhodesia (Zimbabwe) and South-West Africa (Namibia). This was emphasised by the presence of British and American Ministers at the United Nations Conference in Maputo in May. The Presidents of both Cuba and the USSR visited southern Africa and encouraged the guerrillas to "liberate" the whole area by force. President Podgorny also signed a treaty of friendship and cooperation with Mozambique. Thus encouraged, the Front Line Presidents maintained their support for the Patriotic Front and, as Mr Smith made clear, though willing to hand over to a Black majority, he would not hand over to a Marxist Government; the deadlock appears complete.

Mr Vorster has been pressurised by the West to withdraw all support from Rhodesia (which had considerably increased since the Kissinger talks) and to hand Namibia over to SWAPO. If he were to do so, Soviet influence would have reached the borders of South Africa itself.

The Rhodesian army in 1977 was probably the best anti-guerrilla force in the world, but it could not go on fighting guerrillas backed by the East and its "friends" from the West. Mr Vorster could have few illusions about American support, as the West seems prepared to sacrifice its influence in the whole of southern Africa for principles they do not apply elsewhere in that continent. South Africa might therefore decide to fight it out in Rhodesia rather than a few years later in the Transvaal. Whatever happens, the ultimate effect on the West and particularly on Western Europe in terms of raw material and world influence could be disastrous.

Conclusions

The appointment of their top expert on Africa, Vasili Solodovnikov (for ten years chairman of the Africa Institute in Moscow), as Soviet Ambassador in Lusaka indicates increased Soviet interest in, and pressure on, the whole of southern Africa. The objective, as in Angola and Mozambique, is to turn first Rhodesia and then South-West Africa into Marxist States by exploiting African nationalism prior to an attack on South Africa. This would enable them to gain control of 60 to 80 per cent of some of the world's key minerals and of the Cape oil route.

Should the worst happen in both Rhodesia and South-West Africa, the West will have to make up its mind whether, for its own security, it is prepared to defend South Africa.

If, however, Zimbabwe and Namibia both obtain a relatively peaceful independence as non-Marxist States, then the process of evolution, started by Mr Vorster's policy of détente, could continue and could lead to a non-racial solution of some of the world's most intractable problems. This will take time and it will be necessary for both sides – White and Black – to moderate their demands and approach the problem in a spirit of give-and-take. Is this asking too much? Probably not if Africans (Black, White, Coloured and Brown) were left to themselves; but they are not. Quite apart from the interference of the United Nations, there are the strategic designs of the USSR and her allies.

If it is true that one of the USSR's strategic ambitions is to remove southern Africa from the Western orbit, then time is not on the side of the Russians. Within the next five years, the strength of the Warsaw Pact will reach its peak in relation to NATO. After that the United States re-armament will begin to redress the imbalance and North Sea oil, together with other alternative supplies, will become available to the West.

The Soviet Union's main design will be to avoid a Super-Power conflict. With this in mind, she will do all she can to conceal her open support for the guerrilla movements by an appeal to African nationalism. If the guerrillas succeed in their aim of taking over Rhodesia and South-West Africa – even at the cost of a later major civil, or inter-tribal, war, she will have succeeded and will then be in a position to undermine the security of South Africa itself.

This, however, is a dangerous path for the Soviet Union to follow and she may be tempted, by the failure of the West to react over Angola, to try the same game in Mozambique and to launch a Cuban-backed attack on Rhodesia. Such a course would inevitably cause South African reaction possibly the cutting off of the Mozambique ports by a coastal thrust. Were the Soviets then to react through their naval power in the Indian Ocean, the scene would be set for a major conflagration.

The parallels with the Second World War are becoming clear: the "tryout" (the *anschluss* with Austria), the takeover of Angola – the "advance" because of Western weakness (as in Czechoslovakia) into Rhodesia, and finally – the "attack" (as upon Poland, which precipitated the Second World War) on South Africa, which could precipitate World War III and would certainly lead to a nuclear response from South Africa.

In 1939 the Western powers belatedly reacted to Hitler's assault upon Poland. If they fail to react quickly should South Africa be attacked, then, later on, they will have to face the might of the Soviet Union deprived of much of their access to raw materials such as gold, uranium, chrome, vanadium, manganese, copper, industrial diamonds, and probably of their main oil-route to the Middle East. Thus, at the best, they will be wide open to "Finlandisation": at the worst to a demand for surrender or face a nuclear war. The United States of America and Canada would then, indeed, be isolated and friendless.

THE RUSSIAN BUILD-UP

Brigadier W. F. K. Thompson

Brigadier W. F. K. Thompson was born into the Royal Artillery in 1909, and commissioned from Royal Military Academy, Woolwich, into that Regiment in 1929. He commanded an airborne artillery regiment in Italy and Holland in the Second World War and a Light Regiment, Royal Artillery, in the Korean War. He describes himself as "militarily over-educated" and is a graduate of four and on the directing staff of one Staff College. He retired into journalism in 1959 and became Military and Defence Correspondent of the *Daily Telegraph* until re-retiring in July 1976. He is President of the Military Commentators Circle and a Member of Council of the Royal United Service Institute for Defence Studies and the Institute for the Study of Conflict.

AS SOON as the Second World War ended Russia renewed her world-wide campaign to destroy the liberal democracies by all means short of war with the United States. Vast expenditure has gone into building up military forces designed to ensure the "inevitable" conversion of the world to Communism, while at the same time serving Russia's age-old imperial dream. The second part of this policy has brought her into competition and conflict with China.

The latest phase of this war between Russia and the West, called "détente", is interpreted by Russia as placing no restrictions on her right to promote "wars of liberation", a right also claimed by China, while both powers deny liberty to their own colonial peoples: for instance, the Baltic States, East European Protectorates and Tibet.

In the course of this campaign against the West, Russia has developed the means for projection of her power overseas, a capability not yet available to China. This has enabled Russia to defeat China in competition for influence in Africa. It has become clear, from events following the withdrawal of the Portuguese, that however much Chinese aid and projects, such as the Tanzam railway, may win African hearts, it is Russian power and ability to supply arms and deliver Cuban mercenaries that wins African minds, and in this struggle it is minds that count.

It is with the increasing Russian threat to the uninterrupted flow, via the Cape Route, of oil and other strategic raw materials vital to the industrial well-being and military potential of Western Europe and the United States that we are here concerned – a threat that stems from Russia's expanding naval capabilities and the number of states flanking the sea routes which either already do, or seem likely to, afford her naval and air operational facilities when required or otherwise act as proxies in the East/West struggle. Let us therefore examine the importance of the Cape Route, Russia's growing maritime power, and political developments in the African-Indian Ocean area which are making that power increasingly effective.

The Cape Route starts at the head of the Persian Gulf around whose shores lie some 60 per cent of the world's proven oil reserves. From here Japan draws over 80 per cent and Australia 67 per cent of their oil and Western Europe 60 per cent, although the latter will, for a decade or two, be reduced to 45 per cent by the development of the North Sea oilfields. The United States also is becoming increasingly dependent on Middle East oil and may in ten years time be importing 30 per cent of her consumption from there. Whatever developments take place, Middle East oil will, for a long time, continue to be the life-blood of Western industry and a vital element in the West's war potential.

Middle East oil reaches the Mediterranean by pipeline or tanker, via the Suez Canal when open. Both routes can be closed by political decision or war, and pipelines are vulnerable to sabotage. All oil from the Persian Gulf must pass through the Straits of Hormuz, $16\frac{1}{2}$ miles wide, into the Indian Ocean.

The Suez Canal was blocked as a result of the Arab-Israeli war of 1967 and remained closed until 1975. As a result large numbers of "Very Large Crude Carriers" (VLCCs) were constructed with displacement tonnages of from 150,000 to 350,000 to carry the oil via the Cape of Good Hope. Even larger ones are projected. The reopened Canal takes ships with a draught up to 38 feet, that is, a laden tanker of 60,000 – 70,000 tons. There is a plan to widen the Canal and deepen it to 100 feet which would allow for the passage of tankers up to 270,000 tons but the economics of such a project are dubious and the reliability of the route must also remain in doubt. Whatever the future of the Canal, the Cape Route will continue to be of the utmost importance for the shipment of oil to members of the North Atlantic Alliance.

At present some 26,000 ships pass the Cape of Good Hope each year, a daily average of 1.5m tons of shipping. Of these some 12,000 call at South African ports, to deliver or pick up passengers and cargo, or for repairs and servicing; more than a quarter are British. South Africa has a number of first-class ports. Durban is the largest port in Africa, and a major tanker terminal is being developed at Richards Bay.

The naval base at Simonstown has been modernised and includes a newly constructed submarine base. South of the Sahara only South Africa has the dockyard capacity and industrial backing for heavy ship repair. An excellently equipped maritime communication and operational centre has been constructed between Simonstown and Cape Town. Only by the use of these facilities could the Cape Route be defended in war.

Southern Africa is rich in minerals and the Republic of South Africa uniquely so. Where the shipping lanes approach the Cape the stream of tankers is joined by ships carrying minerals. Should the day come when South Africa is a client state of Russia, not only would all routes from Europe to Asia be dominated by

Russia except those via the Pacific, but the mineral wealth of the Republic, added to her home resources, would give Russia control of 90 per cent of the world production of platinum, 80 per cent of gold, 60–80 per cent of diamonds (including industrial diamonds), and 50 per cent of chrome and copper.

Clearly the ability to threaten seriously or interrupt the flow of shipping using the Cape Route would be a very powerful, and possibly decisive, diplomatic card at a time of international tension. In the event of a shooting war between NATO and the Warsaw Pact the importance of the Cape Route would depend upon its course. If short, in accordance with NATO's conventional wisdom, the effects of severance can be offset by stockpiling. Should, however, a prolonged period of conventional war ensue, its denial would, at least, ensure the defeat of Western Europe. In any such war the Simonstown base, despite Britain's termination of the Simonstown Agreement, would surely be at NATO's disposal so long as a pro-Western government was in power at the Cape.

The graver matter is the increasing ability of Russia to threaten the Cape Route and to promote acts of sabotage against it in circumstances short of general war. This ability stems from the interaction of her expanding naval capability and her increasing political influence in the Indian Ocean area and in Africa, which has been greatly enhanced by British withdrawal from East of Suez, announced in 1968, and by the collapse of the Portuguese Empire in 1975.

Russia has no need to use the sea lanes in war. Yet over the past decade Russia's maritime power, in terms of both the number and quality of her warships and their increasingly forward deployment, has been remarkable. When Hitler turned on his ally and invaded Russia on 22nd June 1941 Russia had a considerable navy, including 180 submarines, three times the number with which Germany entered the war. It was, however, a navy designed for coast defence and subordinate to the army. It proved to be singularly ineffectual.

After the war the Russian Navy was reorganised and rapidly expanded, so that by the 1950s it was second in size to that of the United States, but its status remained the same until the 1960s, since when it has become a "blue water" Navy with an ever-widening deployment. In 1960 Russia had, on any day, only a very few warships cruising in the North Atlantic and Mediterranean, and none in the South Atlantic or Indian Ocean, while in the Pacific few cruised beyond the vicinity of the Russian coast. Her merchant fleet included some 250 ocean-going ships.

Today Russia deploys her navy world-wide, maintaining fifty or more navy ships in the Mediterranean, up to thirty in the Indian Ocean, a permanent patrol off the West African coast where she has the use of the port and airfield at Conakry, and a more or less permanent naval and air force presence in Cuba. Her ocean-going merchant fleet has increased to 1,700 and is still increasing; she has some 6,000 ships in excess of 100 tons, of which 2,700 are trawlers and 372 fish-carriers and factory ships, the world's largest fishing fleet. Moreover, Russia deploys a greater hydrographic effort than all other countries together. All these aspects of maritime power are centrally controlled and coordinated by the Ministry of Defence through the Naval staff.

The speed with which Russia's Navy has been modernised is equally remarkable; she is replacing diesel with nuclear-propelled submarines at twice the NATO rate. In the past decade eight new designs of missile-armed cruisers and destroyers have come into production and seven new classes of submarine. Russia is now, for the first time, building aircraft carriers. The first of the new class *Kiev* 35,000 to 40,000 ton carriers is undergoing trials. These ships, equipped with VTOL aircraft, will, unlike the big American carriers, be able to pass through the Suez Canal. Most Russian warships are capable of mine-laying. What lies behind this revolutionary change in Russia's maritime power which has taken place under the Admiral of the Fleet of the Soviet Union, Sergei Gorshkov?

To keep the matter in perspective it should be remembered that whereas the United States has to maintain two fleets, one in the Pacific and one in the Atlantic, Russia has to maintain four – in the Pacific, Black Sea, Baltic, and Murmansk; that both the Baltic and Black Sea fleets have to pass through narrow straits not under Russian control and that 80 per cent of Russia's shipbuilding and repair facilities are still in the Baltic.

Some analysts, of a sanguine nature, would have us believe that the successively more forward deployment of the Russian Navy is a defensive response to the deployment of American missile sub-marines armed with nuclear missiles of increasing range, combined with the Russians' liking for fish caught in distant waters. They argue that when the Americans brought the Polaris A2, with a 1,600 mile range, into service in June 1962 and negotiated with Spain for a base at Rota, the Russians responded by establishing a permanent presence in the Mediterranean. When the A3, with a range of 2,500, was introduced, all targets between the western frontier of Russia and eastern Siberia, as far north as Leningrad, came within range of nuclear-armed submarines in the Indian Ocean. Russia's response was to establish a permanent presence in the Indian Ocean and advance her forward stationing positions in the Atlantic to Conakry and Cuba.

Without denying that this could have been a factor in deciding on a forward deployment, it should be pointed out that the deployment that has taken place is quite inadequate to counter the threat posed by the modern submarine.

For interpretation I prefer to rely upon Admiral Gorshkov. Three of his utterances are particularly relevant.

The Soviet Navy has been converted, in the full sense of the word, into an offensive type of long-range armed force . . . which could exert a decisive influence on the course of armed struggle in theatres of military operations of vast extent . . . and which is able to support State interests at sea in peacetime. . . .

The disruption of the ocean lines of communications, the special arteries that feed the military and economic potentials of those countries (who else but the 'imperialist aggressors'?) has continued to be one of the fleet's missions.

The Soviet Navy is a powerful factor in the creation of favourable conditions for the building of Socialism and Communism.

By 1975 the Russian Navy had acquired a capacity far in excess of that needed to protect a merchant fleet with no overseas role in war.

Political events in the past ten years have greatly enhanced the influence which Russia has been able to exert in Africa and the Indian Ocean through the development of her maritime power. Events which she herself has promoted and abetted through subversion and support for "wars of liberation".

The Cape of Good Hope first acquired strategic value when, in 1497, Vasco de Gama rounded the Cape on the way to India. Within a few years, to protect the Cape Route, the Portuguese established military posts to control the entrances to the Indian Ocean from the Red Sea (Aden and Socotra) and the Persian Gulf (Hormuz and Muscat). These have remained strategic points of maritime control ever since. From the beginning of the nineteenth century until the end of the Second World War the Indian Ocean was a "British Lake".

Even after independence had been granted to South Africa,

India, Pakistan, and Ceylon, Britain retained a degree of maritime control in the Indian Ocean. Through the Simonstown Agreement South Africa provided her with naval facilities at the Cape on a reciprocal basis; she retained control in the Persian Gulf and control of the Red Sea exit through her possession of Somaliland, Aden and the islands of Socotra and Perim.

The first break came in 1960 with the granting of independence to the Somali Republic, but the big break came in the significant year 1968, when a British Labour Government announced their intention of withdrawing by 1971 from British commitments east of Suez. The islands of Masirah, belonging to Oman, and Gan in the Maldives were to be retained as staging posts on the way to Hong Kong.

In consequence of the Indo-Chinese war Russia gained considerable influence in India and later acted as arbiter of the cease-fire which ended the Indo-Pakistan war of 1965. In the spring of 1968 a Russian cruiser, accompanied by two destroyers from the Far East Fleet, paid a goodwill visit to India and went on to visit Pakistan, the Gulf and Somalia. The only previously recorded visit of a Russian warship was in 1966 – to Massawa for Ethiopia's Navy Day.

From now on Russia proceeded to establish a permanent presence in the Indian Ocean, mainly by rotation from her Far East Fleet, though in 1969 a cruiser, a destroyer, a large amphibious ship and a tanker visited Somalia from the Black Sea before going on to the Far East. The size of the task force Russia keeps in the Indian Ocean has not greatly increased over the years. A typical presence is two destroyers, two frigates, two minesweepers, five or six assault craft, one or more submarines and a variety of support ships. What have greatly increased are both her ability to support far larger forces and her control over the Red Sea exits.

The tasks of Russia's Indian Ocean Squadron are to show the flag – one Russian ship appearing for the first time in an area which for generations has seen only the navies of France and Britain makes a considerable impact – to track and monitor space satellites; and to act as a stand-off force in case of a threat of direct American intervention in a local dispute.

Though the size of the Squadron has remained fairly constant, Russia's ability to support much larger maritime forces in the Indian Ocean has greatly increased, while, with the reopening of the Suez Canal in 1975, the speed with which this can be done has also increased greatly. Before the opening of the Canal the distance to the Persian Gulf from the nearest home base was for the United States 11,000 miles and for Russia 11,500 miles; now it is 8,000 and 3,200 miles respectively. Russia has been quick to fill the vacuum left by Britain's withdrawal. She has armed and trained the forces of the Republic of Somalia and the People's Democratic Republic of Yemen, with whose Marxist-controlled governments Russia has treaties of friendship. In exchange she has acquired exclusive rights in the deep-water port of Berbera, which can berth all classes of Russian warship except her fixed-wing and helicopter carriers.

Near Berbera are: an airfield being developed for handling Tu 95s; long-range maritime reconnaissance aircraft; an operations centre, linked to Moscow, for control of maritime forces in the Indian Ocean and Persian Gulf; housing including barracks for 1,500 Russian personnel; workshops for missile maintenance and minor ship repairs; storehouses and oil storage tanks with capacity for some 175,000 barrels. The Russians have also improved other harbours and airfields in Somalia, and have built a military airfield near Mogadishu.

In the PDRY the Russians have use of the former Royal Navy facilities in, and the RAF airfield near, Aden; Russian personnel are stationed at both. They have the use of the oil refinery and storage farm at Little Aden and are reported to have constructed a submarine base. Fleet anchorages have been established at several places near the PDRY island of Socotra.

Russia's success in establishing Somalia and the PDRY as client states has put her in a strong position to control the Red Sea approaches. It looks, however, as though her growing influence over the Marxist government of Ethiopia will not be compatible with retaining her hold over Somalia, Ethiopia's traditional enemy. Moreover France has granted the Territory of the Afars and Issas (TFAI) independence and may withdraw from the Djibouti base. Since both Somalia and Ethiopia lay claim to the TFAI Russia proposes it should be administered by the UN.

Russia has also made a bid to establish her influence by proxy on the western shores of the Straits of Hormuz, by supporting the Popular Front for the Liberation of Oman (PFLO) with bases in the PDRY. Fortunately British withdrawal from west of Suez in 1971 did not include the withdrawal of support for the Trucial Oman States or the Sultanate of Muscat and Oman, or from the RAF staging post on Masirah Island.

After a prolonged but skilfully conducted political and military campaign, with the Sultan of Oman's forces commanded and led by British officers, and in alliance with Iran, the insurgency was defeated. In 1974 the Shah and the Sultan declared their intention of cooperating to ensure "the free passage of ships and freedom of movement through the Hormuz Straits and adjacent seas".

In 1970 Russia signed a treaty with Mauritius giving her landing rights for Aeroflot and berthing rights for her trawlers at Port Louis. Russia has established fleet anchorages, with permanent buoys, off Mauritius, the Seychelles and other locations in the Indian Ocean. After signing a treaty of friendship with Iraq in 1972 Russia has improved the facilities of the naval base at Umm Qasr, at the head of the Persian Gulf, to which she has access.

The United States has also moved to fill the vacuum. Since the 1940s she has maintained, by treaty, a flagship at Bahrain, augmented by two destroyers or frigates on rotation and called the Mideast Force. When, on occasion reinforced by a carrier task force from the Pacific Fleet a serious strain was put on her logistic services. In 1971 the United States therefore took a lease on Diego Garcia in the British Indian Ocean Territory to establish a communication centre, and has since decided to construct a forward support base there.

At Diego Garcia the lagoon is being deepened to take an aircraft carrier and her escorts; the airstrip is being extended to 12,000 feet for maritime reconnaissance, accommodation is being built for 600 servicemen, and warehousing and oil storage tanks are being built. Britain has a right to the joint use of these facilities, which have become more important after the recent decision to withdraw from the staging posts at Gan in the Maldives and from Masirah Island. The United States has been reported as having approached the Sultan for the use of Masirah which is 400 miles from Hormuz, whereas Diego Garcia is 2,000 miles.

The United States' other response to Britain's withdrawal has been to support a massive build-up of the Iranian forces: this also has Britain's support. Iran has emerged as the dominant power in the Persian Gulf and the Shah is establishing a deep-water navy to protect his sea communications as far south as Malagasy.

The Royal Navy still contributes to a Western presence in the Indian Ocean by regularly despatching self-contained task forces to take part, with the navies of the United States, Iran and Pakistan, in CENTO manoeuvres.

France also intends to maintain a permanent presence. She has given up her base at Diego Suarez in Malagasy, and has granted independence to the TFAI, where she will retain some naval support facilities. At the time of writing her permanent forces consist of a guided-missile destroyer, a commandship tanker, four small frigates and an assortment of afloat support ships. This force is augmented by heavier units on three monthly tours of duty, usually an aircraft carrier, a missile frigate and a replenishment tanker.

Britain's decision to withdraw from east of Suez has assisted Russia to bring her maritime power southward to a line of forward posts from Cuba to Conakry to Mogadishu. A new leap southwards towards the Cape is now taking place, following the collapse of Portugal's African Empire through left wing revolution at home and under the pressure of Russian-sponsored wars of liberation abroad. Independent governments under Marxist leadership have been established in the Cape Verde Islands, Guinea-Bissau, Angola and Mozambique.

In Angola, President Neto's Marxist MPLA prevailed over the rival FNLA and UNITA parties only through the support of Russian arms shipments and 12,000 Cuban regular soldiers transported by Russia. All four territories provide first-class airfield and port facilities from which the Cape Route can be threatened. In 1976 Aeroflot established regular services to Conakry, Accra, Luanda, and Maputo. The main strategic implication, however, was the turning of both flanks of the Zambezi Line. Rhodesia and South Africa now have Russian-supported Marxist dictatorships on their frontiers.

The speed with which the situation in southern Africa has changed is well illustrated by a study published only five years ago. Discussing the possibility of a Russian blockade of the Cape, the author points out that the nearest port that might prove friendly is in Mauritius, 2,000 miles away; that Russia has no aircraft carriers and her nearest airfields are in Egypt. Today Russia has one aircraft carrier in service and one nearly completed; the use of first-class airfield and port facilities in Mozambique and Angola is reportedly seeking facilities in Grand Comoro Island in the Mozambique passage.

On the other hand, and significantly, Russia has lost her airfields in Egypt. It is ironic that the one European power which has not only maintained but expanded her empire, Russia, should be able to exploit anti-colonialism, expanding her own sphere of influence through Marxism. Newly independent nations, even when led by Marxists, will accept the position of a client state only so long as they see this as the lesser of two evils. Western diplomacy must act on the assumption that those who are not against us are for us, in working to roll back Russian influence south of the Sahara.

The outstanding importance to the Atlantic powers of the free use of the Cape Route and assured access to the mineral resources of South Africa is clear. What is less obvious are the circumstances under which these might be denied.

Russian interference, direct or by proxy, with the Cape Route could take many forms: piracy or hijacking; sinking by limpet mine or unidentified submarine, as in the Spanish Civil War; the declaration of a blockade, possibly under cover of a large-scale exercise. All these have been suggested, but it seems to me that all either fall into the category of acts of war, or are open to retaliation in kind, or would be politically counter-productive. A possible exception would be the sinking of a giant tanker by saboteurs in the narrow deep-water channel through the Straits of Hormuz.

The present crisis in southern Africa needs to be seen in a much wider context. Russia does not want war by victory. Her strategy is to undermine the will and morale of the West while building up an ever stronger position from which to work her own will. To preserve its freedom the West must act with boldness toward Russia. No possible Russian interest can be served by a shooting war with the United States; therefore, whenever freedom is challenged, the West must demonstrate the will and capacity to go to the brink of war, and if necessary beyond. In that way we need neither have war nor surrender, for Russia will back down.

I agree with those who argue that, had NATO moved ten divisions toward the frontier when Russia mobilised vast forces in eastern Europe in 1968, there would have been no invasion of Czechoslovakia and no war. Had the will of the American people not been undermined by Vietnam, Russia would never have moved Cubans into Angola.

Russia aims to establish client states in Rhodesia, and South Africa. The former soon, the latter later.

Should the Russians succeed, their power to blackmail Western Europe will be almost irresistible. They respect spheres of influence: the North Koreans were given the green light only after Dean Acheson had declared South Korea to be outside the United States' sphere of strategic interest. It is essential, therefore, that the Atlantic powers make clear to Russia that under no circumstances can they allow South Africa to pass into the Soviet sphere of influence.

The dilemma facing the West is that such a declaration is not enough on its own to secure Western interests in the long term. These can be safeguarded only in cooperation with a government in South Africa which not only leans toward the West but represents a system acceptable to the great majority of the people of South Africa. How to hold off Russia, yet bring sufficient pressure to bear against the Government of South Africa to achieve timely and adequate reforms, while maintaining the economy, is the greatest challenge facing the Atlantic community, and time is short.

THE SOUTH AFRICAN RESPONSE

Admiral H. H. Biermann

Admiral Hugo Hendrik Biermann was born in Johannesburg in 1916 and was educated at Jan Van Riebeeck High School in Cape Town and on the *General Botha*. He joined the South African Seaward Defence Force in the Second World War and was appointed Chief of Staff in 1952. He became Chief of the South African Navy and its first Admiral and subsequently was created Commandant-General of the South African Armed Forces in 1972.

Extracts from a speech made by Admiral H. H. Biermann, SSA, OBE, Chief of the South African Defence Forces, in August 1972.

For many years South Africa has been involved indirectly in the world power struggle, and the White governments in southern Africa – particularly the Republic of South Africa – have been the targets for condemnatory resolutions in the United Nations and threats from many sources. Latterly however we have entered more sharply into the international limelight on account of, on the one hand, the change in the pattern of relationship between the Republic of South Africa and the other African states, and, on the other, the obvious increase in interest shown by Communist powers in the Southern Hemisphere, and more specifically in the regions of the Indian and Atlantic Oceans. Communist penetration into the Southern Hemisphere, and the threat that this portends, have caused the Southern Hemisphere, and particularly the Indian Ocean, to emerge dramatically from a position of relative obscurity and to assume a conspicuous position in the East-West power struggle. The focal point in this changed perspective is occupied by southern Africa – and the Republic of South Africa.

This statement may appear to be exaggerated, and it is a fact that in many circles the threats referred to are watered down or even denied. Rational investigation demands that the facts should not be manipulated as statistics only, but that they should be interpreted against a valid background. In the present case, the basic elements of the background in point are the current world conflict, the enemy strategy and the ambient climate on national and international levels. In Western circles one finds a certain hesitance to accept the assertion that the increasing Communist influence in the Southern Hemisphere – and more specifically in southern Africa and its oceans – is threatening more than just Western trade and economic interests. The latest publications, however, indicate an augmenting conviction that this expansion is an integral part of Communist strategy in pursuit of world domination, and that, as such, it is aimed at the very heartlands of the West. However this may be, the simple facts of this penetration and presence will probably be accepted generally as constituting a threat to the states within the Southern Hemisphere. The Republic of South Africa, being one of these states, must therefore deliberate on the manner in which this threat is to be faced. Obvious questions which arise are: To what extent could individual states counter this threat on their own? Would the indicated solution perhaps lie in one or other form of coordinated action amongst the states concerned, as for example, a treaty organisation or an alliance? Thirdly, the question arises as to whether a solution could in fact be found in the Southern Hemisphere alone or whether it would be necessary to look further afield.

We live in an era of global conflict which, towards the end of the Forties, became polarised as a struggle between East and West. It was at this stage that Communism was identified as a monolithic world power in the hands of an aggressive USSR, and the Western powers then decided on the establishment of the North Atlantic Treaty Organisation as a counter. Since then it has become customary to refer to the conflict between East and West. Over the years the Communist world has experienced many movements: centrism had to yield to a degree of polycentrism; Communist countries were divided into ideological *blocs* and a schism developed between Russia and China. Nevertheless Communism, and especially Communist influence, continued unremittingly to expand and to penetrate new areas. In spite of the domestic divergences within the Communist world, the East-West conflict continues unabated, and the Communists maintain a united front as far as it concerns the conflicting interests of East and West.

In the meantime the "Third World" emerged. This Third World with its posture of "non-alignment" has developed into a cardinal element in the East-West conflict. Black Africa, with the OAU as its mouthpiece, is probably the biggest coherent element of the Third World. The OAU charter specifically provides for the inclusion of the Third World principle, namely, ". . . a policy of non-alignment with regard to all *blocs*". This manifesto also explicitly states one of its goals to be "to eradicate all forms of colonialism from Africa". It is a fact that Communist powers never had colonies in Africa, and consequently the OAU does not harbour a residual grievance against them. This provides the East with an initial advantage, *vis-à-vis* the West, in respect of relations with African states. Black Africa identifies colonialism, imperialism and racism with the West, and not with the East, to such an extent that in many cases anti-colonialism has assumed the form of anti-White racism. In general, Black Africa looks upon any Western assistance either as an attempt at neo-colonialism or as the delayed settlement of colonial debts. Although most African leaders do not speak Russian or Chinese and although they are not Communists, their vocabulary is Communist and their idiom is permeated with Communist clichés and Communist jargon. Geographically southern Africa is an integral part of the Third World, and politically the prime target of the OAU.

After the Second World War the West was in a favourable position strategically because it enjoyed an undisputed lead in nuclear weaponry, and because its military, economic and political power embraced the globe. Besides NATO, several other defence agreements came into being, such as CENTO, SEATO, ANZUS and the Rio Pact. The United States established mutual agreements with Japan, Taiwan, South Korea and the Philippines, as well as with the Protocol States of Laos, Cambodia and South Vietnam. The centre of gravity of all these agreements was in the Northern Hemisphere.

Notwithstanding these initial advantages, the West witnessed the strengthening and the entrenchment of the USSR in the once-free countries of eastern Europe, the USSR retaining the initiative and continuing to extend its influence outwards. Instead of repulsing Communism, the West in turn was obliged to entrench itself; all this to no avail, because Communism has breached the Western defensive perimeter and is now outflanking the West from the south.

There have been signs that the West is beginning to take note of our Government's continued warnings in respect of Communist penetration into the Southern Hemisphere and particularly into Africa, and the Indian and South Atlantic Oceans. At present there is evidence of anxiety amongst Western students both of Communism and of strategy concerning the rapid development of the Soviet Union's maritime forces, its changed maritime strategy and its increasing presence in the Indian and Atlantic Oceans, and, to a lesser extent, the Chinese presence and activities in southern Africa. A number of symposia on the subject have been conducted in the United States and the United Kingdom, and almost every periodical on international affairs has published articles on it. A mass of recent literature on the subject is available.

The nuclear weapon and its terror have become the dominating strategic factor in the global struggle. As a consequence total strategy in the indirect mode has assumed a decisive role in modern conflict. While the USSR and the People's Republic of China possessed few or no nuclear weapons, there was little

73

danger that the East would risk a point-blank conventional confrontation with the West; this situation however spurred them to greater exertions to intensify their indirect strategy on all fronts. In due course Russia acquired nuclear weapons, and soon the USSR and the USA were locked in a technological struggle to achieve undisputed nuclear superiority. The philosophy of nuclear strategy was evolved and adapted to numerous permutations in an effort to keep abreast of the rate of development and the changes in weaponry which invalidated one concept after another. Passing through all the different stages from "first strike" and "massive retaliation" to "graduated response" and several other variations, the situation has developed to the present state of deterrent balance between the two Super-powers – the United States and Russia. In the field of deterrence the two Super-powers have reached a situation of stability, because either side disposes of a reaction capacity of such magnitude that its assured destructive response is unacceptable to the other, no matter what the stake may be. Consequently neither side dares launch the first strike. A simple increase in the number of nuclear weapons on one side or the other is therefore in itself no longer decisive. General Beaufre contends that, in spite of the apparent paradox, it is true that a classical arms race leads to instability whereas a nuclear arms race leads to stability, because the former encourages the illusion of victory while the latter strengthens the conviction of mutual destruction. This bilateral nuclear stability is a decisive consideration in all global strategic planning. It is clearly discernible, for example, in the statements of the United States Government about foreign policy. Consequently all other strategic planning must continuously take into account the danger of escalation which could lead to a nuclear war. Besides the danger of escalation there are two other possible contingencies which could jeopardise this bilateral stability. Firstly, there is the possibility that one of the Super-powers might achieve a technological breakthrough which could neutralise the other's retaliatory capacity; the other is that one of the lesser powers, also in possession of nuclear weapons, could precipitate a global nuclear war. In this latter respect one thinks especially of Communist China.

While the nuclear stability obtains, both the Super-powers will attempt to avoid direct confrontation because they are afraid of escalation. The scope for Communist expansion without confrontation in the Northern Hemisphere has been largely exhausted or is already being exploited. Hence the surge towards the Southern Hemisphere to involve the Third World and to encircle the West, and hence the increasing strategic importance of South Africa in the global conflict. Communist expansion is being realised on different fronts. Amongst others we identify the following: the exertion of influence on states at the expense of the West by means of diplomatic representation, cultural and trade agreements, economic aid and the supply of arms; the establishment of a presence by means of "specialists" in connection with such aid and with defence; infiltration of trade unions, universities and other social institutions; military presence; maritime presence in the shape of commercial and naval vessels. The following examples are quoted to illustrate the nature and rate of this expansion:

In 1956 there were only two diplomatic missions from Communist countries in African states; in 1961 there were twenty-one; in 1966 there were 155. In 1971 the various missions from different Communist countries in 37 African states, including the Malagasy Republic and Mauritius, added up to 273.

A comparable expansion also took place in Latin America. In 1962 the USSR had diplomatic relations with only two states in Latin America, while at the present time they are represented in almost every state on the American continent.

The Soviet Navy maintains an impressive presence of up to fifty naval units in the Mediterranean. They are afforded free passage through the Dardanelles. They enjoy port and base facilities in Syria and along the north coast of Africa, where they also have airfield facilities. This enables them to cover a major portion of the Mediterranean without overflying other countries.

Apart from the fishing fleet permanently operating off the coast of South-West Africa, they maintain – since 1970 – a permanent presence along the bulge of Africa in the Atlantic Ocean off the coast of Guinea. They have fishing agreements with various littoral states and points of call in Guinea, Senegal, Nigeria, Congo (Brazzaville) and Zaire.

In the Indian Ocean the Soviet Navy has points of call at Mauritius, Mtwara, Dar-es-Salaam, Zanzibar and Mogadishu. It has anchorages at the Seychelles, in the region of Diego Garcia and the Cargados. There are persistent reports that

Russia is constructing a military base on Socotra. The Red Chinese are building a naval base for Tanzania in Dar-es-Salaam and a portion of this base is being reserved for their own use; they use Mtwara for delivery of arms to the terrorists and they have naval repair facilities at Zanzibar.

The USSR has concluded a treaty of peace, friendship and cooperation with India and a similar one with Iraq. It has signed a trade agreement to the tune of R (Rand) 320 million with Bangladesh. It has naval points of call along the coasts of the Red Sea, the Arabian Sea and the Bay of Bengal.

Aviation Week and Space Technology summarises the Soviet naval expansion as follows:

Continuous operations in the Mediterranean, long dominated by the US Navy's Sixth Fleet, were begun in 1964, leap-frogging NATO's southern flank and providing Russia with an additional political-economic wedge into the African and Asian littorals of that sea. Soviet influence, particularly within the United Arab Republic, was further accelerated by the Arab-Israeli war in 1967. The consequent tensions and economic-hardware needs of dependent Arab nations have increased to a point where Russian influence is dominant in several countries. At the height of a potentially explosive Arab-Israeli reconfrontation a year ago, the Russian Mediterranean fleet numbered seventy combat vessels as opposed to sixty for the US. A recent internal Soviet document evaluating that country's worldwide strategic pluses and minuses noted happily, 'We now control the oil in the Middle East.' Militarily and economically, West Europe is dependent upon receiving the bulk of its oil supplies from the Middle East.

Periodic naval operations into the western Pacific were begun in 1965, primarily surface-ship exercises in support of submarine operations.

Extended support operations in the central Atlantic were initiated in 1967, with deployment to West Africa and Communist Cuba in the Caribbean beginning in 1969.

Continuous, if limited, naval presence has been maintained in the Indian Ocean since 1969 after a probing which began in 1968.

The Red Chinese, too, have a bridgehead in southern Africa. It is common knowledge that, for the past decade and more, they have been attempting to expand and establish their influence in this part of the world. In Congo (Brazzaville) they have achieved some success. In Zaire and Burundi they have suffered setbacks, but have by no means abandoned their efforts. On the contrary, there are positive signs of a resumption of their attempt to establish a presence in Burundi after the recent bloody massacres. Their most evident successes, however, would appear to be in Tanzania and Zambia. By means of the Tanzam railway, as well as a number of other projects, they have found a justification for their admittance and presence in large numbers. Public media estimate the numbers of Chinese at present in Tanzania and Zambia as being of the order of 20,000 to 30,000. Furthermore, it has been mooted that all these Chinese workers and specialists are members of Red China's People's Army or that, at least, they have been trained as soldiers. We are aware that the Chinese are giving assistance to Tanzania in the training and organisation of its defence forces, which are organised according to the pattern of the Chinese People's Army; that they are providing arms to Tanzania as well as to the anti-White terrorists; and that they play a prominent part in the training, planning and military leadership of terrorism against White-controlled southern Africa. Their entry into southern Africa by way of economic aid, delivery of arms, association with Black hatred against the Whites and participation in the struggle against the White régimes in the south, bear a marked resemblance to the Russian strategy in the Middle East.

At present many observers in the West aver that drastic changes have recently occurred in Communism, and from this they deduce a softening in Communist attitudes and a reduction of the Communist threat to the West. This, in itself, is perhaps the greatest Communist victory of all time. Other strategists and students of Communism, however, insist that these internal per-mutations have in no way altered the Communist aim of world domination or its hostile attitude towards all non-Communistic norms of living and, therefore, the threat to the West, inherent in Communism. Claude Harmel, an authority on the subject, sum-marises the situation as follows: "It is true that something has changed in the dominion of Communism, and it would not be unduly hazardous to predict that further changes will occur in the years ahead. But amongst that which changes there is that which remains, and what remains – analysis confirms this – is the nature of Communism and its anatomy. That which changes and which has changed are only the less important aspects." If this is so, and if we bear in mind the way in which the Communists apply Marxist dialectics in practice, then history should provide us with a reliable gauge of what the Communists aim to achieve and how they are likely to set about it.

Forrestal's dictum in 1946 about Russia has been vindicated repeatedly and is still valid today for Communism as a whole. "Russia is always pushing," he said, "receding when rebuffed, but, like a great tide, surging in elsewhere if there is an opening." Communism is a centralised machine in which the armed forces are integrated with politics and which exercises absolute control over all the resources and means of the state and society. The fact that all economic resources, without exception, are directly subservient to politics provides Communist régimes with a mighty weapon in the execution of their indirect strategy.

We are well aware of the fact that Communism pursues its goals by the employment of the indirect strategy of infiltration, intrigue, propaganda and subversion, including direct support to subversive and terrorist movements. The obvious objectives of these strategies are to cause chaos in non-Communist countries, to undermine moral and cultural standards, to incite and encourage internal unrest, to gain control of key positions in government and social institutions, and so on. An objective, however, which is not so obvious, and which is often ignored, is that of establishing a prior presence. The term "prior presence" denotes the establishment of a significant presence in the target area *before* a confrontation is provoked. This strategy of prior presence is indubitably one of the goals of the Soviets' increasing maritime activity in the South Atlantic and Indian Oceans.

Referring to history once again, I believe that it would not be far-fetched to assert that the Nixon doctrine of negotiation and the SALT talks suited the Communists admirably. They are, after all, only slightly different versions of Stalin's strategy (or should it be stratagem?) of "disarmament" and Kruschev's "peaceful co-existence". History tells us that these phases of the conflict in no way inhibited the USSR's onslaught on the West or their efforts to outstrip the West in the arms race. The present situation, dominated by the fear of nuclear war, presents a golden opportunity for the Communist powers ostensibly to relax the tension on the nuclear front while stepping up their initiatives in the indirect mode. The West, in its anxiety to maintain a détente on the nuclear front, would be inclined, for this very reason, to be more accommodating on other fronts, where the West might consider that its vital interests are not so directly threatened. Forrestal quoted Stalin as having said "We do not want a war with America, but they want it even less than we do, and this makes us the stronger."

The Southern Hemisphere, and in particular southern Africa, presents an attractive target for indirect strategic assault by Communist forces. Communist efforts of this kind would be facilitated in southern Africa by, amongst others, the following considerations: the West does not yet generally accept that it is being threatened in this part of the world; the Communists have a ready-made front in the terrorist organisations and the OAU, behind which to dissimulate their true intentions; the White governments in southern Africa are so unpopular in the international community that Western powers are loath to be associated with their defence.

Physical Characteristics: Southern Hemisphere

Looking at the map of the earth, we notice that the centre of gravity of the land masses lies north of the equator, while the Southern Hemisphere is dominated by ocean areas. Take as example a line running along the latitude of 60° North. Notice that at this latitude the girth of the earth consists, for approximately two-thirds of its length, of land masses, while latitude 60° South does not touch land at all.

There are three large fingers of land reaching from north to south demarcating the Atlantic, Indian and Pacific Oceans. South America stretches from north of the equator down towards the Antarctic Circle and constitutes a continuous barrier, for the whole of its length, between the Pacific and Atlantic Oceans. The passages for shipping between these two oceans are around the southern point of South America through the hazardous Drake Passage around Cape Horn, and through the Panama Canal north of the equator. This canal, with Cuba on its doorstep and the awakening nationalism of the states to the north and south, is very vulnerable from the Western point of view.

Africa is the land barrier between the Atlantic and Indian Oceans. Ships can pass from the Northern Atlantic to the Indian Ocean via the Mediterranean and the Suez Canal. The vulnerability of Suez has been demonstrated so convincingly on two occasions recently that it does not warrant further comment. The only secure passage, for all practical purposes, between these two oceans, therefore, is the route around the Cape of Good Hope.

The Indian Ocean is separated from the Pacific by Australia and the chain of islands to its north. Although in this case the barrier is not a continuous land mass, the trade routes through the Malayan and Indonesian islands are limited and vulnerable from both the political and physical points of view. The alternative passage is the long route around the south of Australia.

It is evident that major bottlenecks for shipping in the Southern Hemisphere exist at Cape Horn, the Cape of Good Hope, Indonesia and south of Australia. Due to the world trade pattern, the route around the Cape is the most important in the Southern Hemisphere and this confers upon southern Africa a key position in any strategy for this part of the world. The geographical location of our continent is such that a strong maritime force based on the Cape would be able to interdict naval traffic between the Indian and the Atlantic Oceans and would be favourably placed to exert a stranglehold on traffic around Cape Horn.

Before the closure of the Suez Canal in 1956 the number of merchant ships which annually called at South African ports amounted to between 4,000 and 5,000. From 1956 onwards these numbers increased steadily even after the Canal was reopened. After the Suez Canal was closed for a second time, in 1967, the numbers increased to some 12,000 ships per year. Apart from these ships calling at our ports, it is estimated that another 11,000 to 14,000 ships per annum pass around the Cape in both directions without calling at South African ports.

The closure of the Suez Canal led to the introduction of super-tankers of 200,000 tons and more. These giants transport oil from the Persian Gulf to Western Europe along the Cape Route more cost-effectively than the previous generation of tankers. (70,000 tons was the upper limit for ships using the Canal passage.) These super-tankers convey approximately 30 per cent of the oil supplied to Western Europe from the oilfields in the Persian Gulf; the remainder is pumped along pipelines rendered vulnerable by the fact that they traverse different states. The monthly total volume of oil shipped around the Cape amounts to some 20 million tons, of which about 90 per cent is destined for European ports.

The Threat: Southern Hemisphere

In our minds there is no doubt whatsoever that the Communist penetration and presence in the Southern Hemisphere constitute a threat, directly and indirectly, to the Republic of South Africa. There are also indications of increasing conviction in Western circles that this threat reaches beyond the countries of the Southern Hemisphere. Unfortunately, however, there is so much confusion about the nature of the threat that intelligent and serious students of strategy often find themselves arguing at cross-purposes and so fail to arrive at realistic conclusions. In order to avoid falling into the same trap, therefore, we should consider briefly certain properties of this threat.

One of the first aspects normally considered is probably the danger of a large-scale war at sea. If, however, we analyse the situation against the background of the predominating consideration of nuclear terror, we may readily conclude that such an eventuality is highly improbable. It would involve too great a risk of escalation. Nevertheless, there are prominent people who do not entirely discard this possibility. For example, Air Vice-Marshal Menaul recently contended that it was conceivable the next war might be decided at sea, without a single nuclear weapon being used against a target on land. In our view, however, this possibility remains unlikely.

The presence of Soviet naval forces in all the oceans of the world could constitute a threat to the deployment of Western submarine nuclear forces. This would be applicable especially in areas and on occasions where the USSR has naval superiority. The major danger in this respect, however, is the submarine-hunter which is itself a submarine, able to accomplish its mission unseen and unidentified. (To the best of our knowledge the riddle of the American nuclear submarine *Scorpion*, which vanished in 1968, remains unsolved.)

In relating Soviet naval presence in the Southern Oceans to the maritime trade routes, one immediately conjures up visions of piracy and disruption of Western merchant shipping. After further consideration, however, one reaches the conclusion that it is unlikely that, in the prevailing circumstances, the Russians would indulge in practices of this kind, apart from rare exceptions. Serious or systematic harassment of Western commerce at sea would inevitably provoke reaction and this, in turn, is fraught with the risk of escalation. The Soviet Navy might occasionally cause temporary disruption of merchant shipping by conducting exercises in international waters; but this also – should it be repeated too often – would lead to confrontation. Nevertheless there is a real danger that Western mercantile interests could be seriously hampered by indirect Soviet action. The safety of merchant shipping along the Cape Route is undoubtedly of primary importance to the West, but this, in terms of the Communist threat in the Southern Hemisphere, is by no means the only aspect which should claim the attention of the Western powers. The most important element of mercantile shipping around the Cape is the transport of oil. Should the Communists therefore wish to interrupt this commerce, they would probably find it easier to do so in the area of the Persian Gulf than on the high seas. Over-emphasis of the importance of the Cape Route on the grounds of commerce alone could obscure other aspects of the threat, and could, in the event, cast doubt on the credibility of the threat as a whole.

An insidious, but none the less real, danger inherent in the Communist presence in the Southern Hemisphere is the expansion of Communist influence to the detriment of Western interests. It has already been pointed out that the so-called "non-alignment" of the Third World – particularly as far as most Black African leaders are concerned – is anti-Western and racist in orientation. The continued presence of Soviet naval forces in surrounding oceans previously dominated by the West, the courtesy calls, the offers of military aid and assistance with development projects, must inevitably enhance Soviet prestige in these countries and provide opportunities for the Russians to exert their influence. It can be assumed categorically that Communist aid always has a political motive and that the expansion of Communist influence always takes place at the cost of the West.

Another, more active and direct, facet of this maritime presence is the creation of conditions favourable to the application of "gunboat diplomacy" – or the use of limited force. Naval forces – more than ground or air forces – are eminently suited to this kind of operation. They retain their freedom of action up to the last moment and are capable of disengaging when things go wrong or when the limited objective has been achieved. In his book *Gunboat Diplomacy,* James Cable provides an enlightening analysis and historical review of this strategy during the past fifty years. His deliberations lead one to the conclusion that gunboat diplomacy is by no means outdated. Given favourable circumstances this strategy could still be employed to advantage in many present-day situations. It could be used for intimidation or blackmail, without the commission of an act of war; it could execute a *coup de force* and present the opponent with a *fait accompli*; it could support, or aid, the suppression of insurgency; it could bring up reinforcements or evacuate refugees. And so on. An inherent advantage of this strategy is that it invariably places the onus of reaction, and thus the risk of initiating an escalation, on the shoulders of the opponent. A basic requirement for a successful operation of this kind is overwhelming local superiority for the duration of the action; this superiority is relative and bears no relation to the absolute capabilities of the opponents. The ambient climate of nuclear stability and the mutual fear of escalation constitute conditions pre-eminently favourable to the application of this strategy because they complicate, to an unprecedented degree, the decision how to react. Action to redress a *fait accompli*, more often than not, requires the use of force. In the present climate the options of reaction are severely limited: threats of the use of force against the perpetrator have largely lost their credibility, because he would already have calculated whether the opponent would place sufficient value on the re-establishment of the *status quo ante* to risk his own destruction for it; economic, political or diplomatic action, in view of the nature of the prevailing conflict situation, would seldom achieve decisive results and would be more likely to increase tensions on other fronts; direct or even indirect action against the target country (especially one of the Third World) would brand the opponent as an aggressor. The logical deduction is that the only effective counter to this strategy must be prevention. In many situations the only valid prevention would be prior presence. This presence need not be overwhelming; it should only be sufficient to place the responsibility for the choice of confrontation on the opponent.

It is unlikely that the USSR would use force against a Black state or would intervene openly in support of an unpopular revolution in such a state. They could hardly have forgotten the lesson of the Sudan. The White-controlled states in southern Africa, on the other hand, present excellent targets for the application of limited force by the Communists. Although most Western countries are aware of the importance of retaining stable governments in these states, the White régimes are unpopular in the international community and any support they may receive from a Western Power is interpreted and proclaimed as an act directed against Black Africa. If, moreover, we consider the elements necessary to cloak almost any Communist action against the White-controlled South in the guise of assistance to the so-called "freedom movements", we must realise that it is virtually impossible for any Western power to react after the aggression has been perpetrated. Should the White governments be overthrown with the support of Communist powers, there is no doubt whatever that Communist influence and Communist presence will move in with the "liberators" and, by the same token, Western influence – as in the Middle East – will be eliminated from that area; southern Africa will have changed sides. The indicated course of action for the West, therefore, is to ensure that this does not happen; and this can only be achieved by the establishment of a modicum of maritime presence in the southern regions of the Atlantic and Indian Oceans.

Strategy: Southern Hemisphere
The existence of ANZUS, SEATO and the Rio Treaty, and the presence of the First USA Fleet in the South Pacific Ocean provides an infrastructure for the defence of this region. Any Western strategy for the Southern Hemisphere, however, which ignores the South Atlantic and Indian Oceans exposes the West to Communist encirclement by land and sea. The first steps in this direction have already been taken as can be deduced from the present deployment of Communist forces, viz: the Soviet maritime presence in the Indian and Atlantic Oceans and the Red Chinese presence in Tanzania, Zambia and the Congo (Brazzaville). It has been pointed out above that the geo-political situation in southern Africa, the islands of the Indian Ocean and Indonesia and, to a lesser extent, South America, is such that it favours Communist infiltration and expansion of influence. Besides this, the countries concerned do not dispose of adequate military means to counter the Communist onslaughts at all threatened points on their own. This is particularly true in respect of maritime defence – and this is the field where the need for defence is greatest.

It has been postulated that Western strategy should be based on prevention and not on reaction; and that, in the given situation, the only reasonable preventative action is to ensure adequate presence at the right time and place. Owing to the political and geographic characteristics of the strategic theatre, adequate presence can be realised only by the employment of maritime forces.

The size of the area to be covered precludes the feasibility of maintaining viable force strengths at all points of possible crisis at all times. This establishes a requirement for efficient and continuous intelligence of enemy strengths and movements, which, in turn, postulates aerial and/or satellite reconnaissance supported by highly developed communications.

In terms of the global conflict, the West still possesses sufficient real and potential means to ensure not only that the Communist penetration into the Southern Hemisphere is arrested but also that the tide is turned. In practice, however, there are serious problems inhibiting the coordination and rational deployment of the available means. The means available comprise the maritime and air forces of the United States and other NATO countries, as well as those of a number of states within the Southern Hemisphere itself, including the base and support facilities existing there. The restriction of NATO's operational competence to the north of the Tropic of Cancer must, in view of the present threat, be unrealistic.

From the operational and strategic points of view, southern Africa is probably the vital ground of the region. Reference has been made to a number of bottlenecks in the area but the loss of any one of these would not disrupt Western strategy completely. The loss of southern Africa, and specifically of the Republic of South Africa, on the other hand, would be a decisive and irreparable setback for the West. The strategic importance of the Republic, accruing from its geographic location, is obvious, and this is enhanced by its supporting capabilities and potential. South African ports are backed up by a highly developed industrial hinterland with a network of excellent communications and by a stable government. In the interior of the country there are heavy industries, while in the ports themselves extensive repair facilities and know-how are available. Good airfields with their supporting services are dispersed throughout the country. Simonstown is a modern naval base, there is a large protected anchorage at Saldanha Bay, there are major modern ports at Cape Town and Durban, and important port facilities at Port Elizabeth and East London. The new maritime headquarters near West Lake in the Cape Peninsula are equipped with a modern sophisticated communication system capable of communicating with any point on the globe; it will also be in continuous communication with auxiliary headquarters in Durban and Walvis Bay.

Should the West adopt the indicated strategy and decide to

establish an adequate maritime presence in the Indian and South Atlantic Oceans, it would immediately be faced with the problem of the immense costs involved. The maintenance of a maritime force at sea for an extended period of time and at a great distance from port facilities is a difficult and costly operation.

The concept that a modern fleet does not require bases in the operational area is only partially valid. It could apply in the case of a conventional war, and, to a certain extent, in the case of maritime operations in a nuclear war. It is, however, unrealistic when applied to the modern indirect strategy of sustained tension and protracted wars of low intensity. It is not valid for maintaining a presence, or for blockading operations, far from the home base. Approximately four ships are required to ensure that one is permanently on station. Long, continuous periods of deployment at sea tend to erode the morale of the crew; shuttle cruises to relieve the crews and to replenish supplies are expensive. Aircraft carriers have the advantage of being able to provide continuous air cover for units of the fleet, but they are very expensive substitutes for land bases, especially when long range reconnaissance missions are involved. All these disadvantages contribute to the fact that the efficiency of a given maritime force operating away from its home base over a period of time is reduced by 60 to 80 per cent. Western planners and policy-makers are aware of the need for land bases as a prerequisite of an effective presence in the South Atlantic and Indian Oceans. Most of them, however, are still inhibited by the present political climate, to the extent that they flinch away from the very thought of involving the White governments of southern Africa in the regional defence.

One must conclude that the West, owing to political pressure, is not prepared to adopt a preventative strategy by means of establishing a prior presence. Hence they are predestined to a strategy of reaction: and such a strategy is apt to be counter-productive.

Conclusions

It would be more appropriate in this context to use the designation "strategic policy" rather than "strategy", since the West is called upon to face a protracted war of low intensity in which victory cannot be achieved by a single devastating action, but which requires a sustained preparedness with the capability of immediate response to enemy initiatives of varied intensity over a wide front. The term "response" (or reaction) is indicative of the fact that the initiative rests with the enemy. This is so, because, in general terms, the West is protecting the status quo in evolution, while the Communists are spreading revolution. The demoralising conclusion emerging from these considerations is that a local victory does not constitute a positive advance for the West – nor a shattering defeat for the enemy. The only valid defensive strategy for us in the present situation is to present a viable front, resisting infiltration and subversion, and to ensure an effective prior presence at vulnerable points so as to deny the enemy the opportunity of achieving local successes by means of blackmail, intimidation or the use of limited force, without the risk of confrontation and escalation. This predicates the need for a deterrent element in our strategy. Furthermore, the political and geographic composition of the Southern Hemisphere would appear to favour the employment of maritime forces as the most feasible means of achieving the desired presence.

There are three separate, but complementary and interacting, levels on which a strategy for the Southern Hemisphere should be considered.

The first is the domestic level. If the component parts are unsound, one can hardly expect a sound whole. Therefore each state concerned must ensure the inviolability of its territory and the maintenance of internal law and order. This imposes heavy demands on every state. We must be prepared and willing to defend ourselves, because no nation which is not prepared to give the utmost for its own security can expect alliance with, or assistance from, another. Furthermore we must be morally viable, and foster this viability, otherwise the nation's motivation is liable to become attenuated, and its will to resist will be eroded. At the same time we must ensure the maintenance of social progress and development in all fields of the community.

In the world of today no state can exist in isolation. This applies no less to major powers. Besides the interdependence of states in the areas of economics, industry and commerce, the power struggle between East and West and the ideological trends, which are no respecters of frontiers, must also be taken into account. The forming of *blocs*, alliances and trade organisations is not a freak of modern society: they are vital necessities of our time. The viability of a state, therefore, is determined to a large extent by international relations. South Africa, in this respect, finds itself in a particularly invidious position. Because of our geographic contiguity with decolonised Black Africa, the ethnological composition of our population, and our conservative way of life, we have become the target *par excellence* for the application of double standards on the international level. As a consequence our defensive task is exacerbated by the need to combat this prejudice, and by the exertions required to convince at least Western opinion and Black African states of the sincerity of our intentions and the validity of our policy. This task demands the participation of government and governed alike, and this, too, demands volition and sacrifice.

In the regional context it is important that the highest degree of cooperation is achieved amongst the countries concerned. In the Southern Hemisphere this cooperation must obviously extend to states having common interests in the region. A certain degree of liaison in the maritime and other fields is already operative. The South African Navy takes part from time to time in limited exercises in which, for example, units of the British and Argentine Navies participate, and it pays courtesy calls on countries in this region. In addition there is significant cooperation in respect of scientific expeditions to the Antarctic. This cooperation is important and efforts should be made to promote and to elaborate it within the framework of the defence of the Southern Hemisphere. No matter how close the cooperation amongst the states in this region, however, it is unlikely that they could effectively provide mutual support by means of the employment of their combined forces outside their respective continents – with the possible exception of operations on a reduced scale in neighbouring islands. The situation in respect of mutual support in maritime operations, however, is somewhat different. Admittedly none of the states concerned would, in the normal course of events, be capable of employing significant naval forces in direct support of a distant ally. On the other hand, coordinated action, especially in maritime reconnaissance and intelligence, could make a major contribution to common defence in the Southern Hemisphere. This could ensure that virtually all activities of enemy surface units in the South Atlantic and Indian Oceans could be kept under surveillance, that surprise attacks are obviated and that, with the benefit of up-to-date intelligence, limited combined maritime operations could be mounted. The combined maritime capability of the countries in the Southern Hemisphere, however, remains limited in terms of time and space, and therefore inadequate to withstand a large-scale enemy infiltration or invasion. A regional treaty or alliance is an excellent goal, and should be pursued with vigour, but in the long term this can only serve as an intermediate objective to the final aim.

This brings us to the third dimension of the strategy, the need for a Super-power to be involved. The signs of our time are global conflict and global strategy. We are part of a game of chess between Super-powers in which the concepts of "local" and "regional" have relative values only – values eventually determined by the global conflict. I have already referred to the deterrent role of nuclear stability in the current global strategy employed by the Communist powers, and to the Communist threats in the Southern Hemisphere. A strategy for the Southern Hemisphere must counter these Communist threats. In the final analysis it is a prerequisite for the successful defence of the Southern Hemisphere that the deterrent strategy based on nuclear terror and fear of escalation should also be applicable in this region. The USA has already on occasion demonstrated that the Monroe doctrine is still in force and that she will not tolerate outside interference in the affairs of Latin America; her interests in the Pacific and South-East Asia could also be taken as a reasonable assurance for the defence of Indonesia and Australasia. It is only southern Africa and its surrounding ocean areas, therefore, that are deprived of this deterrent umbrella and where there is a vacuum in Western prior presence.

Our task is clear. We must secure our own territory and ensure domestic order, and we must promote good neighbourliness and friendly relations with Africa and the countries in the Southern Hemisphere. We must persuade the West that Communist penetration into the Southern Hemisphere is a direct threat to Western Europe and to the rest of the Free World. As soon as the West realises the seriousness of this threat, it will also realise that it cannot effectively counter the threat without the cooperation and the supporting capabilities of the Republic of South Africa.

Admiral Biermann wrote an article in January 1975 for the Journal of Social and Political Affairs, *from which the following paragraphs are taken:*

The Republic of South Africa views with considerable misgiving the apparent tilting of the balance of power against the West and therefore in favour of the East. This tilt can be discerned in the Communist victories in South Vietnam and Cambodia, the slide to the left in Portugal and Italy, the weakening of NATO's south-eastern flank, the ever-growing strength of the Warsaw Pact forces, the constantly expanding Russian Navy, and, nearer to home, the change in the regional balance of power brought about by Portugal's withdrawal from Angola and Mozambique....

... Early in 1974 observers noted that: "The standard Soviet line has been, and continues to be, that 'the real alignment of forces in the world arena' has shifted against the US and has left US leaders with no choice but 'to concern themselves with ensuring that foreign policy objectives, methods, and the doctrines for achieving them, are proportionate to dwindling (US) resources.' "
Since then the Communist camp has notched up some very significant successes and feels that the balance of power has moved irreversibly in their favour to the extent that they have now achieved a considerable freedom of action in pursuing their goals.

It is quite clear to the Republic of South Africa that the Soviet naval build-up in the Indian Ocean is part of the Soviet long-term strategy for world domination. Whilst the significance of this build-up was for a long time either denied or ignored by the West, there are fortunately positive indications that this is changing. President Ford, in May 1975, said: "... We must take into account some dramatic changes in the global balance of power.... There is no doubt about it. The Soviet Union understands the importance of seapower. The Russians built up their navy while we permitted ours to shrink, and they know how to show their flag."

President Ford's words were happily backed up by action, in that the decision to go ahead with US naval facilities on the British island of Diego Garcia surmounted the various obstacles which have been strewn in its path. It is nevertheless a sad commentary that the infinitely superior naval facilities at Simonstown, which could have been placed at the disposal of the US, have not, for political reasons, been taken advantage of.

The British too, appreciate the significance of the Russian Indian Ocean build-up, but this has had to be said by the Leader of the Opposition, Mrs Thatcher, since it could not be said by the Government after their decision formally to abrogate the Simonstown agreement. The French, who have always been very pragmatic in these matters, are clearly aware of the Soviets' maritime aims and, in spite of their rapidly shrinking Indian Ocean naval facilities, contrive to show the flag as often and as powerfully as they can.

The Russian Indian Ocean presence — first established in 1968 — has no doubt a number of aims in the maritime strategy of the

Soviet Union. One aim is probably to keep its Communist partner, China, under surveillance from the southern flank. Another – having consideration for the Soviet naval and military build-up round the "Horn of Africa" and in the Persian Gulf area (and in conjunction with its Mediterranean naval strength) – is the control of the Suez Canal and the Red Sea, and the control of the Middle East's oil upon which most of the West depends. Her third main aim would be related to the political influence which can be achieved by the use of seapower. Admiral Gorshkov, Chief of the Soviet Navy and Deputy Minister of Defence, has referred to "the special features of the Navy as a military factor which can be used in peacetime for purposes of demonstrating the economic and military might of states beyond their borders and which is capable of protecting the interests of a country beyond its borders".

Contrary to popular belief, South Africa is not so much concerned about the military aims of the USSR's Indian Ocean, presence, as about its political and ideological aims. It is not, for example, anticipated that the Soviet Navy would risk a confrontation with the West by physical interference with tanker traffic or other merchant shipping in any situation short of war. What South Africa is concerned about is the gradual but steady infiltration of the African continent by both the main Communist powers and by their satellites, using the "freedom from colonialism" and Black-White hatred themes as stalking horses from behind which they can move in and spread their influence.

It is gratifying to see that the South African view is confirmed from other quarters. Speaking in February 1975 at the Royal United Services Institute, Admiral Means Johnston Jr, US Navy, Commander-in-Chief, Allied Forces Southern Europe, said of the threat as he saw it: "While recognising its dynamic and multifaceted qualities, I believe it is principally a Soviet political threat with which we must be concerned today ..." He goes on to observe that indices of Soviet interest and design are readily evident not only in the Eastern Mediterranean area but in the African littorals, and points out that the substantial Russian naval presence in the Indian Ocean provides an imposing military potential which is quite at odds with the Soviets' vocal endorsement of the Indian Ocean as a zone of peace. He concludes by observing that expanding Soviet seapower poses a whole series of challenges to NATO's southern region and beyond.

For South Africa to be seen in the defence context against this background of global conflict, it is necessary therefore to see her

91

as playing a positive role in the fundamental struggle between East and West, between the two great social systems of Communism and Capitalism. This role is manifested by South Africa's geographical situation, Western orientation, uncompromising stand against Communism, her long history of sound government and stability, her economic and industrial strength, her highly developed communications system of ports, airfields, roads and railways and the strength of her armed forces.

THE ECONOMIC DIMENSION

Major-General D. H. V. Buckle

Major-General D. H. V. Buckle CB, CBE was born in Cape Town in 1902. He served in the British Army for thirty-five years in Malaya, China, Ceylon, north-west Europe, Egypt and Cyprus. He was Chief Administrative Officer to the Allied Commander-in-Chief in the Suez Campaign 1956 and Major-General in charge of Administration, Middle East Land Forces, 1956–1958. He was ADC to King George VI and Queen Elizabeth II, 1950–1953, and Colonel Commandant, Royal Army Service Corps, 1959–1964. After retirement from the Army his appointments included: Director of United Kingdom – South Africa Trade Association, 1965–1968, and administrative member of Southern Africa Committee of the British National Export Council. He has been resident in Cape Town since 1968.

THE WESTERN countries have a giant investment and two-way trade stake in the Republic of South Africa. According to the latest South African Reserve Bank census, foreign countries' investments in South Africa total R10,380 million. Of that total, the European Economic Community owned 64 per cent, remaining European countries 9 per cent and North and South America 17 per cent. Direct foreign investment at the end of 1973 was R5,616 million, of which R5,451 million was invested in the private sector. Indirect investment was assessed at R4,764 million, of which R3,712 million was in the private sector. Foreign investment in South Africa was distributed among activities in the following proportions:

Manufacturing	39.7 per cent
Finance, insurance, real estate and business services	24.9 per cent
Mining and quarrying	14.7 per cent
Wholesale, retail and accommodation	11.3 per cent
Electricity, gas and water	3.6 per cent
Transport, storage and communication	2.0 per cent
Other activities	3.8 per cent

The natural mineral resources of the Republic, together with those of South-West Africa and Angola, are of prime importance to the Western World, and the waters around South Africa's coasts carry a large proportion of the West's vital supplies. The Republic could emerge as an agricultural supply base for much of the African continent.

Although it occupies only 0.6 per cent of the continent and only 15 per cent of the country is arable, South Africa produces 20 per cent of the African continent's agricultural output.

Vast irrigation projects now under construction and scientific methods of agriculture are increasing this output. The Republic will be capable, in the future, of feeding her rapidly growing population and will still have surpluses for export to less developed African countries.

Her principal agricultural assets are maize and other cereals, wool, sugar, fruit and fish with their associated products. She is currently a major exporter of all these commodities.

Owing to her range of climate and soil conditions, crops normally produced in the temperate or sub-tropical zones will thrive.

The difficulty will be to prevent further drift from country to cities and towns, of both management and labour, Black and White, and indeed to encourage an increase in the agricultural community. This problem will be particularly acute because of the pressure to expand in every field of the economy.

Finally South African skills and economic power are essential to the development of much of Black Africa, in whose natural resources the West has also a vital interest.

In fact the economic importance of South Africa to the West is not in dispute, except in fanatical ideological circles. There has always been agreement on the desirability of separating economic interests from political objections. The problem has been to decide how far it is possible to pursue this pragmatism without forfeiting too many votes.

Strategic and economic importance are inextricably connected. But the strategic aspects of the Republic's importance have, in the past, been controversial. Many tended to think very narrowly in the context of Simonstown, neglecting the importance of the whole complex of the Republic's infrastructure and of its resources, because of the political difficulties involved. However the Angolan War and its aftermath, including the infiltration of Soviet influence in Mozambique, have confirmed and accentuated it. Western nations now perceive that stability in South Africa is the key to stability in southern Africa.

The Question of Confidence

During the early critical months of 1976, a large number of prominent industrialists from many Western countries visited South Africa in connection with their existing or projected interests. The great majority expressed confidence in their investments or plans for investment despite the turbulent conditions in bordering countries and the internal political problems which have to be tackled.

Also of interest are the latest available immigration figures. The number for 1975 was 50,000, the largest ever recorded. In January 1976 over 6,000 arrived, compared with 3,600 in January 1975. In particular the numbers of managerial and professional immigrants are noticeably increasing.

The situation is really not remarkable considering the threats around the world, in the Middle East, in the Far East affecting Australasia, in South America and indeed in Western Europe with the superiority of Russian military strength and the internal instability of many NATO countries. The South African Government's handling of all its recent problems, with one exception at an exceptionally difficult juncture, has been cool, calculated and helpful to the West.

In South-West Africa, there are signs of acceleration towards a possibly acceptable situation. In the Republic itself there is slow progress, some frustration but increasing pressure for change from quarters which count.

It is hard to look ahead with complete confidence in the future security of the majority of countries and areas in the world today. It is a matter of comparison and calculation on the number of years' assurance which one's capital investment demands. For example, people are still investing in Hong Kong.

It is worthwhile examining some of the attractions and safeguards which induce and, I believe, will continue to induce Western investment in the Republic.

The South African Government favours foreign investment. It encourages but does not insist on local participation. Although there are restrictions on the repatriation of capital, earnings on investments can be freely withdrawn and these are, on the whole, highly satisfactory. Foreign companies are taxed on exactly the same basis as local companies. Despite recent increases, taxes are still among the lowest in the world. Unlike many others, the South African Government is wedded to the capitalist system and will not enter any field of endeavour providing private enterprise is available and can effectively handle it.

As regards the future, by the year 2000 the Republic's population may well have grown from twenty-one to fifty million. The Black and Brown population, which will predominantly cause the growth, are yearly earning more money, and, as their education improves, the quality and quantity of the goods they demand will grow.

The urge to develop the full potential of the economy will force the Republic to expand all its basic services including transport facilities, telecommunications, electricity and water supply. Secondary manufacturing industries to provide for the growing population will also have to be undertaken and experts believe that there will be a faster growth in the mining industry than in any other.

Like most countries, South Africa is suffering from severe inflation and a balance of payments problem. The former disease she caught rather late from her trading partners and the latter trouble is mainly due to an over-confidence in the rising price of gold which induced lavish public spending and a failure to develop her export trade. Now that recovery in the Western World is on its way and the hard facts of life have been brought home to her business community, there is reason to hope that 1977 will see the beginning of a return to her long-term prosperity.

Included in any assessment of justification for confidence in the Republic must be a consideration of her internal political strengths and weaknesses. Essentially South Africa's future depends upon whether she can adjust her internal policies to convince all her peoples that South African society is worth defending.

Despite serious weaknesses and warts in the separate development policy, it has had one undeniable success. Over the past twenty-five years, it has trained up a generation of Black and Brown politicians and administrators. By reason of their appointments, however limited their responsibilities may have been, Black and Brown politicians have been given a platform from which they can publicise their views and exert pressures, both through the media and increasingly in direct contact with White Ministers and civil servants. They have become national personalities who are generally accepted in all national activities – in Associations, in seminars, as lecturers and socially at their own level.

But before weaknesses and warts can be eliminated and meaningful negotiations between White, Black and Brown leaders can take place, it is essential that there should be a very high degree of accord and consensus between the two White groups.

The antics in the House of Assembly, where an overwhelmingly strong and entrenched Nationalist party plays at politics with two weak and squabbling oppositions, have become irrelevant to the future of the Republic. Some kind of reorientation of parties is certain to occur which may well influence relations between the Afrikaans- and English-speaking groups.

It would be a gross exaggeration to suggest that there is hostility between them, but there is still mistrust. Apart from the legacy of South Africa's eventful and turbulent history, there are a number of reasons for this sad state of affairs.

Nationalist Ministers and Members of Parliament are almost exclusively Afrikaans and, although there are many Afrikaans Members in the two opposition parties (particularly in the United Party), they tend to be regarded by the majority of their group as

97

renegades. The attitudes of the two groups to the Rule of Law and Security are completely at variance. This fundamental difference is, of course, the result of history and background.

The separation of the two groups throughout their school and University education (despite some minor mixing at Stellenbosch and Port Elizabeth) is a symptom of mistrust and a bar to closer understanding. As a corollary, the living areas of the two groups in the cities are largely separate.

The very nature of political debate in the White House of Assembly adds fuel to the embers of mistrust. The points on which the opposition parties (particularly the Progressive-Reformists) mount their attacks coincide with overseas attacks. The opposition criticism and "disclosures" must be emphatic and highly coloured to be politically effective. These are naturally prominently reported and commented on by the English-language press and used to effect by overseas critics.

The opposition parties (and again particularly the "Prog-Refs") are obviously pressing for approximately the same things as the Blacks and Browns are demanding. So the Nationalist Afrikaner accuses his English-speaking (or "renegade" Afrikaner) political opponent of a lack of patriotism, of undermining confidence and encouraging subversion.

Another cause for mistrust is the hesitation of many British immigrants who have been here for more than the five years necessary to take South African nationality. I believe one of the main reasons for their hesitation is the extreme limitation on travel imposed by a South African passport. Except for very special reasons dual nationality does not entitle a citizen to possess two passports.

But the mistrust is far from being one-sided. The English-speaker realises that, for one reason and another, he no longer has any direct influence in the government of the country and that he is unlikely to have any as long as the present White political line-up persists. For a comparatively short but very unpleasant period, he was blatantly discriminated against in the country's Permanent Defence and Public Services (as indeed the Afrikaner was prior to 1948). Consequently his participation in these has since been minimal, except in the Navy, which has a long British tradition. Despite encouragement to participate, he finds himself isolated in professions which are predominantly Afrikaans. As one English-speaker who is a post-graduate in an Afrikaans University said to me, "I get on excellently here in all my student activities, but I want to live my life in my own group, however many Afrikaan friends I have." Not a bad advertisement for separate development!

The expansion of National Service in the Defence Force, the accentuation of common danger and the economic hardships which all Whites will have to share in the immediate future may combine to shorten the time required for the healing process, providing some extreme crisis does not spark off a White reactionary backlash. The most effective hastener would, in my opinion, be a system of combined secondary and higher education for the two White groups, whatever the attendant but temporary drawbacks and setbacks might be.

Many Afrikaans leaders in the industrial, professional, academic and ecclesiastical worlds are pleading for the kind of changes which most English-speaking South Africans feel to be essential. Several Afrikaans-language newspapers have joined in these pressures and certain Nationalist Ministers and backbenchers are spelling out the need clearly enough.

As yet, action is halting. No Nationalist Prime Minister would seriously risk dividing the Afrikaans *Volk*, but I am convinced these pressures are gradually producing a climate in which the Nationalist leaders, who are themselves convinced of the need for change, can take the necessary action without that risk.

Deadlock between the Labour Party representing the majority of Cape Coloureds and the Government persists, although there is some dissension within the party between those who want to negotiate and the militant majority. Sonny Leon, the anti-cooperation leader, is reported to be a sick man. The opposition Federal Party wants to negotiate on the basis of a Coloured Cabinet linked to the White Cabinet proposed by the Prime Minister. The long-awaited recommendations of the Government-appointed Theron Commission on the Coloured problem have only been partially accepted. The most important and far-reaching recommendations were rejected.

Indian evolutionary problems are similar to those of the Cape Coloureds, but the Indian community is closer, more advanced, and more fortunate materially than that of the Coloureds. It has stronger traditions behind it. The Indians of whatever religion and race regard themselves as essentially South African and take advantage of their Indian Council to press their aims. Recently there has been talk of closer cooperation between the Coloured and Indian Representative Councils. The future of both groups is

99

inevitably bound together with the Whites.

One factor which is, to put it mildly, imperfectly understood in the Western World is the degree of difference in the interest and outlook between the various colour and ethnic groups of the Black and Brown populations.

Vocal political elements among the Brown peoples (in particular the Coloureds) are apt to claim partnership and ideological empathy with the Blacks when facing up to White supremacy. But, in fact, any idea of Black control of South Africa is, and with reason, terrifying to them. Furthermore, the differences between the outlooks of, for example, Chief Matanzima of the Transkei, Chief Mangope of Boputhoswana and Chief Buthelezi of Kwa-Zulu have been well publicised in the Western press. At lower and less instructed levels, the tribal faction fights in places where the various tribes are brought together, especially in the mines, are relevant.

Matanzima has a reasonably consolidated territory which can be administered. Mangope and Buthelezi's Homelands are hopelessly fragmented. Mangope has asked for independence but Buthelezi has not. From the Government angle Buthelezi is the *enfant terrible*.

Ignoring moral rights and wrongs, these basic differences do tend to balance the differences in the White camp to which I have referred. They also complicate negotiation.

As regards the "illegal" and admittedly subversive African organisations, the African National Congress is manipulated by the Eastern European Communist world and the PAC by China, a situation which is hardly calculated to produce unity in militant African opposition. The internal troubles of the ANC with regard to Rhodesia and in SWAPO have also been exhaustively covered in the Western press.

In South Africa, the ANC is more active than PAC and probably slightly less wedded to Communism. Its influence is mainly among the Urban Blacks in White areas, although its external leadership has claimed that its influence will be felt in the Transkei and other Homelands once they have attained independence.

Both ANC and PAC were banned by the Republican Government in 1960. It was not until 1970 that the "Black Peoples Convention" emerged. Since then, this very radical organisation has held "Annual Conventions", and the last one at Kingwilliamstown in the Eastern Cape was extremely outspoken.

However the Government is unlikely to ban it. Their experience has probably taught them that banning merely sends people underground and that it is better to recognise and watch.

The Transkei

The very recent independence of the Transkei is certain to have its effects on confidence once the extent and nature of its independence become apparent. Prime Minister Matanzima has announced that his country will be a non-racial state in which anyone irrespective of colour or country of origin will be eligible for citizenship on application, providing he gives the country his loyalty. He has refused to accept the Pretoria Severance Act as applicable in his country. Only the Transkei's population, including its migrant workers, will be automatic citizens. Those who live in South Africa and have no roots in the Transkei will have the right to choose Transkeian citizenship if they want it. He has also made it clear that, as long as Transkeians have no rights to property ownership in the Republic, Whites cannot expect them in his country. Although welcoming Whites to help his country, they will have to sell their land to his Government and rent it back again. He has announced his intention of repealing all laws in his constitution which are repugnant, including the immorality and mixed marriages acts. Although Transkei is dependent upon the Republic economically, its dependence is no greater than that of many African states and its potentialities are better than those of many other independent countries. Matanzima's behaviour since independence is certainly not that of a puppet. Maintenance of this independence will depend on his continued internal authority and his ability to convince outside opinion in Africa and overseas that investment and technical help is worthwhile as a guarantee of genuine independence. Meanwhile, pressures of all kinds, including those from the heart of Afrikanerdom, are forcing the South African Government step by step to alter their attitude towards permanent Black dwellers in the White areas.

South-West Africa

The solution of the South-West African (or "Namibian") problem is a priority if bloodshed is to be avoided and confidence maintained. The Western countries associate themselves with the United Nations and the OAU in a refusal to accept any solution which fragments the territory.

Constitutional talks have for some time been proceeding in

Windhoek, attended by representatives from all the National Groups in this very multi-racial territory; from the independent territory of Ovamboland (by far the largest entity) on the borders of Angola, from the Ovambos, Kavangos, Damaras, Hereroes and Bushmen in the northern half of the territory, and from the Basters (mixed racial group) and the Hottentots in the south. The very fact that representatives of all these peoples are discussing matters comparatively amicably around a table with the White group seems no mean achievement to anyone who has travelled in that country, even a few years ago. But this is all geographical representation and none of the Black political parties is represented at the talks.

In particular the South-West African Peoples Organisation (SWAPO), which the United Nations and the Organisation of African Unity regard as the legitimate successor government of "Namibia", is excluded. This organisation is split into an internal faction and various feuding external factions, now attempting, so far without success, to reconcile their difficulties with the help of Kaunda in Lusaka. Several of their representatives have been taken into "protective custody" there. The internal section is allegedly not in favour of violence. It has its major influence among Ovambos and is therefore suspect by the other groups. However, although its following in other parts of the territory is problematical and will remain so unless elections are held, it is certainly the biggest political party. There is also no doubt that, if an agreement was reached without their participation, the new government, whatever its nature, would be subjected to external attack and internal subversion. Mr Vorster has announced that he would not oppose any proposal from the Conference for talks with SWAPO or an inclusion of its representatives. His attitude has always been that it is for the various groups to decide on their future and on the methods of arriving at their decisions, even though his personal inclination is still to exclude an organisation which he inherently mistrusts.

It seems to me that, once the national groups can agree on the substance of a constitution among themselves, an approach must and will be made to the internal leadership of SWAPO.

Conclusions on Confidence
Despite the complexity of her internal problems and the weight of external hostility and pressures, the Republic's long record of comparative economic and political stability cannot be

discounted, nor should the extent of racial goodwill be minimised, any more than the injustices and the bitterness. Black and Brown leaders are far from insensitive to the tragic results of so-called successful violence in Mozambique and Angola and, so long as they can see signs of movement away from discrimination and towards genuine negotiation on Urban African, Coloured and Indian problems, I believe they are sufficiently far-seeing (and self-interested) to prefer gradual change to violent revolution and chaos.

I also believe – and have always believed – that the West can help by active cooperation and diplomatic persuasion, whereas continuous condemnation and attempts to interfere can only frustrate and delay progress. In a very confused situation it seems to many South Africans that the Angolan affair has gone some way to convince the West that cooperation with the Republic in the solution of southern Africa's problems is essential, that "Majority Rule" seems a doubtful formula in the light of what has happened in most other African countries, and that its implementation without violence and resultant economic chaos in Africa is at least unlikely.

All these considerations suggest that confidence in South Africa is justifiable, assuming that the critical threat in Rhodesia can be averted and the South-West African problem resolved.

Effects of Marxist States in the area
The influence of the appearance of Marxist régimes in neighbouring states on the indigenous populations of the Republic has to some extent already been covered.

Initially when the Lisbon revolt led to Portuguese evacuation from Mozambique and Angola, the impact must have been traumatic to the Black peoples of South Africa. To them, Black "victory" over the colonial White man on their borders must have spelt the beginning of the end of White supremacy in Africa, particularly when the mounting pressures on White-governed Rhodesia were noted. They must have felt that their bargaining position was immensely strengthened by the threats of force from across the South African borders. But as the drama subsided and they observed developments, it is probable that, particularly among the Homeland leaders approaching independence, there was a more sober appraisal of the future. The frightful slaughters in Angola, followed by a foreign invasion, the harsh dictatorship and consequent unrest in Mozambique and the chaotic economic conditions in both countries, caused largely by the wholesale exodus of the Whites, has been observed and no doubt compared with the plums of office peacefully handed to them. But it is the potentially stateless or virtually stateless Blacks in the townships who are obviously most liable to be influenced by the heady calls for freedom born out of the barrel of a gun. The proximity of these Marxist-oriented states must inevitably facilitate subversive infiltration.

The influence of these threats on the White population is much harder to assess and no generalisation can be realistic. Those who have been pleading for change in both groups have been convinced of the added urgency of doing what they press for. Some of those who were adamantly against change are seeing the red light and wavering. Some Nationalists now speak up in parliament and elsewhere in public to advocate measures they would have decried before the Portuguese collapse and the Rhodesian crisis. A number of recent immigrants and some South African-born English-speakers, particularly those with young children, are showing signs of escapism. The majority of Trade Unionists are still more frightened of losing their jobs to Blacks than they are of the political results of failing to train and accept them as skilled and supervising partners. Finally there are those who live in isolated areas, who do not understand what is happening and do not contemplate a change in their way of life. I am certain, however, that inroads are gradually being made in the reactionary sections of the population, and that already there is a definite majority in the White population which realises the necessity for change and would accept it from its present leaders.

In these complex times, and particularly in Black Africa, so much will depend on the extent and probable duration of the "domination" and in the type of "Communism" involved. Basically the aim of most emergent Black leaders is nationalistic and help in realising their aims is welcome from any source. Because revolt against foreign or minority rule is essentially Left and militant, the contacts of potential leaders who take refuge, and are educated, overseas are inevitably on the far Left, and thus Marxist ideology naturally becomes a major tool in their political campaigns. If material assistance is made available from a Communist power, this ideology becomes at least temporarily inescapable. But personal power and nationalism are, in most cases, predominant aims.

The problems which face such men when they assume power

can be seen very clearly in Mozambique and Angola. The economy is in ruins, they are faced by hostile elements and they have no knowledge or experience of large-scale administration. They are therefore in no position to embark immediately on further external military adventures nor can they afford to endanger their own essential economic interests. The closing of the Rhodesian border and the declaration of a "state of war" by Samora Machel is no exception to this general rule. In this case, Machel had the backing of the United Nations and the Commonwealth because of the "illegality" of the Smith régime. Furthermore Mozambique's internal situation was so unstable that some kind of "patriotic" appeal to the emotions of his dissidents was urgently necessary.

It would therefore be possible for Communist-inspired Black Nationalist governments to live amicably with a South African government which was well on the way to solving the South-West African problem and was seen to be moving towards policies acceptable to its own Black and Brown populations.

Should Angola become directly and effectively dominated by Russians, their control of its mineral wealth and the threat of their control of the mineral wealth of the whole of southern Africa could hardly be accepted by the West when combined with the strategic threats to shipping in the South Atlantic from Angola and to the Indian Ocean from Mozambique.

As I write, Mozambique seems to be moving further towards internal unrest and economic chaos and further into Soviet control, as Samora Machel and his Government become increasingly insecure. However, it suits Machel to remain, at least temporarily, on pragmatic terms with the Republic and relations are at present impeccably correct and mutually advantageous. But the reports of businessmen visiting the country are the reverse of reassuring regarding conditions there and its future. The effects of having lost almost one hundred per cent of the White population with their "know-how" are a warning to the Blacks in Rhodesia, but not one which is likely to be heeded by the ANC.

A Cuban withdrawal from Angola, if genuine and Russian-inspired, could have an adverse effect on South Africa, should it remove the fear of Marxist colonial interference. It could halt the recent American move towards cooperation with the Republic on southern African problems. Another imponderable is the ability of UNITA seriously to embarrass the present Angolan Government.

So far as Rhodesia is concerned, now that talks with Nkomo have broken down, Russian dominance could be established, given the will to dominate. Russia has however denied any interest in that country. If there is a reunited ANC uprising against the Whites or factional tribal warfare, it is difficult to imagine an absence of interference from outside. The West would then be faced with a tricky political problem and so would the Republic.

There is one particular danger to the Republic entailed in any serious threats from across her borders, and Russia is obviously well aware of it. South Africa cannot afford to keep proportionately large bodies of troops mobilised for any length of time. The absence of management material and skilled labour would jeopardise the economy, the strength of which has for so long been responsible for maintaining peaceful conditions among her Black and Brown population. For the same reason she cannot continue year after year to increase her military expenditure, even though that would be a help with any unemployment problem which might arise.

Some people are beginning to think that the build-up of Russian naval and military forces is so great that the Soviet Government, which may be facing serious effects from the two-year grain famine and dissident elements, will not be able to avoid using them. Are Solzhenitsyn and various American personalities right in thinking that Russia is now preparing for a non-nuclear or even a nuclear war? Should this situation arise, even South Africa's sins would be temporarily forgotten, and when, if ever, the world re-emerged from chaos, those sins would no longer exist!

Avoidance of Conflict

What are the chances of creating conditions within the Republic which would avoid conflict with Marxist-oriented neighbours?

Although Angola and Mozambique are both considerably dependent economically on South Africa, as would be a Black Rhodesia, there will always be deep-seated hostility and potential danger from guerrilla activity so long as there is a dissatisfied Black population in the South. White politics in the Republic are becoming ever less relevant to future events. The two opposition parties are at each other's throats. The United Party is disunited and indeterminate. The Progressive-Reform Party's policies and opportunist composition have no appeal to the Afrikaner and little to many English-speaking voters. The effects of their pressures on the Government are therefore reduced, although valuable when added to those of the English-language press, sections of the Afrikaans press, Afrikaans academics and businessmen and organisations such as the South Africa Foundation and the Institute of Race Relations.

The last Annual Report by the Director-General of the South Africa Foundation, an increasingly influential organisation whose trustees and members are drawn from the highest level of all race groups, all professions and callings and all political persuasions, contains the following impressive passage:

> We believe that the average White in this country has no conception of the depth of resentment that is felt by Blacks in the rest of Africa about the colour discrimination in South Africa, which they see as a totally inexcusable insult to Black people everywhere.
> The foundation sees it as a duty to convey these attitudes to White South Africans in whose hands total political power is still held.
> They must know that without adjustments to changing conditions the ultimate obstacle to better international relations for their country will remain.

The Black and Brown leaders are gaining in experience and influence as the result of the separate development machinery which the Government itself has created. The future will be decided by direct consultation between the Government and those leaders. The Government could obtain a mandate in the House of Assembly, with the aid of the opposition parties, for any reasonable progressive action it might contemplate. But it would not be prepared to do this at the expense of splitting the National Party and Afrikanerdom. The question therefore is how far it can go without that risk.

A retired Afrikaans High Court judge has recently suggested that there is now far more support for the most urgently needed measures than is generally realised. He recommended that a referendum should be held on compulsory free education for all races up to a certain age, complete removal of all discriminatory legislation regarding racial employment and rates of pay, votes for the Coloureds on a phased programme, full home ownership for permanent Urban Blacks and the establishment of an all-racial "Parliament of Debate". He believed the result of such a referendum would be favourable. A recent poll conducted suggested that a majority of Whites now favour closer relations between the White and Coloured communities.

All that can be said with certainty is that pressures from within the White, Black and Brown populations will rapidly increase and, combined with outside pressure and economic influences, will ultimately prove irresistible.

As regards South-West Africa, present signs indicate an appreciation by all concerned in that territory of the urgency of decisions on a constitution which will give birth to an independent territory, capable of surviving tribal and political antagonisms. The problem of whether the internal branch of SWAPO should be drawn into the discussions is contentious and akin to problems of this kind in Rhodesia. The South African Prime Minister does not favour this course but has clearly stated that he would not oppose it if it is recommended to him by South-West Africans.

The future of southern Africa depends on how far Russia is prepared to go with interference and infiltration in that part of the continent in furtherance of her long quest for world domination. Unknown factors are her ability to control the vast military machine she has built and is still building up, the extent of economic troubles and dissensions within her own borders and the degree of success or failure in her subversive campaigns.

Obviously, if the Politburo is still in control and its subversive efforts are meeting with success, it will not wish to embark on large-scale military adventures. But should things go the wrong way for her in Portugal, Italy, France and Britain, and if internal troubles, such as the two-year grain harvest failure, should lead to unrest, the decision might be quite different.

The position of China has also to be considered. Presumably she is not yet ready to try conclusions with the Soviet Union. For Russia, if a clash has to come, it would be to her advantage if it were early. But she would not want to take on China and the West, however unprepared, together. That situation might conceivably arise if she were to precipitate a major struggle in Africa, which would almost certainly spread to the Middle East and ultimately become global.

Nearer home, a peaceful settlement of the Rhodesian problem and the ability of the Republic to disengage herself creditably from South-West Africa and to gain the confidence of all her racial groups could be vital factors.

Conclusions
If South Africa's stability can be maintained, her considerable economic importance to the West will increase. The South African industrial and communications complex is itself of great

strategic importance, in fact, an area which will have to be denied to an enemy of the West, particularly as its resources and skills are essential to the development of Black Africa, in which the West has a big stake.

Providing Black Marxist-oriented governments on her borders are not directly controlled and actively supported by Moscow, and providing the Republic can be seen to be making definite progress towards self-government in South-West Africa as well as towards conditions within her own borders acceptable to all South Africa's peoples, stability can be maintained.

If Russia decides to equip and actively support Black African states in military adventures outside their own borders, it will probably mean that she is preparing for major war, whether nuclear or non-nuclear. In that case, the West can hardly fail to become involved in southern Africa. Even if Russia gained control of Angola's mineral wealth and threatened the mineral wealth of other southern African states while dominating the sea routes round southern Africa, the West could hardly stand aside.

The hazards of stepping up military aggression will probably discourage Russia, historically and understandably scared of major war, from such a course. However it is possible that the disturbing build-up of military strength, combined with internal pressures and the failure of external subversion plans, might outweigh Russian prudence.

A Brief Analysis of Racial Problems in South Africa
THE WHITE GROUPS
The two White groups – Afrikaans- and English-speaking – are educated separately and, to a great extent, live separate social lives in different areas. Their attitudes to certain basic political principles such as the relative importance of security and the rule of law, and indeed to race relations generally, are at variance. There is top level cooperation combined with competition in the business world. In general there is still mistrust, yet a high level of White solidarity must be established before the Black and Brown problems can be successfully negotiated. Common danger and austerity combined with expanded National Service may hasten this solidarity. But a common system of education from Standard Five onwards would be the best long-term solution.

THE CAPE COLOUREDS
The Coloured Labour Party, which has a majority in the

Coloured Representative Council, refuses to participate in the Council's deliberations, rejects any form of parallel development and demands direct representation in the White Parliament. But the Party is showing signs of division on this approach. The Opposition Federal Party favours negotiation with the Government on the basis of Coloured Cabinet Ministers in direct liaison and on a level with the White Cabinet. This is Government policy.

THE INDIANS

Their interim Constitution follows the same lines as that of the Coloureds and the proposals for the immediate future are similar. The Indians operate the Indian Council and negotiate with the Government. They have a degree of tradition, culture and community spirit which the Coloured by virtue of their history cannot possess. The future of both Brown groups must inevitably be with the Whites. Their combined populations number approximately seven million, a third of the total.

THE AFRICANS

The Transkei became an independent nation in October 1976 and may soon be followed in this course by Baputho-Tswana. There are disputes in most of the Homelands regarding territory and a disinclination to accept independence while their territories are fragmented by White pockets. The most outspoken opponent of Government policy is Chief Buthelezi of Zululand. He is an able politician but the extent of his influence and security within Kwa-Zulu has been questioned. He certainly has enemies.

The problem of the permanent and long-established African residents in the White cities and rural areas is unsolved. The government policy of making them citizens of the Homeland of origin as it·becomes independent is a fantasy in which I do not believe the majority of Nationalists themselves have faith. One long-term policy which they may possibly have in mind is the gradual evolution of "City States" in African complexes such as "Soweto" (Johannesburg). These would however have to have some kind of central representation eventually.

SOME NOTES ON FUNCTIONAL RACE PROBLEMS

1 *Job Reservation.* Theoretically continues. The practice steadily phasing out.

2 *Equal pay for equal work for all races.* Very slow but definite progress towards narrowing the gap. Finance rather than

ideology is the major impediment. The recession does not help either in the public or private sector. The intent is acknowledged.

3 *Education.* Compulsory for Whites, Coloureds and Indians. Not so for Blacks owing to impossibility of providing sufficient teachers or schools. Numbers at school are steadily increasing. Free issue of books now established government policy.

4 *Petty Apartheid.* Some progress, e.g. Nico Malan Theatre and selected hotels and trains now for all races, sporting concessions. No segregation in shops, parks and gardens or private office blocks except for restaurant facilities. Beach notices still stand but tend to be ignored in some provinces. Buses and non-selective trains still segregated, also all public buildings including Post Office.

5 *Migrant Labour Group Areas and Pass Laws.* Attempts at top level to mitigate hardship and administer more humanely. Do not often permeate to lower bureaucratic levels. But some improvement.

6 *General Attitude of Government.* Government will not allow any moderation to threaten the general policy of separate development. The Prime Minister has often said publicly that so far as he is concerned there is no such thing as "petty" apartheid. Presumably he meant that such aspects are inextricably entangled with the overall plan. Yet he and other Nationalist Ministers continually stress the importance of recognising the dignity of individuals of all races and condemn affronts of this nature. There is undoubtedly a conflict of view on this whole aspect of race relations among Nationalists themselves. There is also a conflict within individual Afrikaners, even those who are most conscious of what needs to be done. An eminent Afrikaans industrialist once remarked "With my head I am uncomprisingly *verligt*. But deep inside me I am incorrigibly *verkrampt*."

THE LONG-TERM PROBLEM

The economic importance of South Africa to the West in the more distant future depends on the ability of all races in South Africa and all states in her immediate vicinity arriving at a workable compromise solution.

So far as South Africa is concerned, whether one foresees a federation of separate territories or a confederation of independent states, it is not possible to envisage the White minority ultimately ruling the whole of the Transvaal, the Free State, Natal and Cape Province, less the Homelands within their present borders, even assuming that the "White pockets" are eliminated. It would seem that the ultimate pattern can only be either a very greatly shrunken White/Brown state containing a Black minority and a series of Black states, or a series of multi-racial states or provinces with a multi-racial central government. The latter alternative seems to be by far the most likely finality.

However, whichever alternative eventually evolves will have to be approached through a series of phases negotiated and agreed — not dictated, if violence is to be avoided.

NATO'S ROLE

Sir Robert Thompson

Sir Robert Thompson KBE was born in 1916 and educated at Marlborough and Cambridge. He entered the Malayan Civil Service in 1938. During the war, as an RAF officer, he escaped from Hong Kong through China and served in both Chindit operations in Burma, being awarded the MC and DSO. After the war he returned to Malaya, where he was almost continuously concerned with security and the emergency. From 1957–1961 he was successively Deputy Secretary and Secretary for Defence in Malaya. From 1961–1965, he headed the British Advisory Mission to South Vietnam. He subsequently visited South Vietnam frequently as a consultant to the White House and the US National Security Council. His publications include *Defeating Communist Insurgency, Revolutionary War in World Strategy* and *Peace Is Not At Hand.*

"There is not a single question of any importance in the international arena that could at present be solved without the Soviet Union or against its wish.*"*

That statement of Mr Gromyko, the Soviet Foreign Minister, could not be uttered, let alone challenged, by any Western leader, not even the President of the United States. It expresses the inescapable fact that the global strategic balance of power has shifted dramatically over the last ten years in favour of the Soviet Union at the expense of the West. That it has not shifted more drastically is due not to any Western response to, or even recognition of, the Soviet threat but to the split between the Soviet Union and China which has led the latter to regard the Soviet Union as its most dangerous enemy and to become seemingly the West's temporary ally. But let it be understood that, whatever happens between Russia and China, whether calculated or miscalculated, concern by China for Western security or interests will not be a factor in its decisions.

The two main reasons for the shift are changes in capability, that is, the Soviet ability to deploy and to extend the reach of its military power, and psychologically the loss of political will in the West to defend its vital interests. Outwardly, at least, intentions on both sides have not changed. There has been no shift of policy. The Soviet Union still believes in world revolution and the ultimate victory of Communism ("Socialism") under Soviet leadership, and the West still adheres to the bankrupt policy of containment.

With regard to capability, the Soviet Union, having had a consistent policy, though a flexible strategy, since the Second World War, has learnt the lessons to give effect to that policy. Ten to fifteen years ago the range of Soviet military power (excluding strategic nuclear weapons) was limited to the continental land mass of Europe and Asia with the main military emphasis on its two fronts in Europe and on the Chinese border, on both of which its massive army of 168 divisions played the dominant role. In Stalin's day the Soviet Navy was little more than a coastal defence force. But, as students of history, the Russian leaders have evidently studies Mahan's *The Influence of Sea Power on History.* They also drew the correct conclusions from the Second World War, in which seapower finally gave the Allies the strategic initiative against both Germany and Japan and in which Hitler came closest to victory when his submarine fleet challenged the main Allied supply artery across the Atlantic. The West drew one wrong conclusion from the Second World War – that aircraft can sink ships. The Soviet Union, however, appreciated that aircraft can only sink enemy naval ships *in a declared war* and that, in time of peace, naval forces can project military power and political influence, which aircraft based thousands of miles from the scene cannot do. The Cuban missile crisis of 1962 and the Vietnam war drove home the point that, if the Soviet Union was to be a global as well as a continental power, naval forces were of paramount importance, with the result that by 1976 the Soviet Union, as part of its relentless build-up of military power, with a steady annual increase of 5 per cent, had 214 major surface combat ships and 231 attack and cruise missile submarines, of which 84 are nuclear. The comparable American figures are 176 surface ships and 75 submarines, of which 65 are nuclear.

At the same time the Soviet merchant marine (including trawlers for reconnaissance and electronic surveillance) has been vastly expanded at the rate of a million tons a year over the last five years. Complementary to this has been an expansion in both military and civil long-range air transport, which are essential to rapid supply in any critical situation. Air transportable weapons, some quite sophisticated such as the SAM 7, were also developed to the benefit of Marxist guerrilla movements. Rapid movement by air transport also enhanced the background threat of the Soviet army's seven airborne divisions. They were not so far in the background during the Middle East War of 1973, when the United States was "persuaded" to stop Israel from annihilating the Egyptian Third Army and to impose a ceasefire.

When subsequently Dr Henry Kissinger, then American Secretary of State, hinted that in the event of a further oil embargo amounting to "strangulation" it might be necessary to use military force, everyone knew that the United States lacked both the capability and will to do it. There were not enough American divisions (out of only sixteen at the time) to spare and no prepared bases from which to operate at such an enormous range. What could two or three divisions have done against the local forces available and what would have happened if the Soviet Union had then alerted her airborne divisions and inserted a preponderant naval force into the Indian Ocean with adequate re-supply bases, including missiles, and air cover in South Yemen and Berbera in the Somali Republic? It was quite unrealistic.

Now several years later there are no operating bases available to the United States, except Simonstown in South Africa, which for political reasons was not even used during the Vietnam war. Naval ships from America's east coast refuelled at Luanda in Angola and Lourenço Marques (now Maputo) in Mozambique (thereby adding considerably to their steaming time). Both these ports are now available to the Soviet Union, not to the United States. In addition, the United Kingdom has given up its staging post at Gan and has withdrawn from the island of Masirah on the Oman coast. Diego Garcia in the centre of the Indian Ocean is both inadequate and vulnerable. The collapse of the Portuguese empire in Africa has now given the Soviet Union naval and air bases in both Mozambique on the east coast and Angola, Guinea-Bissau and the Cape Verde Islands on the west coast, well forward of those in Aden and Berbera. Few appreciate that geographically, through the Mediterranean and Suez Canal, the Soviet fleet from its Black Sea ports is closer to the Indian Ocean than any other naval power.

The position in 1977 is, therefore, that the Soviet Union is now the only power capable of deploying military force in the whole area of the African continent, whether directly or through proxies like the Cubans. That this was one of the Soviet Union's strategic objectives was forecast as long ago as July 1967, when Admiral S.G. Gorshkov, the Soviet Naval Commander-in-Chief, stated: "The Soviet navy has been converted in the full sense of the word, into an *offensive* type of long-range armed force ... which can exert a decisive influence on the course of an armed struggle in theatres of military operations of vast extent ... and which is able to support state interests at sea in peace time." He did not confine the objective to the expansion of Soviet influence and domination but recognised a further objective when he later said: "The *disruption* of the ocean lines of communication, the special arteries that feed the military and economic potentials of those countries (i.e. 'the aggressive imperialist countries'), has continued to be one of the Fleet's missions." But the Soviet Union's stated intentions have been ignored by Western leaders, as were those of Hitler in the 1930s.

When in April 1975, the Soviet Union conducted on a global scale the most extensive naval manoeuvres, "Exercise Okean", that the world has ever seen, the full extent of Soviet capability and intentions should have been understood. Over 200 surface ships and 100 submarines were deployed in the Atlantic, Mediterranean, Pacific and Indian Oceans and the Sea of Japan, supported by intercontinental Tu-95 bombers flying out of bases as far afield as Cuba and Guinea-Bissau. The operation was fully coordinated and synchronised and its message to NATO was clear.

In the event of war, even in a preliminary conventional stage, American reinforcement of Europe by sea would be costly and minimal. Secondly, the whole of NATO's Southern Command, stretching 3,000 miles from Gibraltar to Italy and round to the Turkish-Soviet border, would collapse because it is absolutely dependent on naval control of the Mediterranean for freedom of movement between its isolated parts. And, thirdly, NATO countries would be almost entirely cut off from their global sources of raw materials, particularly minerals from Africa and oil from the Gulf.

The shift in the global strategic balance has not been caused solely by the change in capability. The fact that the Soviet Union has applied its resources to achieve its strategic objectives could always be countered by the West with its far greater resources and experience in the maritime field. The other major factor contributing to the shift has been the lack of political will in the West to defend its vital interests. This has stemmed mainly from the failure of the United States in Vietnam and the failure in all Western countries to understand the basic nature of that struggle both as a means of expanding Communist domination and Soviet influence and as a test of will over the policy of containment. The consequences are becoming apparent not least in the extent to which all countries and peoples, outside NATO and the Warsaw Pact, now regard the Soviet Union as the rising global power and the more reliable ally and the United States as the declining global power and the less reliable ally.

Other factors have been the decolonisation process, which has meant not just the retreat from Empire but a reluctance to assume any responsibility for enabling successor governments, either militarily or to a lesser extent economically, to survive in an unstable world, even though vital strategic and economic interests are at stake. In fact Britain, for example, did intervene east of Suez twenty-five times in the more immediate post-war years, but any such action would be inconceivable now. NATO countries in Europe are far too obsessed with their domestic economies and the illusory promises of socialism to worry about their survival. Moreover, the threat to survival, if not ignored by politicians, is brushed aside or recognised solely on the central front in Europe.

All other issues are either obscured by double talk and emotive phrases (especially in southern Africa) or elevated to the realms of wishful thinking for solution. Finally, the artificial restriction of NATO's territorial interest to the area north of the Tropic of Cancer is a convenient excuse for all NATO's political leaders to shut their eyes to what is happening strategically in the rest of the world.

One of the great tragedies of the war in Angola (the greatest is the suffering of the Angolan people) was that with an ounce of political will the Cubans could have been warned off and the forces of the pro-Western UNITA would have defeated the forces of the Marxist MPLA. Apart from the loss of Angola itself the failure of the West to respond when it had such a golden opportunity of halting the expansion of Soviet influence has reinforced the psychological consequences of Vietnam in many other countries which have so far inclined to the West. President Ford and Dr Kissinger understood the importance of Angola but were overruled by the flabbiest Congress in United States history. Socialist leaders in NATO, such as Herr Helmut Schmidt, the German Chancellor, have indulged in mere wishful thinking by drawing parallels between Angola and Egypt, from which the Soviets have been expelled for the third time. They fail to recognise that Egypt is not a Communist state and does therefore have some freedom of action whereas Angola is now under the virtual control of Soviet advisers and their Cuban proxies. No Marxist state, other than China, has yet expelled the Russians, and no Marxist state has yet been liberated.

Even in the case of Portugal, itself a member of NATO and, with the Azores, vital to Atlantic defence, the threat of a Communist take-over elicited negligible Western support for the moderate majority and was thwarted solely by a few courageous men and the peasants of the north. If there had been a Communist state on its border, this resistance would have collapsed and the Communist party, representing only 13 per cent of the electorate, would have taken over.

But a classic and still more blatant example of the West's loss of will has been the case of Zaire. President Mobutu's Government may leave much to be desired but it is no worse than others in Africa and better than some. At least he supported, in the Western interest as well as his own, Holden Roberto and the FNLA, which was allied to UNITA against the MPLA and the Cubans. Now he has paid the price. Rebel Katangans, trained, equipped and logistically (if not more directly) supported by the MPLA government of Angola and the Cubans, and with the connivance of the Soviet Union, invaded Katanga province, on which Zaire depends for its copper revenue. King Hassan of Morocco has sent troops to his aid with the assistance of air transport courageously provided by the French President. The United States continued their limited economic aid and military supplies but did not respond to a request for further arms and ammunition. There has been no concerted Western protest. There are other trouble spots, such as the Western Sahara, Uganda and Ethiopia, where, if cross-border adventures occur, the Soviet Union can be expected to meddle. As Dr Kissinger put it: "If attacks across sovereign borders are supinely accepted by the international community, sooner or later events will get out of control."

Over the last thirty years and particularly since Vietnam, the Soviet Union has been allowed to establish three ground rules. The first is that Communist countries (or Socialist as defined by Moscow) are off-limits while the rest of the world is a free-for-all. Eastern Europe, North Korea, Cuba, Vietnam and now Angola and Mozambique have all established that. Secondly, in a free-for-all the Communist party (or a Soviet ally) only has to win once. This law was laid down by Mr Brezhnev as part of his doctrine when he stated: "Experience shows us that, in the present conditions, the victory of the socialist system in this or that country can be regarded as final and the restoration of capitalism can be regarded as precluded." In other words neither the ballot-box nor revolt can ever throw the Communist party out. These two rules also mean that in all its adventures the Soviet Union is in a can-win can't-lose position. There may be setbacks and defeats (as in Egypt) but these are temporary. Only victory is final. Thirdly, revolutionary parties know that they will be supported by the Soviet Union or its client states, whereas threatened governments and peoples know that they are unlikely to be supported by the West. The rapidity with which, after Angola, the front-line Presidents of Zambia, Botswana and Tanzania came to terms with their Marxist neighbours and the Soviet Union (with President Podgorny's visit) was remarkable. There is no talk now of the Soviet "tiger and its marauding cubs".

The policy of containment originally conceived by Mr George Kennan in 1947 and adopted by the United States and its allies as a means of checking further Soviet expansion was never more than a temporary expedient. As James Burnham pointed out in his book *Containment versus Liberation* in 1953, the policy was purely defensive and was bound in the end to lead to drift, appeasement and a steady erosion of the Western position. Its only lasting achievement was the establishment of NATO at a time when the West had overall military superiority and the United States a nuclear monopoly so that the West's political will and its unity were at their strongest from the point of view both of security and of economic recovery after the Second World War. In that atmosphere there was no problem in getting the signatories to state: "They are determined to safeguard the freedom, common heritage and civilisation of their peoples, founded on the principles of democracy, individual liberty and the rule of law" – but not, it will be noted, the freedom of anyone else.

Now, more than twenty-five years later, the Soviet Union and its allies have overall military superiority and at least nuclear parity and, in the intervening period, the Soviet Union through the varied instruments of proxy forces, wars of national liberation, united front tactics, trade and aid has so bankrupted the policy of containment that even NATO's capability and will to defend itself on the European front is being called in question. Elsewhere, in South-East Asia, the Mediterranean, the Middle East and Africa, the West has lost both the capability and the will to defend its interests. The Soviet Union is now poised to create a north-south *bloc*, centred on the Indian Ocean, which will cut the world vertically in half.

Four major threats to NATO's stated objective are being steadily developed. First, NATO's southern flank in the Mediterranean is starting to crumble, with cracks in the alliance appearing in Turkey, Greece, Cyprus, Malta, Portugal and even Italy. The erosion would be greatly accelerated if a Moscow-oriented régime is installed in Yugoslavia after Marshal Tito's death. Moreover, with a powerful Soviet fleet in the Mediterranean and strong Soviet influence in Libya and Algeria on the North African coast, the Mediterranean is no longer a secure Allied "lake". The strategic importance of North Africa to the security of Europe's southern flank is as valid today as it was from the time of Carthage to El Alamein.

Secondly, and perhaps as important strategically in the context of NATO and Africa, the Cape Route now carries 80 per cent of Western Europe's oil supplies and a growing proportion (about one-third in 1976) of those of the United States, in addition to nearly 70 per cent of other strategic materials required by NATO.

While the Suez Canal was closed, over 26,000 ships annually (about seventy a day) rounded the Cape. Nearly half of these required servicing and bunkering facilities in southern Africa. A very high percentage are super-tankers which could not use the Suez Canal anyway. The Suez Canal is in reality no longer a substitute, being even more vulnerable and also inadequate for many of the vessels now being built. The threat to the Cape Route is therefore threefold: Soviet naval control of the Indian Ocean, which could at a time of crisis impose a blockade (as President Kennedy did over Cuba in 1962); sporadic attacks on shipping by a Marxist state on the African coast, of the same type as the Cambodian attack on the *Mayaguez*; and the loss of servicing, bunkering and maintenance facilities on the African littoral.

Thirdly, Africa (and particularly southern Africa) is a repository of some of the world's greatest mineral resources including vanadium, platinum, uranium, chrome, antimony, copper, gold and diamonds, most of which are vital to Western industry and for some of which Africa is the West's only or major source.

Fourthly, as the first two threats develop gradually and insidiously, they must have some political effect on the course of events within the Middle East oil states themselves, thereby raising for NATO the alarming question of whose hand will be controlling the tap in ten to fifteen years time, or even less.

These threats to NATO cannot be divorced from the great dilemma facing the West, particularly Britain and the United States, in Rhodesia and South Africa. Neither problem can be solved without, or at the expense of, the other. The dilemma has been intensified by the failure of the containment policy, one cause of which has been the proclivity of the West for double standards in requiring its natural friends and allies to be immaculate on such issues as freedom, democracy and human rights, while tolerating the complete disregard of them by the other side. If the West had made a concerted stand for these virtues for all peoples over the last twenty-five years (a policy of liberation), it would not have been faced with such a dilemma now. It is the great irony of our time, and a measure of the West's decline, that the Soviet Union can pose as the champion of national liberation.

Whatever historical parallels may be drawn from the past, such as the alliance with the Soviet Union in the Second World War, the argument that, when survival is at stake, moral considerations must be abandoned cannot be justified. Whatever the vital interests or the strategic requirements, they cannot be safeguarded either morally, nor in practical terms, by outright support for the present governments of either Rhodesia or South Africa, if that means the continuation of White minority rule in Rhodesia and apartheid in South Africa. At the other extreme the campaign to end both by any means and at any cost runs the grave risk that not only will Soviet influence eventually expand right through southern Africa but that the cause of freedom for its peoples will be irretrievably lost. The final outcome could be that the repression (as in Cambodia and Vietnam, for example) would be far worse and that the standard of living of the peoples in southern Africa would be lower than it is now.

There is the further risk that, in South Africa, the Afrikaner, who has nowhere else to go and whose claim to most of the territory is legitimate and whose resources are by no means negligible, would fight to the last, even to the extent of using nuclear weapons with incalculable consequences for the West.

The situation in Rhodesia is more immediate and predictable. If no solution is found, the Marxist guerrilla movement (the Zimbabwe People's Army – ZIPA – under Robert Mugabe), based in Mozambique with reliable Soviet and other support, whether direct or indirect, must eventually succeed. It is a classic situation where the strategic initiative is held by the side with the secure base (in Mozambique) against a side whose base (in Rhodesia) is constantly threatened, and where the guerrilla movement, at a cost which is indefinitely acceptable both to itself and to its supporters, can impose costs on Rhodesia which are not indefinitely acceptable. It can suffer innumerable setbacks and failures but remains in a permanent can-win can't-lose position (like a continuous penalty shot at goal). In the end it must win and only has to win once.

This has great implications for any attempt at a negotiated settlement. The "Patriotic Front" will not accept a negotiated settlement except on terms of absolute victory, because any compromise settlement involving elections might jeopardise its succession to power in Rhodesia. The real struggle (as in Angola) is not between the Patriotic Front and Mr Ian Smith's Government but between the Patriotic Front and those nationalist forces in Rhodesia which do not want a Communist government. The Marxist element is using Mr Smith and racialism as a means of capturing the whole nationalist movement and of destroying the base of more popular leaders, such as Bishop Muzorewa, who might in electoral terms command a majority. Black minority rule could be worse than White, and the "bloodbath" will not be of Whites who can get out but of Blacks who cannot.

The key feature in a solution has always been the establishment of an independent government through the ballot-box, not the gun, whether by way of a referendum or of elections, preferably under outside supervision. The pre-condition of a new written constitution has become a luxury, which time, after Angola, will not allow, because the prospect of all-party agreement has proved to be negligible and constitutions anyway have a habit of being swiftly and capriciously amended or suspended. The new government, hopefully a cohesive African majority to which more may be attracted, can later draft the constitution in its own time. This approach does require that there should be broad agreement between the Smith Government and the leaders of the elected African majority, fully supported by Britain and the United States, on the retention of essential existing institutions and laws to enable the new government to function. A legal basis for this could be provided in the British Parliament Act granting independence.

The chances for a more peaceful, gradual and tidy solution were lost long ago and were finally destroyed by the speed with which the local strategic situation deteriorated after Angola to the advantage of the Soviet Union and its clients. Even the solution now proposed will stand no chance (and no one can then be criticised for not taking it) unless it has the unequivocal support of Britain and the United States, backed by other NATO leaders. That support must obviously be political and economic on some scale but there must also be a guarantee, otherwise, as Dr Kissinger said, "events will get out of control".

The days of supine diplomacy are over, and upon the outcome in Rhodesia will depend the course of events in Namibia and South Africa. More than that is at stake. Now is the time for the present leaders of NATO to endorse their predecessors' determination "to safeguard the freedom, common heritage and civilisation of their peoples", before it is too late, by recognising and matching the expansion of Soviet power and by adopting a realistic approach to the solution of issues which threaten our very survival.

THE VIEW FROM WASHINGTON

William Schneider Jr

William Schneider Jr is a Congressional staff member, and a consultant to the Hudson Institute (New York). He is an economist and a defence analyst, and is author of *Food, Foreign Policy, and Raw Materials Cartels* (Crane, Russak, 1976), and is co-author of *Arms, Men, and Military Budgets* (Crane, Russak, 1976) and *Why ABM? Policy Issues in the Missile Defense Controversy* (Pergamon, 1969). He holds a PhD degree from New York University in economics, and is a member of the American Economic Association and the International Institute for Strategic Studies.

AMERICAN POLICY in Africa has been an episodic affair since the period of rapid decolonisation by the West European powers in the late 1950s and early 1960s. Before the rush of independence-granting, the US's economic autarky, coupled with the isolation of sub-Saharan Africa from Super-power conflict, provided few opportunities for diplomatic initiative. The unsuccessful experience of the Kennedy and Johnson administrations with the rapidly changing cadre of leaders of the new African states further undermined official interest.

This was in spite of unambiguous signs of Soviet-*bloc* intelligence and subversive activity in several African nations. For example, Soviet Russia and its satellites were active in Guinea and Ghana in the late 1950s, in Congo-Leopoldville (now Zaire) in 1960-61. East German intelligence officials and military personnel were active in Zanzibar (1961–63), Soviet personnel were significant participants in the guerrilla organisations in Angola, Mozambique, Rhodesia, South-West Africa (Namibia), and now play a dominant role in the régimes of several African nations including Angola, Mozambique, the Congo (Brazzaville), Ethiopia, Equatorial Guinea, and elsewhere.

Minimal American political and diplomatic interest in Africa was maintained directly through several foreign aid programmes sustained on a modest scale, and indirectly through the activity of American corporations involved in Africa. The latter focused on extractive industries and tropical agricultural products. As of 1976, 350 American corporations or subsidiaries operated in Africa with a direct investment of $4 billion – 38 per cent of it in the Republic of South Africa. American non-military aid to Africa is twice that of the Soviet Union: over $1.5 billion in the 1971–75 time period. Programmes include economic assistance from the Agency for International Development (with two-thirds of the assistance going to eight "development emphasis" states – Ethiopia, Ghana, Kenya, Liberia, Nigeria, Tanzania, Uganda, and Zaire), the PL-480 surplus agricultural products programme, the Peace Corps, Export-Import Bank loans, and Public Safety Assistance (lately cut). The Soviet Union instead focused upon military aid to Africa; over the same period it was $2.2 billion – considerably more than the American military aid figure.

Not until open warfare in southern Africa broke out in 1975 was there a substantial change in American policy. This policy shift occurred as a consequence of Soviet intervention on behalf of Communist forces in the Angolan civil war. The stark character of Soviet forces at a time when détente was a bilateral article of faith between the United States and the Soviet Union came as a substantial shock to officials in every Western capital, including Washington.

Initially, American policy provided covert assistance to the anti-Communist faction in Angola, to offset Soviet military assistance to the Communist MPLA faction, which was pouring into Pointe Noire in the People's Republic of Congo (Brazzaville), the staging point for shipment to Angola. American military equipment was shipped to Zaire covertly by the Republic of South Africa at American request by way of South Africa and elsewhere. The improved effectiveness provided to the Communist forces in Angola by the employment of Cuban cadres against the poorly trained and led anti-Communist (UNITA) forces prompted direct South African intervention – again, at American urging. The Cuban forces proved to be incompetent, and in some cases even cowardly, in the face of South Africa's well-organised offensive sweeps through southern Angola to the outskirts of Luanda.

As a consequence of the possible failure of the Cuban foray in Angola, the prospect of a wider conflict became greater. Evidence of a willingness on the part of the Soviet Union to support the deployment of additional Cuban forces (the regular Cuban Army disposes of 90,000 troops plus reserves) to the theatre became apparent. This proved to be a troubling prospect for the American Congress; fearing "another Vietnam" the Congress in December 1975 approved an amendment proposed by Senator John Tunney, a Democrat from California, appended to a military appropriation Bill which prohibited further overt or covert military assistance to forces fighting in Angola. There was a (wishful) belief in the Congress that foreign intervention was not sustainable in Africa – even if initially welcomed – and therefore little would be gained by anti-Communist intervention. The collapse of American efforts precipitated the most important full-scale change in policy since the mid-1960s.

Senator Tunney, incidentally, was defeated for re-election in November, 1976. In the Senate debate on his Angolan amendment, he stated that the rival movements were "basically pro-Angolan, socialist, and highly nationalistic". Senator Tunney was shocked when President Agostinho Neto told him in an interview that the Cuban troops were in Angola to stay. Upon Tunney's return to the United States, he was unable to meet with Secretary of State Cyrus Vance with this information, but it was passed on to a subordinate. Tunney's warning was ignored in subsequent statements by the Secretary of State as well as President Carter.

Recent American Declaratory Policy toward southern Africa
The first changes in American policy under the Ford Administration were announced in a series of speeches by Secretary of State Henry A. Kissinger in Africa and the United States between April and August of 1976. The new American policy announced by the Ford Administration attempted to come to terms with the African states in their insistence upon "majority rule" ("majority" only in the sense of rule by Black Africans, not in the sense of majority rule by consent of the governed) by applying economic and diplomatic pressure to Rhodesia, South-West Africa, and the Republic of South Africa to undermine their régimes and force them to give way to Black African rule. Application of these pressures against Rhodesia would initially be subsidised by the American Treasury by assuming the economic costs of the trade embargo of the so-called "front line" states of Zambia, Mozambique, and Botswana against Rhodesia. Arms sanctions, travel privileges, and trade access for the Rhodesian régime (in particular the right to sell chrome ore to the US) would be severely enforced to the disadvantage of Rhodesia. More veiled threats against South Africa were raised to imply complete abandonment of the South Africans in the event of war unless their policies changed.[1] The policy was reinforced by Mr Ford's Presidential

[1]The key documents from this period are Secretary of State Henry Kissinger's remarks in Lusaka, Zambia, on 27 April 1976, reprinted in *Survival*, Vol.18, July-August, 1976, p. 171-6; 30 April 1976 in Monrovia, Liberia, 1 May 1976 in Dakar, Senegal, and 6 May 1976 in Nairobi, reprinted in the *Congressional Record*, 13 May 1976, pp. S7197-206; in Boston on 2 August 1976 (National Urban League), and Philadelphia (Opportunities Industrialisation Centres) on 31 August 1976, reprinted in the *Department of State Bulletin*, Vol. 75 pp. 257-265 and 349-357. More recently, the possibility that the government-supported financing of exports to South Africa through the Export-Import bank may be withdrawn as a "punitive" measure has been raised by the Carter Administration, see M.T. Kaufman, "U.S. Policy Toward South Africa Under Review; Symbolic and Punitive Options are on the Agenda," *New York Times*, 15 May, 1977 p. 3. The despatch also suggests that the "ending of exchanges of intelligence information" is being considered. Since the United States gains more information than it dispenses, it is difficult to know who is punishing whom. The campaign statements of President Ford and other 1976 Presidential candidates relating to Africa are contained in F.A. Kornegay, Jr., "Africa and Presidential Politics," *Africa Report*, July-August, 1976.

campaign where he emphasised his support for majority rule.

The rhetoric of both Secretary Kissinger and President Ford appeared to accept the use of the term "majority rule" to imply identification only with rule by Black Africans without reference to majority status in terms of tribal allegiance. This policy left the United States with little room for manoeuvre in African politics when such an objective became embedded into the fabric of American foreign policy. A policy stated in such terms as "the US unequivocally upholds the principle of majority rule, condemns apartheid policies, and urges the peaceful solution of these difficult problems by peaceful means" was a weak statement compared to, say, Tanzania's view that "where freedom can be obtained only through violence, we have to and must support that cause" (as expressed by Foreign Minister Ibrahim Kaduma to Secretary of State Kissinger, and reported in the *Chicago Tribune*, 26 April 1976). The overt change in US policy toward southern Africa was coupled with a change in American policy toward the economic relationship with Africa and the under-developed world as a whole. In short, the Ford-Kissinger policy toward Africa attempted to usurp the Soviet posture by articulating similar goals, while seeking to obtain results through diplomatic efforts and economic incentives or threats alone.

The election of President Carter has led to changes in policy toward Africa, particularly southern Africa. Responding to a question from a journalist during the 1976 election campaign, President Carter said:

We should also realise that the Russian and Cuban presence in Angola, while regrettable and counterproductive of peace, need not constitute a threat to United States interests; nor does that presence mean the existence of a Communist satellite on the continent. The Communists have given military assistance in many African nations, but have never been able to remain there once independence is achieved. The OAU policy of non-alignment is so strong in the African tradition that it is reasonable to assume that an independent Angola would continue in that tradition. Furthermore, since Angola's survival economically depends on the sale of oil and other natural resources to the West, there will be some economic ties with any government which emerges.

This policy reasserts the notion implicit in the Ford-Kissinger policy that independent African nations would not long tolerate

Top: *A map at Simonstown in which each tag represents a ship. On this particular day there were 1,245, excluding those in harbour.*

Above: *British-built Buccaneers of the South African Air Force. The Labour Government has refused to replace them.*

Left: *With a deck cargo of military vehicles, including tank transporters, the freighter* Dmitry Poluyan *passes along the Natal coast on its way to an unknown destination.*

Above: *The new Soviet aircraft carrier Kiev, photographed from an RAF Nimrod soon after passing through the Bosphorous from the Black Sea. Other Kiev-class carriers are now under construction.*

Heavy Russian equipment captured in Angola: below left *a wrecked Mk III Amphibian;* below *a 122mm rocket launcher, with a range of 20,000 metres.*

PARTE MATERIAL DEL FUSIL AUTOMATICO M-52

Above: *Some of the military handbooks used by Cubans during the Angolan Civil War. The Cubans sought to conceal the origin of the books by trying to erase the word "Cuba".*

Right: *Angolan refugees, October 1976.*

Opposite: *Men of the British South Africa Police and tracker dogs, working with the Rhodesian Army, during an anti-terrorist operation in the Zambesi valley.*

Amphibious forces of the Royal Iranian Navy, seen here on beach reconnaissance exercises, are active in the Persian Gulf and Indian Ocean.

An Argentinian Air Force plane was sabotaged by terrorists while taking off. Five people were killed.

Above: *The USS* Leahy, *one of the 15,000 ships which sail through the Panama Canal each year.*

Below: *An Australian heavy landing craft, HMAS Balikpapan, operating in support of the army.*

Soviet domination, but goes somewhat further and implies that, even if Communist domination does take place, it will not be significant to the West, because of President Carter's belief that the way to avoid alienating Marxist-oriented régimes in Africa is to continue to provide such a country with access to Western raw materials without requiring it to oppose Communist domination.

The essence of the Carter policy toward southern Africa is clearly described in the statement:

> For almost a decade, the United States had no positive policy toward South Africa. The Angola situation is a result of this policy vacuum. The United States should move immediately toward using leverage on South Africa to encourage the independence of Namibia and the beginning of majority rule in Rhodesia. There is no question that independence will come in the near future. The only question is whether it comes through armed struggle sponsored by the Soviet Union or through an aggressive diplomacy of peace encouraged by the United States. (*Africa Report*, July-August 1976).

The Carter policy as of mid-1977 strongly suggests that the new Administration will work actively toward a change in (non-Black African) governments in the region. Moreover, unlike the previous Administration, no lip service is paid to the idea of American or Western interests in the region. Indeed, the current American Ambassador to the United Nations, Mr Andrew Young, has suggested that the United States should send armed forces to southern Africa to participate in the overthrow of the existing White régimes. While Mr Young's erratic behaviour makes it difficult for an observer to take his intemperate rhetoric seriously, the fact that he is tolerated − if frequently rebuked − cannot be overlooked.

Observing the statements (and behaviour) of the Carter Administration on southern Africa, one can deduce a few hypotheses about their policy preferences in the region which may provide some guidance to future policy.

1 South Africa is the linchpin of the Administration's strategy, for it alone can bring about an overnight change in the prospects for early Black rule in South-West Africa, and can exert a powerful influence on the policy of the Smith régime in Rhodesia.

2 Should the United States take a strong and active role in achieving or facilitating Black rule in Rhodesia and South-

West Africa, the United States may claim the mantle of Super-power leadership assumed by the Soviets after their victory in Angola. Such leadership would make it easier to achieve a peaceful settlement of Black African claims against South Africa than if leadership of the Black African guerrilla movements were held by the Soviet Union as is now the case.

The adoption of the rhetoric of the Black African terrorist movement in Rhodesia by describing nations with a Black leadership contiguous to Rhodesia as "front line" states, the championing of aid requests in the Congress for purposes of facilitating the guerrilla campaign against Rhodesia, and the diplomatic efforts to influence the course of negotiations between South Africa and the tribal organisations in South-West Africa aiming at independence, all indicate a well-developed policy with substantial Presidential support. The issue not yet faced by the Administration is the character of the régimes likely to emerge as a consequence of these manoeuvres. South Africa (with Britain as colonial power) was able to negotiate independence arrangements with Botswana, Lesotho and Swaziland suitable to the taste of most of the world (though they have not been successful in the case of South-West Africa or the Transkei) — all of them states moderate enough not to be active participants in guerrilla activities or a source of serious terrorist activity. Today the prospects for the emergence of further moderate régimes in southern Africa look poor.

While the Black nationalist movement in Rhodesia is split among several factions, it is prevailingly Marxist in character and rhetoric. Even the more "moderate" of the factions (e.g. the Nkomo group) make it clear that the new régime will be a radical socialist state with little or no commitment offered to the racial minority as to the protection of their human, civil, and property rights. The models of Mozambique, Tanzania and Angola are more appropriate to the likely evolution of South-West African and Rhodesian (Zimbabwe) régimes than the Ivory Coast, Kenya or Liberia. That is to say, the new régimes can be expected to be basically hostile to the nations of the West, and to the West's associated economic and security interests.

The likelihood of a future régime in South Africa under Black African auspices is much more difficult to predict. The reason for this is the ethnic character of the White minority. The ancestors of the Afrikaner — the majority of the White population — were the first settlers in South Africa. Black Africans moved southwards into the region after the Afrikaners' arrival in the seventeenth century. Unlike many of English descent who may return to the United Kingdom, the Afrikaner has nowhere to flee. Thus the introduction of majority rule to South Africa might not be accomplished without serious warfare. Unlike many modern states, South Africa is not vulnerable to urban terrorism on a significant scale, due to the lack of co-location of Black and White residential and business areas; Mozambique is the only state with suitable overland access to South Africa to support guerrilla movements, but is itself too vulnerable to South African retaliation to make assault sensible. South Africa recently announced plans to construct a new air base near the Mozambique border. The location of this air base makes it possible for the South African Air Force to deliver more bomb tonnage on Maputo (Lourenço Marques) with the fifty Kfir aircraft the SAAF is buying from Israel than the Allied Air Forces delivered on Berlin in a 1,000-plane raid in the Second World War. The arithmetic of these circumstances cannot be lost on the current Communist régime in Maputo. The only serious threat to the South Africans is from foreign intervention. Cuban military forces are not competent for the task without substantial improvement in their training and equipment as well as augmentation in numbers. However, the introduction of Soviet *bloc* forces cannot be excluded.

The Soviet Union has a massive presence of intelligence personnel in sub-Saharan Africa. More than one-third of their "diplomats" in the region are intelligence personnel – either from the KGB or the GRU (military intelligence). The Cuban ambassador in Angola is a senior official of the Cuban intelligence service, the DGI, itself a subsidiary of the KGB directed by a Soviet General from Moscow. The KGB has established an intelligence service for the new Communist régime in Angola, the DISA, along Soviet lines managed by DGI personnel. A similar institution is now being established by the Soviets for the Machel régime in Mozambique. Moreover, the DGI is engaged in a direct operational role in Brazzaville, where 300 Cuban troops are now deployed, as well as others in Somalia, Mozambique, Ethiopia, and with rebel forces in southern Zaire. In each case, Cuban intelligence officials are supervised by resident KGB officers assigned to embassies or Soviet front organisations such as Aeroflot. With a significant intelligence-oriented infrastructure throughout Africa, it would not be difficult to imagine an augmentation of this presence with the introduction of East German, Czech or Soviet military personnel. While some commentators have explained the observed surge of Soviet activity in Africa as a consequence of intra-Communist *bloc* competition for the leadership of the Third World, Soviet activities are too narrowly focused toward the elimination of Western influence from southern Africa for this to be a sufficient explanation, even if it has some relevance under specialised circumstances.

A wholly new initiative of the Carter Administration in the region has been the proposal, raised during the Vance mission to Moscow (March 1977) as part of a wide-ranging set of bilateral policy proposals (including such diverse subjects as strategic arms limitation, human rights issues, and mutual force reductions in Europe), to demilitarise the Indian Ocean. Though the United States has but a single facility in the Indian Ocean area (on Diego Garcia Island in the Chagos Archipelago), France has a considerable basing structure in the Malagasy Republic (Diego Suarez), and several Indian Ocean Islands including Réunion, and has access to several small islands in the Mozambique Channel (Europa, Tromelin and the nearly independent Comoros) as well as small installations on Kerguelen and Amsterdam Island in the southern Indian Ocean. In addition, the United States is able to make use of Oman's Masirah Island for the northern leg of patrols by maritime aircraft originating from Diego Garcia (as does the UK).

The existing facility at Diego Garcia is the most significant, because it permits the United States to sustain the deployment of surface naval combatants and submarines, drawn from the Seventh Fleet in the western Pacific (stationed at Subic Bay in the Philippines), to the western Indian Ocean and the Red Sea without having to operate a 5,500 n.m. line of supply from Subic Bay. Moreover, the P-3C Orion and British Nimrod maritime aircraft operating in the region permit high-quality surveillance of Soviet naval operations. The Soviet Union now must operate from either Vladivostok or the Kamchatka Peninsula in eastern Siberia or from Black Sea ports (via Suez) to support its naval operations in the Indian Ocean. The recent acquisition of deepwater facilities in Mozambique, however, permits an increase of the level of Soviet naval activity in the region.

The Carter proposal to "demilitarise" the Indian Ocean has several forms. In its most comprehensive expression, it would deny bases to either side on the Indian Ocean littoral, while less expansive versions of the proposal relate to negotiated limits on the number of "steaming days" (one "steaming day" equals one day of operation at sea by a single vessel) each side could operate in the region as a step toward ultimate demilitarisation of the Indian Ocean. The Soviet view that it maintains no bases outside its own territory raises doubts about the outcome of this Carter initiative. The proposal places the United States at a diplomatic disadvantage for it can only reduce America's regional naval capability to ensure the right to transit the Indian Ocean: it would surrender or curtail America's naval presence, thereby enabling the Soviets to achieve an important component of their foreign policy in the region, namely denial of access to the Western powers. It is not yet clear whether the Carter Administration will "link" its southern African policy with its proposal to demilitarise the Indian Ocean. There is some evidence to suggest that the Carter Administration views the problem of a Soviet-American naval competition in the Indian Ocean as a separable issue from the dispute over southern Africa. It may find, however, that Soviet domination of southern Africa will make Soviet-American naval competition in the Southern Oceans inevitable.

Implications of Current American Policy for the Future Security of the Southern Oceans

There are many perspectives from which one can assess the potential consequences of current American policy in southern Africa and the Indian Ocean. One of the clear consequences of the unfolding events in the region is the effect the developments will have on the whole security of the Southern Oceans. The harvest of allies the Soviets have reaped with the installation of Marxist régimes in Africa is remaking the politico-military configuration of the South Atlantic and Indian Oceans. To appreciate the significance of these developments, it is important to recognise the differences in Soviet and Western attitudes toward bases on foreign territory. Western nations obtain bases that provide for a permanent presence in support of political and diplomatic objectives in the region, as well as improving the support structure for conducting military operations in the area. Western bases therefore tend to be well-developed affairs with dry-dock and repair facilities, supply depots, and a large personnel complement to support anticipated needs in a time of crisis. As a consequence, Western bases in Africa have been few and of major importance. Simonstown near Cape Town, and Walvis Bay in

South-West Africa, have been the two most important in southern Africa, although, through self-denial by British and American policy, these bases have not been used. Minor facilities have been maintained elsewhere in east Africa (e.g. Djibouti) and just one of significance in west Africa, apart from American and British use of Ascension Island, and limited French deployments and naval manoeuvres in the region.

The Soviet Union, by contrast, does not establish a base to support a permanent military presence. Soviet bases are available to support a "surge" of combat support activities in the event that such forces are needed. Otherwise the facilities serve only for emergency repair purposes and support of intelligence collection activities such as reconnaissance aircraft or electronic intelligence vessels. Soviet naval forces are often characterised as "one shot" navies because of their very limited shipboard magazine space, and their inability to reload at sea. Thus, their (now) well-known base in Somalia was primarily a missile-handling facility to reload Soviet surface-to-air missiles and cruise missiles should they expend them in time of war. The Somalia facility supported Soviet naval operations in the north-western portion of the Indian Ocean and the Red Sea. The Soviet Union has acquired the following deep-water facilities in the three years since 1974: Cape Verde Islands; Luanda, Angola; Maputo, Mozambique; Beira, Mozambique; Nacala, Mozambique; Porto Amelia, Mozambique; and Berbera, Somalia.

Soviet reconnaissance flights (primarily by long-range Tu-95 Bear bombers) are now regularly made from Conakry, Guinea and Luanda. Operations normally cover the Atlantic to Cuba, although the US Air Force recently intercepted a Tu-95, flying from Conakry, near the US East Coast. From these bases (spares and maintenance services are supplied by Aeroflot "technicians") the entire Atlantic south of the NATO boundary can be placed under observation or aerial attack. All of the South American continent is now vulnerable to attack from bomber missions flown from Soviet air bases in West Africa. It also places at risk seaborne traffic via the Cape Route. It is insufficiently appreciated that 80 per cent of the West's oil imports pass the Cape Route, as do 70 per cent of NATO's strategic raw materials. While the Cape of Good Hope remains the most efficient base from which to interdict seaborne traffic, the long range of modern aircraft undermines the security of all the Southern Oceans.

The events since 1974 have opened up to the Soviet *bloc* the means by which they may now threaten Western trade lifelines, not only to Europe, but to the dynamic economies of east Asia as well. Western failure to take resolute action in Angola has resulted in a series of events which now make forthcoming decisions on southern Africa crucial. Southern Africa will be the most important source of raw materials for Europe and Japan for the balance of this century and well into the next, a detail not overlooked by the Soviets. Soviet strategy with respect to southern Africa, at least in part, is directed toward the denial of access by the industrialised West to southern Africa rather than to any urgent requirements in the region for their own economic or security purposes. To this end Soviet tactics are well suited, as they have achieved entry to most of the important coastal nations of Africa for their naval and air forces without the burden of either occupation or administration. Moreover, the character of developments in Africa is now well suited to increasing pressure for change in Rhodesia and South-West Africa, paving the way for a final assault on South Africa itself, perhaps a decade from now.

American policy has unwittingly played a supporting role, aimed, as it is, at achieving peacefully what the guerrilla leadership is determined to gain by violent means. American policy undermines the ability of the existing leadership to resist a change in government, and Soviet policy is most effective at surfacing radical Marxist régimes out of the leadership of the anti-White-rule opposition.

CONGRESSIONAL ATTITUDES

Representative Bob Wilson

The Hon. Bob Wilson is the Representative of San Diego, California. He was born in Calexico, California in 1916, was educated in public schools in California and later studied in San Diego State College and at Otis Arts Institute in Los Angeles. During the Second World War he directed a cooperative "Conship" and served in the Army. He is now a Lieutenant-Colonel in the Reserve of the US Marine Corps. He was President of the National Republican Committee of Congress from 1962 to 1973. He was first elected to the 83rd Congress and has been returned at all subsequent elections.

THE REPUBLIC of South Africa at the present time is a fortress country, much in the same way that Israel is a fortress country. It has been ostracised from the world community because of the world's perception of its racial policies. Its claim of separate development has been rejected for a multitude of reasons, the primary one being a world-wide propaganda campaign decrying "White supremacy".

The Government of the Republic of South Africa recognises, as do the people living within its borders, that it is a country peopled by several nations, with different cultures, languages, backgrounds and histories. In recognising this, the Republic of South Africa intends to see that each nation develops on its own, in its traditional homeland, with its own sovereign government. To this end, the country has set up the "homeland" concept and sees in the future a South African Commonwealth, composed of the many diverse nations and peoples that inhabit the area. In such a commonwealth, each nation will exist as a separate entity, deciding its own course of action on what is best for its citizens, but interacting for the good of the whole.

If South Africa is allowed to continue to progress in its own way and at its own pace, the transition should be fairly smooth, with little or no economic disruption. It will take time, but the vast majority of South Africans, Black and White, believe that this is the best way to resolve the question of nationalities.

However, with the victory in Angola by Russia and its Cuban army, with Mozambique now a pro-Soviet country and with a violent upheaval being threatened in Rhodesia, the Republic of South Africa feels increasingly surrounded. This attitude is not without foundation. The United Nations has pointed an accusing finger at the country, severely criticised it for its allegedly discriminatory policies and has set forth a list of items – most of a military nature – which its member countries are enjoined from exporting to the Republic of South Africa. The United States has turned its back on South Africa, refusing military aid to one of its best friends in the United Nations.

In the face of these circumstances, the Republic of South Africa still maintains that its policies will remain in effect and that it will determine its own destiny, going it alone if necessary. The possibility remains that, if Rhodesia goes under, either through internal dissension and coup or through outside intervention launched from either Mozambique or Angola, South-West Africa will be the next target, with the ultimate goal of a Communist take-over of the Republic of South Africa itself.

If the present day is any indication, the United States will remain on the sidelines, watching whatever events transpire in southern Africa without offering assistance and, indeed, through non-interference, will accelerate and exacerbate the rate of aggression and take-over.

South Africa would, of course, resist any such attempts – if necessary, by force. It has the finest fighting force on the sub-continent and is fully capable of defending itself against external encroachments. However, the possibility of such events occurring seems some years away, and, by that time, South Africa's Homelands should be well on their way to independence, thereby negating much of the White domination-Black suppression argument that would undoubtedly be the *casus belli*.

Internationally, the Republic of South Africa is one of our staunchest allies, but because of its internal racial policies the United States persists in not recognising those close ties of friendship. Again, the cause goes back to our perception of the Republic of South Africa as a country where a White minority subjugates a Black majority, ruling over it in almost feudal fashion.

The United States is completely simplistic in its judgement of the country. The social, economic and political atmosphere that exists in South Africa is much more complex and needs to be studied. Our government is judging emotionally, rather than rationally, and has not thoroughly examined all the circumstances and conditions that make up the Republic of South Africa.

There seems to be an ingrained guilt complex in the United States which, for decades, imported Blacks as slaves. Upon emancipation, the Blacks were technically freed but still had not the rights and privileges of free men. That struggle has taken another century and has yet to be fully resolved. In the meantime, over the three hundred years of living in America, our Black people have completely lost their former tribal identities and become a homogeneous society, unlike that of the Republic of South Africa, where nationalities are separate and distinct.

In our new-found self-righteousness, the United States has accelerated its recognition and integration of our Black population (and not without violence, either) and in our rush to atone for our past sins, we insist that every other country with a racial imbalance follow suit.

If the Republic of South Africa were left alone to complete its goal of separate but equal nations in a Commonwealth of South Africa, the United States would probably, and reluctantly, concede that in the end the South Africans were right. However, should the Communist world, through subversion or through active conflict, attempt to oust the current White minority and install a Black majority government, the United States in all probability would continue its bench-sitting policy. Only a massive invasion by foreign troops or other atrocities might reverse the current US position.

However, there is still a little "Yankee Trader" in most Americans, the sense of what constitutes a good deal. I suspect, therefore, that the policy of the United States toward the Republic of South Africa is that of the governing few, rather than the general will of America's private citizens. Should the question of our relations with South Africa, together with the region's advantages and disadvantages, be put squarely to the American people, their innate common sense could cause them to demand a reversal of our policy of non-recognition and that, instead, we should get on with the business of the day. But until that happens, the United States will continue to shun South Africa, treating it like an ancient city's belled leper.

If the track record of the majority of other Black African countries is any indication of the future, the collapse of Rhodesia would almost certainly result in an oppressive government with ties to Moscow. Rhodesia could then become the base (along with Angola and Mozambique) for guerrilla raids into South Africa. As these guerrilla bands become stronger and should they gain strong support among the Black population of southern Africa, these raids could escalate into ruinous all-out warfare, a war the South African Government has no intention of losing.

There would, of course, be some public concern in the United States, but whether it would be enough to produce a change of policy toward South Africa is debatable. If such conflict did escalate to the point of wholesale killing of Whites, burnings, rapings and lootings, we might be shocked enough to see that, by refusing to sell defensive arms to the South Africans, we helped to create the problem; and we might then step in at the last minute and try to alleviate it. But it is frankly doubtful, even in those circumstances, that the United States would intervene.

On the other hand, outright invasion by a Pan-African army would really excite America. The United States, though not committing itself, made a number of strong protestations about

Cubans being used as foreign troops in Angola. If that kind of activity were to be continued, America would certainly re-examine its whole policy toward Africa and toward détente with Russia. But it seems at the present time that nothing short of such an invasion would trigger any sort of a positive response toward any future difficulties the Republic of South Africa might have.

Not since the Second World War has the USSR participated in any invasions or sent any real troops to fight any battles. In Korea there were no Russian soldiers. The Soviet Union provided enormous quantities of equipment and perhaps some pilots and technicians, but only at the start. The same held true in Vietnam. The USSR lets others do its fighting and seems not likely to alter that policy in Africa today. They will finance, they will supply and they will outfit others but will stay out of the actual battle. In other words, it is hard to conceive of an invasion of southern Africa by Russia. But if Russia were actually to send in large numbers of technicians to fight a war, the United States would have to be very much concerned.

A peaceful solution in the Republic of South Africa is as vital to the United States as it is to the country itself. A progressive and aggressive country, South Africa's strategic position makes it important to world economic and military security. The loss of South Africa to Soviet domination would deal the United States and the rest of the Free World an enormous blow.

South Africa holds a commanding position regionally, continentally and world-wide because of its high standard of living, wealth of resources, thriving economy and scientific development. It occupies only about 5 per cent of the total land mass of Africa and houses only 6 per cent of Africa's population, but its industrial output is nearly half that of all Africa combined, and it accounts for more than 20 per cent of Africa's agricultural production.

Half of all foreign investment in Africa goes to South Africa. It generates 60 per cent of all the electricity on the continent and its railways carry 60 per cent of all railway freight. The United States, Canada and the Republic of South Africa together are responsible for more than 30 per cent of the world's annual mineral production.

South Africa's goldfields are the largest in the world. From 1884 to the present, its contribution to the gold production of the Free World averaged more than 49 per cent. Together with Russia, South Africa controls the gold production of the world.

Of major importance to the United States is the fact that southern Africa has the largest reserves of chrome ore in the Western World. The reserves are estimated at more than 2,000 million tons, or about 75 per cent of the Free World's reserves. The United States has very little chrome ore and must import nearly all of the chrome used in the production of stainless steel, a most important alloy to the economy of the United States. No chrome, no stainless steel.

Should the USSR assume dominance over southern Africa, it would control the world's gold supply. The Republic of South Africa, Rhodesia and Russia produce almost all the world's supply of chrome ore. If the worst were to happen, Russia would be in a position to dictate the price of chromite, or to withhold it.

All this, of course, is not to mention the loss of the citadel of South Africa that guards the shipping lanes around the Cape of Good Hope. Were the USSR to attempt to interdict the sea routes, it would *ipso facto* be an act of war and would be dealt with in the harshest of terms. But through bases in Angola and Somalia, Russia would be in a position to threaten those routes.

The Republic of South Africa is a stronghold of extreme importance to the West. It is paramount for the future, not only of Africa, but of all the Free World, that this position be maintained. As Anthony Harrigan says, in geopolitical and strategic terms South Africa occupies the focal point between the energy riches of the Persian Gulf and the Arabian Peninsula and the industrialised, oil-consuming nations of the West.

The reopening of the Suez Canal only emphasises the strategic location of South Africa. The reopened Canal cannot handle the giant oil tankers of today. What it does afford is an opportunity for the Russian fleet to gain quicker access to the Indian Ocean.

Most of the oil from Saudi Arabia, Kuwait, Iraq and Iran exits through the Persian Gulf and finds its way by sea to Europe or Japan or to the United States. Those tankers which come to Europe, with the exception of the very small ships which can pass through the Suez Canal, have to go round the Cape of Good Hope. The same holds true for ships *en route* to America.

Since its discovery early in 1488, South Africa has been a replenishment point for mariners. In modern times, more than 12,000 ships call at South Africa's ports annually. In addition, anywhere from 11,000 to 14,000 sail around the Cape heading either east or west. On the major shipping routes of the world, 45 per cent of traffic goes round the Cape of Good Hope annually, while the lanes from South America to European waters handle 20 per cent of the traffic. The lanes around southern Australia accommodate 12 per cent; between Australia and the Indian Ocean, 12 per cent; and around Cape Horn, 11 per cent.

In oil alone, the Cape Route transports 57 per cent of Europe's requirements. 20 per cent of the United States' oil requirements are routed around this southern tip of Africa and that figure is expected to rise to 60 per cent by the 1980s. 25 per cent of Europe's food supplies are also carried around the Cape.

Were the Soviets in a position to interfere with such shipping as a part of some master plan for world domination, the consequences for the United States alone would be dire, not to mention Western Europe. These shipping routes must remain open and a pro-Western Republic of South Africa is the only way to ensure that they do.

One of the major problems the United States has with respect to a policy in the Indian Ocean is the fact that the American people do not want to recognise that there really is an energy shortage which affects them. The Arab oil embargo of three years ago has been largely forgotten and Americans are again used to a ready supply of petroleum products – at a higher cost, but nevertheless a full supply.

Government officials, Congressional representatives and the public at large have little understanding of the importance of either the Indian Ocean or the Cape oil routes. They cannot relate these areas to what happens at their local gasoline station. What is desperately needed is an increased awareness by the American people of the United States' position in the international community and how it depends on sources abroad for a large amount of its manufactured goods and services. As much of our supplies come by sea, an understanding of the dangers we face from the recent massive build-up of the Soviet fleet must be impressed on the citizens of the United States.

Since the British receded from the Indian Ocean within the last decade, there has been only an occasional Western presence in those waters. Recently, when the Soviet Navy began sending large numbers of warships into the area through the newly reopened Suez Canal, the United States realised the importance of a refuelling base on Diego Garcia Island. As it stands now, the closest US Navy bases to the Indian Ocean are at Norfolk, Virginia, and at Subic Bay in the Philippines. The South African port at Simonstown, which had been used by the British until their departure, is closed to the United States by its own self-imposed policy of non-cooperation militarily with the Republic of South Africa.

In order to effect some presence in this critical area of the world, a decision was made several years ago to build an American base somewhere in the Indian Ocean. The island of Diego Garcia was selected, but not without a great deal of opposition. Senator Edward F. Kennedy of Massachusetts fought against the base, charging that it would ignite a "naval presence race" in the Indian Ocean. The United States Congress itself was torn over the issue until it was disclosed that the USSR was building a naval base at Berbera, in Somalia. After these revelations and after a joint House-Senate Armed Services Committee toured the area and returned with a report that a large number of Russian warships routinely navigated the Indian Ocean, Congress voted to provide the funds for the base at Diego Garcia. Construction is now under way.

The Diego Garcia base gives the United States a definite naval capability in the Indian Ocean, with its sea-lanes of vital importance for the transportation of oil. But liberal elements of Congress still contend that if we develop a sizeable presence in the Indian Ocean area, it will only trigger an equally large response by the Soviets.

There has always been a general anti-defence spending attitude by liberal Congressmen. The liberals, of course, want to divert money from national security into programmes to better the American life-style and to help our own people. National security is an intangible, a concept difficult to measure until the need arises and one knows or does not know if the expenditure was sufficient.

The simplest and most reasonable solution to the Indian Ocean question would be for the United States to accept South Africa's offer of the use of the modern naval base at Simonstown and other ports.

The Republic of South Africa's strategic importance, stemming from its geographical location, is further enhanced by its supporting capabilities and potential. The military aspects of this importance are centred at Simonstown, the modern maritime headquarters at Silver Mine and the sub-headquarters at Durban and Walvis Bay. These facilities, together with the country's support capability, make South Africa ideally suitable as a base for naval operations, both in the Indian Ocean and the South Atlantic.

However, because of the United States' view of the Republic of South Africa and its policy of separate development, the Simonstown Naval Base is off-limits to the American Navy. Our Navy would like nothing better than to make Simonstown a port, but the State Department has said no. The US Chief of Naval Operations, Admiral James Holloway, has indicated that it would take a very serious emergency before a US ship would put into any South African port. Although the Navy and the United States are counting on Diego Garcia to serve the purpose, it will be nothing compared to the facilities readily available at Simonstown.

The gigantic build-up of their navy by the Russians, their construction of a naval base to service those ships in Somalia and their confident naval operations in the waters of the Indian Ocean should all have been indicators to the United States that the USSR has a large role in mind for Africa and the Indian Ocean area. Now their arrogant interference in Angola, utilising puppet Cuban troops, has served as a clear signal of their great interest in Africa.

The American public was shocked by the use of the Cubans, and Angola's loss was an important one for the Free World. The State Department probably blundered by not bringing to the attention of the American public that control of Angola by the Soviets would provide a base for Russian submarines to operate in the South Atlantic. As a result, Congress cut off all aid to Angolans fighting for freedom. The American public would have understood that Russian-dominated Angola would be able to provide a base from which it would be possible to intercept the supply routes on the west coast of Africa, just as the Russian base in Somalia serves this function on the east coast. The Russians are now in a position to operate conveniently in the Indian Ocean on the one hand and the South Atlantic on the other.

The unmistakeable intent of the Communists to take over Africa through force has never been more obvious than in Angola. Angola was a signal to the rest of Africa, as indeed to our allies, that the United States would probably waffle in the face of Soviet determination. There is also the probability that, given the same set of circumstances in another country, both Super-powers would repeat their actions in Angola – the Soviet Union, through the use of foreign troops, would intervene, and the United States would remain on the sidelines, protesting loudly and promising ruination, but refusing to run on to the field.

In 1938, both Britain and France, in an effort to appease Nazi Germany, agreed to Germany's absorption of a portion of another country – Czechoslovakia – on the grounds that it was relatively unimportant in the overall scheme of world politics. A year later, Britain was at war with Germany.

What makes the US decision to keep hands off Angola so lamentable is that the necessary determination would have been much easier for the United States now than for Britain in 1938. At that time, a firm stand could have meant war. For the United States, it meant little more than financial aid that would have been trifling in terms of its overall budget. No one asked the United States to fight – only to make forcibly clear that it disapproved of such adventurism. Yet Congress overwhelmingly turned down the Administration's plea for funds to support Angola.

Alexander Solzhenitsyn has observed about the West, "You have entered the era of calculation. For the old spectre of freedom you are no longer capable of making sacrifices, only compromises", a statement highly relevant to the US attitude toward the Angolan conflict.

Although Soviet use of naval and air facilities in Angola would not immediately pose a substantial threat to the United States, in the long run it could diminish America's security in many ways.

1 It would mean an immediate threat to the area south and east of Angola.

2 Russian ships and planes based in Angola could threaten the Cape oil route.

3 Angola will most certainly provide bases for forays and adventurism in south and east Africa, and perhaps across the Atlantic to South America.

The Soviet intervention in Angola demonstrated a whole new range of intentions and capabilities which had previously only been subjects of speculation, and which reflect the USSR's emergence as a Super-power capable of sustaining a major military operation anywhere in the world.

What the world saw in Angola was not a "liberation" but a military conquest, in which Soviet-supported Cuban troops forced the rule of a minority group down the throats of the majority of the Angolan populace. The risks of any such actions in the future are minimised by the relative uninterest of the United States Congress.

While the action in Angola was occurring, the United Nations stood by, refusing to censure the obvious aggressor, but severely criticising the Republic of South Africa for sending in troops to help those on the side of the West. The then-United States Ambassador to the United Nations, Daniel Moynihan, inveighed against the selective morality being applied by the UN to the Republic of South Africa and the use of the "big lie" to suggest that only South Africa was involved in Angola without a word being said against the flagrant aggression of Russia and Cuba.

Because of its strategic position and wealth, South Africa is a coveted prize for Communist imperialists and their collaborators. Through surreptitious propaganda, the USSR to a large extent has succeeded in portraying the struggle being waged on the subcontinent as purely a Black-White confrontation. Numbers have become one of the mightiest factors in world politics, and because of its numerical situation – the White minority and the Black majority – South Africa has drawn the short end of the stick.

The heart of the matter is that anti-racism and the numbers factor have become welded together in a cry for "human rights", no matter the ideals, conditions and ideology of the community concerned.

This brings to mind an interesting aspect of the propaganda levelled at the Governments of the Republic of South Africa and Rhodesia over the past decade (and, in the case of South Africa, for the last thirty years). Majority rule is clamoured for by the Russians, the Cubans and others, but the overwhelming majority of the other nations in Africa do not have real majority rule. Of the forty-nine independent nations in Africa, fifteen are ruled by the military and twenty-nine have one-party civilian governments. Only five have multi-party political systems, two of these being Rhodesia and the Republic of South Africa. There is much justification for the cynical comment, "One man, one vote, once".

In almost every case, the other nations in Africa have totalitarian rule by a Black minority élite. Should the same "Black majority rule" be effected in the Republic of South Africa or Rhodesia, it would undoubtedly end the freedoms and democratic processes of those countries, however imperfect those two democracies may now be, and would probably lead to mass eviction or the voluntary exodus of the

White Africans who have developed both nations. But the State Department does not condemn Black minority governments and herein lies the hypocrisy of America's split-level ethic.

The Republic of South Africa has a policy of separate development. This is universally recognised and denounced at the same time, either through misunderstanding or malice. Within this policy of separate development, each nation identifies the others as nations. Each considers itself different from the others, not on the basis of colour, but as separate entities. The Zulu is different from the Xhosa, who is different from the Tswana, who is different from the White, in culture, language, background, history, heritage, in all the aspects that go to make up a nation and its people. Each is as different and as separate as the Danes from the French and the French from the Italians.

Therein lies the problem. Americans, like the other peoples of the world, tend to see things in terms of their own history and background. We see the separateness as a matter of Black against White, when in actuality this is anything but the case.

The southern African area has in general been condemned by the outside world because of this tendency to think in Black and White terms. It is being pulled violently in all directions, by friends and foes alike, while trying to continue to grow and improve at its own pace.

Another basic difficulty the United States finds in dealing with Africa is that for a long time it has had one "African" policy, which makes no more sense than having, say, a European or an Asian policy, and actually not as much. Africa covers eleven and a half million square miles, with a population of some 305 million, speaking over 800 languages and dialects. To be viable, the policies which govern our approach to southern Africa must recognise the hugeness of the continent, the diversity of its peoples, and the multiplicity of its problems.

The United States takes the position that if White South Africa can be persuaded to abandon its present course, the Russians will have no reason to intervene. In actuality, if White South Africa were to accede to America's wishes it would precipitate a Black power struggle of unbelievable proportions, with all southern Africa, the entire continent, and the Free World coming out the losers.

As a first step toward forming any sort of a workable African policy, the United States should immediately and unilaterally, without any discussion with the United Nations, remove sanctions from Rhodesia and the arms ban from the Republic of South Africa. The United States could supply them with everything they want as quickly as possible. This is no time to continue to quarrel with our friends. To throw southern Africa to the wolves because we do not understand or appreciate just what the Republic of South Africa is trying to accomplish is patently ridiculous.

The best hope for the Western world is for Black-White cooperation in southern Africa, attained in an evolutionary manner. Only in that way will democracy have a chance to grow. Only in that way can the abundant minerals and enormous agricultural resources of southern Africa be used to the benefit of all its citizens, both Black and White. Only in that way can the Black South Africans realise their rising expectations.

However much we want to see a speedy solution, it is not for the United States, the United Nations or any outsider to determine the tempo of southern Africa's policies. Encouragement, even the absence of opposition and criticism, would definitely contribute to a smoother and more rapid achievement of a harmonious internal development.

The southern Africans are extremely pro-West, but prefer to conduct their countries' business in their own way and at their own pace. They recognise the need for a resolution of their difficulties, but they also believe that it is they who know best how to approach them. The best help the Western nations could offer would be to support them passively, but in an active way, that is to say, letting the southern Africans do what they have to do by themselves, but also warning others who might be contemplating interference to keep out.

The South Africans to a certain extent feel that the Western world relies on them, that the West is happy to have the South Africans where they are. But the West does nothing to ensure that South Africa remains strong. Therefore the South Africans must plan on the basis that, should a crisis arise, they would have to go it alone. They would be happy to accept aid, but they are realistic – almost fatalistic – about America's seeming reluctance to understand or assist a friend.

The southern African countries are of immense value – both now and in the future – to the United States of America, and it is time we realised that very simple fact. South Africa wants nothing from us but our friendship and support. America should come off the sidelines and get into the game.

THE STRATEGIC STAKES

Anthony Harrigan

Anthony Harrigan is a former newspaper editor and the author of seven books on military and national affairs, including *Defence Against Total Attack* and *A Guide to the War in Vietnam*. He is a former Research Associate at the Georgetown University Centre of Strategic and International Studies and former Managing Editor of the American Security Council's *Washington Report*. He has contributed widely to professional military journals in the United States and in allied countries. He has lectured at the US National War College, South African Defence College and other academic institutions. Since 1970, he has been Executive Vice President of the United States Industrial Council.

Behind the smokescreen of the vocabulary of détente, Moscow opened through its naval build-up a whole spectrum of new possibilities of direct – but principally of indirect – strategy to the hegemonial aspirations of Soviet imperialism.

IN THIS sentence, Wolfgang Hopker, the West German naval strategist, succinctly describes what has happened in the 1970s in the Indian Ocean, the South Atlantic, and the adjacent land areas of the African continent – chiefly south-central Africa.

Alexander Solzhenitsyn, in his interview with the BBC, reminded Europeans and Americans of disturbing truths, among them that in the past two years "the West has become much weaker than the East" and that our capitulations "move very quickly". Witness the shocking events in Angola.

"Today you don't have to be a strategist to understand why Angola is being taken," he said. "What for? This is one of the positions from which to wage world war most successfully: a wonderful position in the Atlantic."

Solzhenitsyn added: "The Soviet armed forces have already overtaken the West in many respects, and in other respects they are on the point of overtaking. The navy? Britain used to have a navy. Now it is the Soviet Union that has the navy, control of the seas, bases. You may call this détente if you like, but after Angola I just can't understand how one's tongue can utter this word."

Though the vast territory of Angola – only recently in the possession of a friendly NATO power – has been lost to the West, the significance of this disaster is still not recognised in the United States at the official level. Indeed former Secretary of State Henry Kissinger's speech in Lusaka was shot through with hostility towards the remaining anti-Communist bastions in the African sub-continent. The massive Soviet-Cuban thrust into Angola, far from enlightening and energising the United States, has produced a curious reaction whereby heavy pressure is put on Rhodesia and South Africa to accommodate themselves to revolutionary forces – in effect to the design for the continent long-favoured by the Soviet Union. More than one-tenth of the Cuban army was deployed in Angola, but Dr Kissinger proposed aid to such leftist régimes as the People's Republic of Mozambique, which intended to launch guerrilla war against Western bastions.

Americans simply do not understand the stake that they have in south-central Africa and the Western Indian Ocean.

They fail to grasp the fact that the resources of the region are an integral part of the industrial system of the West, including Japan, and contribute to the overall strength of our civilisation. They do not realise that the United States is increasingly dependent on south-central Africa for strategic materials – it imports more than a hundred minerals, sixteen of them in very large quantities, from various areas. If these resources were lost to the West, it would give the Soviets the biggest boost that they have ever enjoyed.

They include – and I speak of South Africa alone – two-thirds of the world's proven chrome reserves; three quarters of the world's supply of gold; one quarter of the supply of uranium; the world's largest deposits of platinum-group metals; and the world's largest known reserves of high-grade iron ore; plus vast quantities of manganese, copper, nickel, zinc and other minerals, as well as colossal coal reserves (between 35 and 40 billion tons).

The failure of understanding also extends to the matter of the West's oil lifeline around the Cape of Good Hope.

It is imperative that Americans should realise that the Cape Route around the southern tip of Africa is now not only the most crowded sea route (24,000 ocean ships a year, or 66 per day), but also the most vital route for fuel-hungry Europe and the United States. According to the United States Strategic Institute, 60 per cent of America's oil imports will be moved via this route in the 1980s and the apparent unwillingness of the US Congress to push for American energy independence makes certain an increasing dependence on Persian Gulf oil and on the Cape Route.

It is in the light of this situation that we should consider the significance of what has happened in Angola. This territory is of course a substantial oil producer, which underscores the importance of the victory Communism has achieved there. The Angola operation suggests the methods which the Soviets are likely to use in Africa and the Southern Oceans in future.

Angola was conquered by a 12,000-man Cuban force which must now be recognised as the Soviet Union's foreign legion. It was a fully-equipped expeditionary force, involving paratroop battalions, artillery with truck-mounted multiple 122-mm rocket launchers, tank battalions, and anti-aircraft artillery units. It also included political police units. Across Africa, in the Arabian Peninsula, other Cuban proxy forces have been deployed. In South Yemen, the Cubans have had a substantial military mission, incorporating an aviation component flying helicopters and MIGs. In short, Cuba is the Soviet Union's surrogate. Cuban forces, supported by the Soviet Navy and transported by plane and ship, can be − and undoubtedly will be − deployed at numerous spots in the Afro-Asian Ocean world. The Soviets, therefore, have a ready and effective means of intervention.

They clearly hope to extend their sway over the African subcontinent. They know, for instance, that Rhodesian chrome is vital for the United States. As economic historian John Chamberlain has written, "much of the communications structure of a modern society would fall to pieces without this metal".

In general, the Soviet approach is to establish control points in Africa. To this end, the Soviets have given more than $3 billion in military aid to African countries in the past five years. With this aid, Moscow has gained access and influence. From their base in Angola, the Soviets will be able to exert pressure against Zaire, Botswana, Zambia and other Black African countries.

Operating out of Angolan and Mozambique ports, the Soviets could effectively dominate both Southern Oceans and gain the ability to intimidate Brazil as well as Australia.

Wolfgang Hopker, in an article in the *Proceedings of the US Naval Institute*, suggested that "the role of Cuba as a Soviet base is connected with the development of Conakry into a naval and air base in West Africa. A control line, patrolled by Soviet aircraft, runs across the narrowest part of the ocean, the 'wasp's waist' from Conakry through the Cape Verde Islands into the Caribbean to Cuba." Thus today the South Atlantic is rapidly becoming a zone in which the Soviets have a strong air-naval capability: and this is a zone across which the oil traffic from the Persian Gulf must move to the industrialised West.

This situation underscores the outdated character of NATO arrangements. The alliance was founded a quarter century ago as a North Atlantic pact which considered only North America and Western Europe as defensive zones. The restriction of NATO to the oceanic region north of the Tropic of Cancer makes no sense now and has not made sense for years. Had NATO been able to make even a modest commitment of arms and expertise to countering revolutionary forces in southern Africa in the 1960s and 1970s, Mozambique and Angola would be under Western control today. Moreover, Portugal would have been spared revolutionary excesses in its metropolitan territory.

While the errors of the past are beyond repair, the NATO Alliance still has an opportunity to adjust to current realities. It is essential, for instance, for NATO countries to realise that the Soviet threat to the Alliance's fuel supplies is in the Indian Ocean and South Atlantic, and must be dealt with in those oceanic regions. But the NATO countries are politically muddled and apparently unable to see the need for a new, realistic approach to oceanic defence and protection of the oil lifeline. Dr Ray Cline, research director of the Centre For Strategic and International Studies at Georgetown University, writing in his book *World Power Assessment*, has rightly said that the United States must offer credible security guarantees to a core group of allies. His thesis is that the United States should adopt an "oceans alliance" policy.

Both in Europe and in the United States, however, there is an unwillingness to come to grips with these strategic realities. Moreover, there is an ideological obsession with eliminating every vestige of European influence on the continent of Africa. Thus, for example, Stephen S. Rosenfeld, *Washington Post* editorial writer, supports the position (20th Feb. 1976) that the United States should attempt to "steal some of the Russians' advantage by coming more openly to the side of the Black-majority Liberation movements in Rhodesia and Namibia (South-West Africa)." In the same spirit, he writes "The United States ought to be more supportive of the black nations just north of South Africa – Zambia, Mozambique, Tanzania." That these nations are committed to revolutionary violence and are openly hostile to America's political and economic system, Mozambique being in fact a self-styled "People's Republic", apparently means nothing to Mr Rosenfeld. He is not alone; this was the official view set out in former Secretary of State Henry Kissinger's Lusaka address.

If America is to achieve security in the Southern Oceans, profound attitudinal changes must be accomplished in the United States. Basic to such attitudinal changes is an accelerated process of education with respect to the Southern Hemisphere, so that the American people understand the stake they have in a continued Western presence and the unimpeded movement of oil and strategic materials to the industrialised countries of the Northern Hemisphere.

Americans must ask themselves what they would do if the oil traffic from the Persian Gulf were interrupted as a result of Soviet action. They must consider what they would demand if the chrome, manganese, tin, cobalt and plantinum group metals of southern Africa were denied to American industry. They must understand the havoc such actions would play with the American economy, with the livelihoods of millions of citizens, and with their own standard of living and physical security. Would they accept drastic rationing of fuel and materials and the adoption of an austerity régime such as has never been known in America even in wartime?

Surely, if the American people understand that their way of life is involved in the strategic manoeuvres in southern Africa, the western Indian Ocean and the South Atlantic, they will insist that their Government adopt a more realistic policy.

The American and European opponents of stronger defence efforts in the Southern Oceans region argue that there is no immediate threat of Soviet naval-subversive war, if indeed there is even a potential threat. They insist that the real danger in the area is of a racial conflict which would damage the interests and image of the Western powers. The danger from the Soviet Union, they say, is minimal. The Angola experience should have destroyed that argument, but its proponents resist realism.

No one argues that the Soviet Union will begin massive surface and sub-surface operations against NATO shipping next week or next year. But the fact is that the capability for such operations has been created. Furthermore, the Western officials and opinion-makers must answer the question: why have the Soviets made the vast expenditures involved in creating a large Indian Ocean naval force, support facilities, and air reconnaissance units which cover the South Atlantic as well? The Soviet Union does not depend on oil moving via the Cape Route. The deployment of naval power into the Indian Ocean and the South Atlantic is difficult and expensive for the USSR, given its geographical position. Nevertheless, the Soviets have made this enormous effort. No sooner had the British begun their pull-out from the Indian Ocean in 1966 than the Soviets began to move in.

The passing decade finds the Soviets with very significant facilities at Berbera in the Somali Republic, which include installations protected by Soviet missiles, and other facilities around the rim of the Indian Ocean – at Aden, Hodeidah in Yemen, Chittagong and Vishakhapatnam and Umm Qasr in Iraq. The Soviet Navy also has anchorages and landing facilities from Mauritius to Socotra Island at the entrance of the Red Sea. Indeed the USSR is well on its way to dominating the principal control points for the Indian Ocean. And on the west coast of Africa, Soviet military aircraft operate out of Guinea on a regular basis, providing surveillance of warships and merchant vessels. It is to be expected that the principal ports of Angola and Mozambique will be fully utilised by the Soviet Navy in the years ahead. In addition, the Soviet propaganda organs have waged a continuing struggle to mobilise world opinion, including opinion inside the Western countries, against America's use of the Diego Garcia atoll in the Indian Ocean and against Western use of the important South African naval base of Simonstown near the Cape of Good Hope. The Soviet Navy's access to a wide range of shore facilities augments its capability of interfering with Western shipping. The application of Soviet seapower in this manner, in an area remote from Western centres but vital to Western interests, is a very real possibility. It could be applied selectively against one or more countries, with little fear that the United States would respond in an effective fashion. The NATO Alliance, which recognises an attack on one as an attack on all, does not extend to the Southern Oceans, although the Cape Route is the oil jugular of the West. To deny the Western countries essential fuel is within the capability of the Soviet Union, if the West is weak in the Indian Ocean and deprived of its power base in southern Africa. The Soviet naval forces also provide essential support and cover for proxy forces engaged in pushing the West out of southern Africa.

An immense furore is created when a Western government attempts to protect its interests in the Southern Oceans region. A global chorus of protest and disapproval was heard when the United States opposed the most extreme revolutionary movement in Angola or favoured the expulsion of a hostile régime in Chile, which has a long frontier on the South Pacific. The elements in America and Europe that are so vocal in condemning South Africa's continued control over the South-West African coastline – and the rich mineral lode of that territory – are eager to supply money and munitions to revolutionary Mozambique. Such activities are a key part of a doomsday scenario for Western civilisation.

The strengthening of Western naval forces in the Indian Ocean and South Atlantic is imperative for NATO and for friendly states such as Japan. The Japanese are especially vulnerable to an interruption of shipping. Japan's lifeline is the chain of tankers transporting oil across the Indian Ocean to the home islands. That lifeline is endangered, not only by the Soviet naval presence but by the growing might of the Chinese Communist Navy. As Fox Butterfield reported in the *New York Times* (10th Aug., 1975), Communist China "has quietly built up what is now regarded as the world's third largest navy".

Some of the most important strategic developments in the area are the result of South African initiatives especially in so far as ports are concerned. On the east coast of Africa, Lourenço Marques (now called Maputo) in Mozambique may cease to be an open port for Western shipping, in which event the Western countries, including Japan, would be seriously handicapped. The South Africans, however, have created a vast new harbour at Richards Bay, which will not only serve Western and Japanese shipping but will provide harbour facilities for Zambia and Zaire if those countries continue to cooperate with the West.

A sophisticated new harbour is also being created at Saldanha – just over 60 miles to the west of Cape Town. This is probably the largest deep-water port between Europe and the Far East, and plans for a repair dock have been made. Such a facility would be ideally situated from the naval standpoint, halfway around the vital Cape Route. Through this port will pass millions of tons of high-grade iron ore needed by Western Europe. The four billion ton iron ore lode at Sishen, which the port will serve, is an invaluable strategic materials source for the West. The direct importance of the Sishen-Saldanha project for the United States may be gauged from the fact that in 1973 the US imported 95 million tons of minerals – a figure which may increase to 160 million tons by the year 2000.

Such realities explain the fierce political-military-propaganda struggles pertaining to the Southern Oceans region. The Soviets are determined to exploit the Western weakness of will and vision and to play upon Western idealism and intellectual confusion.

Dr Paul Eidelberg, research professor at Claremont College, in an essay entitled *Beyond Détente* (United States Industrial Council Educational Foundation, 1976) notes, in this connection, that there "has long been a moralistic aversion" in the United States to defending foreign policy on economic grounds. He has pointed out that "American statesmen have been reluctant to inform the public" that the foreign policy of a democracy "must be vitally concerned with securing foreign markets and sources of energy and raw materials – and not simply for the sake of maximising wealth, but for extending equality and the blessings of liberty to all its citizens". Regard for the economic interests of Western nations, which are dedicated to the values of our civilisation, is perfectly compatible with moral purposes. To put it another way, Western nations are under no moral obligation to commit suicide by denying themselves access to what is essential for their security.

Other nations besides Japan and the NATO countries have a vital stake in the security of the Indian Ocean, the South Atlantic and southern Africa. These include Iran and Saudi Arabia, which must sell their oil in Western markets if they are to survive and complete their modernisation process. Indeed their stake is likely to increase inasmuch as they are gradually acquiring their own fleets of tankers. Iran, with its growing navy and strong air force, could already contribute significantly to any joint defence against Soviet moves in the Western Indian Ocean. These forces, the Shah has indicated, have a mission that extends far beyond the Persian Gulf. Far to the south, maritime aircraft and ships based at Simonstown logically have a mission of protecting ocean traffic round the Cape and in zones extending for hundreds of miles along the eastern and western edges of the sub-continent.

A vital key to security in the western Indian Ocean, however, is the construction of US naval communications and supply facilities, including a landing field, on Diego Garcia, which is 3,200 miles from Durban and 2,700 miles from the entrance to the Persian Gulf. Further delay in constructing these facilities would be very costly in terms of Western security. On the west coast of Africa, it would be immensely valuable if the Cape Verde Islands and the Azores remained available to the West and if ways were found to add military capabilities in those islands. The key to this is an improvement in the political situation in Portugal and continuation of Portuguese participation in NATO.

It is not at all clear that official and public opinion in the West is prepared to take cognisance of these facts. The manifest truth of the Angolan situation has been obscured by the propaganda war waged against the remaining European elements in southern Africa. As Dr Milton Friedman, the prominent American economist, wrote in *Newsweek* (24th May, 1976), "we seem to be going out of our way to alienate southern Africa, to make its position untenable, and to drive it into the arms of the Soviet Union." In so doing, America makes its own position untenable and threatens its national interest and that of its allies in Europe and Japan. The ideological conflicts which have rent the fabric of American society since the mid-1960s live on, having an impact on US foreign and military policies and impairing America's ability to respond to Soviet aggression in the Southern Oceans region.

Nevertheless, there are signs that many Americans realise the nation must concentrate anew on security and protect sources of energy and strategic materials. There seems to be a growing awareness that the Soviets must not be allowed to seize and control the resources of southern Africa. Time is running out, however, and must be used constructively. Otherwise, the United States and its allies will make one of those enormous, tragic capitulations to which Alexander Solzhenitsyn referred. This would come perilously close to being the ultimate capitulation for the West. Certainly, it would set the stage for the final showdown.

THE FRENCH PRESENCE

General Jean Callet

General Callet has had a varied career in the Army. After leaving Saint-Cyr in 1935 he served in the Foreign Legion, the Marocains Goums and air o.p.s. During the war he served in the Second Armoured Division under General Leclerc in Normandy, in the liberation of Paris, and in Germany. Later he served in Indo-China, Algeria and in the Western Sahara. In 1965 he became military commandant of the Colmar sub-division and in 1969 Commander of the 4th Mechanised Division at Verdun. From 1972–1974 he was the Director of L'Institut des Hautes Etudes de Défense Nationale and is the author of *Légitime Défense*, published in 1976.

IN FEBRUARY 1976, Michel Debré, for many years Prime Minister of France, an earlier Minister of Defence, and latterly Deputy for Réunion, published an article in the *National Defence Review* called "Indian Ocean 1976, French presence, pledge of peace and hope." The article emphasised the point that France was still present (in the Indian Ocean) and "is keeping her options open for the future. She is prepared to recognise her chances and to take them." A similar view prevails with the French Government of the present day (1977): one may assume that it is trying to keep its options open for the future by maintaining a French presence wherever this may be feasible.

For one thing, France is not strictly an external power in the Indian Ocean. Because Réunion is regarded as French territory, France counts as one of the nations of the area, and in any case the level of her forces is not high enough to disturb this "peace zone". "Réunion," comments Monsieur Debré, "is for foreigners the land of freedom and the development of man; expression is free, the press is free, television is open to all, new buildings are multiplying ... Our country is an example of a Western nation concerned also with the Indian Ocean, with no imperialist ambitions, and with no military aims ... France is the only power of the West which is in the Indian Ocean for a reason other than tourism or the maintenance of a military presence."

Moreover, to keep open options for the future, France must hold on to her means for freedom of action and preserve her interests. The question raised by Admiral Labrousse in the October 1976 issue of the *National Defence Review* was whether the Indian Ocean would remain a peaceful zone. "The crucial points," he added, were the "organisation of communications and of the economic, political and other ties which hold the countries together, and which will allow them to have relations with each other and to exchange their products in reasonable freedom."

Let us now turn to the extent and character of the various French interests in the area. It was for purely commercial reasons that the Indian Ocean became important in French history. Hard on the heels of the Portuguese came intrepid French sailors who were active in the Indian Ocean from the beginning of the sixteenth century. The first record of a French ship was in 1527, when the *Marie-de-Bon Secours* called at Madagascar, Sumatra and Diu; the next occasion was in 1529 when a merchant from Dieppe, Jean Ango, sent the *Pensée* and the *Sacre* there. Until the beginning of the nineteenth century French seamen followed the

"*Carriera do India*", the Cape Route, which led them to all the wealth of India and China. The ports of Nantes, Bordeaux, and Lorient owe their importance largely to the Cape Route; Lorient even owes it its name, originally L'Orient, since it was the base of the French East India Company ("Compagnie des Indes Orientales") which was founded by Colbert in 1664.

What remains of French possessions after a long history of involvement in the area is all in the western part of the ocean or in the open part to the south, and consists of several islands.

The island of Réunion, formerly the Isle of Bourbon, is the most important of them and is the most closely attached to France because of the origin of her population and her status as French overseas territory. Her surface area of 2,500 square kilometres and her 500,000 inhabitants qualify her to send three Deputies to the French Parliament. The island is almost entirely round and most of it consists of a volcanic mountainous area, which reaches 3,069 metres at Piton des Neiges, and which occasionally shows a tendency to be active. The arable area is relatively small (1,000 square kilometres) and is given up largely to cane sugar (430 square kilometres). Coffee cultivation has almost ceased altogether, but another speciality has been developed in the shape of aromatic plants: ylang-ylang, geranium, vetiver and vanilla.

When the French arrived the island was deserted, but it is now somewhat overpopulated (200 inhabitants to the square kilometre), and the population is increasing considerably (2.2 per cent in 1976). The people's nationalities make up a mosaic with very imprecise outlines. It is estimated that there are 130,000 descendants of the original European colonisers, some of whom have a very low standard of living. A fifth of the total are Indians whose forebears came from Madras and Calcutta to work there in the nineteenth century; 12,000 to 13,000 are Muslim. The Chinese number 25,000, while the rest of the population are halfcasts, many of them the descendants of black slaves brought there in the eighteenth century. The main problem of the population on Réunion is that the average age is very young; 60 per cent are under twenty.

The major products are sugar (235,000 metric tons per year), which is guaranteed a certain price and a market within the European Community, rum, and methylated spirit (8 million litres per year). With external support the GNP per inhabitant is quite high (7,000 francs in 1975, compared with 825 per inhabitant in

Madagascar), but three-quarters is probably money from France, and social security funds for the people of Réunion amounted to 200 million francs in 1974.

The capital of St Denis has 90,000 inhabitants. The prefecture is in the marvellous building put up in the eighteenth century for the French East India Company. Eleven kilometres away there is a large airport which can accommodate Boeing 747s. The port, Port-des-Galets, is quite small; it has forty hectares of docks with eleven berths for trading ships and eleven for fishing vessels. It is impossible to enlarge it since the hills around are very steep. It can be dangerous during cyclones.

Not far from Port-des-Galets stands the vast pylon (427 metres) of the transmitting antennae for the OMEGA radio navigation system, built with the financial collaboration of the United States. The road network is worthy of the capital and has 2,325 kilometres of asphalted roads.

There are two groups of islands which can be included with Réunion despite their being some distance away. The nearest group is known as the "scattered islands" (*iles éparses*). Three of them (Europa, Juan de Nova, and Bassas da India) are in the Mozambique Channel. The fourth, Les Glorieuses, has a meteorological station and is to the west of the Cap d'Ambre, at the northern point of Madagascar. Tromelin Island, the fifth, is to the east of Madagascar. Except for Les Glorieuses they are all uninhabited.

The southern possessions (Terres Australes) are those islands lying between the thirty-eighth and the fiftieth parallel. The most important of these French possessions is the Kerguelen archipelago, whose 300 islands have a total area of 7,000 square kilometres. The French navigator by whose name they are now known discovered them in 1772; they are swept by the great westerly winds and are distinctly inhospitable. At Port-aux-Français there is an establishment of about a hundred technicians and researchers.

The small Crozet archipelago has an area of only three hundred square kilometres and there is a small base on Ile de la Possession. The two islands of St Paul and Amsterdam are smaller still, the former being only fourteen square kilometres in size and uninhabited, while the latter is a volcanic island covering eighty square kilometres, and with a population of about fifty people. These islands are important for their fish – crayfish and shrimps – and Japanese and Soviet trawlers often call in there.

The Territory of the Afars and Issas (TFAI), now Djibouti, was a French overseas territory, until independence was formalised in June 1977. The Republic is situated on the east coast of Africa which flanks the Gulf of Aden. It is surrounded by Ethiopia to the west, Eritrea to the north and by the Somali Republic to the south. It covers 23,000 square kilometres, with a population of 125,000, of which 62,000 live in Djibouti. 80,000 are Afars or Issas, 35,000 are of mixed racial origins, and 10,000 are Europeans. The Afars have the north, the west and southwest, while the Issas live in the south and south-eastern part of the country. The Republic is in a semi-desert area where the climate is tropical, the soil very poor, and the rainfall slight and irregular. Fishing could be a source of income if fish formed a greater part of the diet.

Djibouti is important mainly for its port. Since 1949 the dependencies of the commercial port and part of the southern port area have been a free zone and the rule of paying indirect contributions in the Republic does not apply. Goods can be left there indefinitely, which is to the advantage of businesses concerned in collection and distribution, revictualling, and the allocation of ships. The port is easily accessible to ships drawing a maximum of thirty-nine feet, and has eleven berths. The outer roads have good mooring facilities where the water is twenty to thirty feet deep. From this port come supplies which go on to the Franco-Ethiopian railway. In 1969–70, 411,000 metric tons of goods were transported by this railway, and 457,000 passengers. The port is essential also for Ethiopia, whose only other port is Assab. Assab has only a road connection with Ethiopia and Djibouti is at the moment being linked to this road system.

The amount of traffic which passes through the port of Djibouti is influenced directly by the Suez Canal. Before the Canal was closed an average number of 260 boats stopped at Djibouti each month. In 1974 this number fell to seventy-two, but rose again in July 1975 to eighty-seven and in September 1975 (three months after the reopening) to 129.

The subject of the French possessions in the Indian Ocean may be completed by a survey of the French military forces which have lately been stationed in these islands and Djibouti. Most of the ground forces are in Djibouti, namely two motorised regiments with armoured anti-tank units, and an artillery regiment. After the evacuation of Diego Suarez the French forces were redeployed in the south of the Indian Ocean around Réunion, where the second regiment of marine parachutists is stationed. Some "roving companies" (*compagnies tournantes*), detached in turn for land intervention, are permanent reinforcements for the forces in Djibouti and in Réunion. One of these companies, which the Legion supplies, guarantees a French presence in Mayotte.

As for seapower, France keeps a small permanent naval force in the area, which in December 1975 consisted of the following: four frigates (aviso-escorts), three patrol boats, a transport boat for lighters, one strategic support ship and an oil supply ship, which carries the ensign of the admiral commanding the naval forces in the Indian Ocean. These permanent forces in the territories are regularly reinforced by an occasional group of two or three major ships, the *Clemenceau* at the end of 1974 and the *Jeanne d'Arc* in 1975, frigates, squadron escorts and even two submarines by the middle of 1976. A sea patrol aeroplane is sometimes detailed for Djibouti.

The French air forces in the Indian Ocean have an air base at Djibouti with a squadron of F100 fighters, which are part of the Tactical Air Force (Force Aerienne Tactique), and an overseas air force group which deals with air transport and consists of six Nord 2501s, two Broussards and four Alouette II and IIIs.

Another air base was opened on Réunion on 1st August, 1973 and supports another overseas group with three Transalls, two Nord 2501s and two Alouette IIs. An air force detachment also exists at Dzuandzi, and it has been decided that the air force establishments on some of the scattered islands should be improved.

The total strength of these three forces is therefore fairly modest, and certainly does not constitute a threat to the peace of the area.

History and national feeling are united on one point, namely that Réunion is as much a part of France as any other *département*, and the French, whether in France or in Réunion, are firmly committed to it. Political opposition in the island concentrates on lobbying for an internal status which would give the island control over the distribution of finances. This opposition knows very well that without French support Réunion would soon relapse into the condition of neighbouring islands and become dependent on another power, probably a less favourable one. How to provide a living for a young population without making intolerable demands on the mother country, in difficulties herself, is nevertheless a problem.

In the lands of this ocean where French ships have ploughed the waves for so long, French cultural interests are by no means negligible. French is still spoken in Mauritius, where descendants of the French colonisers are still numerous; it is also spoken in the Seychelles, although here there has been a certain amount of language degradation, to which the instructions on how to use the telephone at Mahé airport bear witness. In our own time France has had strong cultural influence in Madagascar through the education of certain individuals; the obvious example is the present head of the Malagasy Republic, the frigate captain Didier Ratsiraka, who was at the French Naval School (Ecole Navale Française). French obviously has a hard battle against English, which is used by traders and technicians, but many French people are coming to realise that culture does not just mean literature. French cannot make its mark through Racine and Molière, nor even Claudel, but through the education of engineers and specialists. Indeed, there are several technicians at the Indian nuclear station at Trombay who speak French, having been educated at Saclay or Grenoble. The University of Réunion plays a role which is still small in the encouragement of French culture because of the small number of students from outside Réunion which it can accept, but there is certainly scope for development.

The Indian Ocean is most important to France, however, by reason of the maritime oil trade, which has not been markedly affected by the reopening of the Suez Canal. At the moment only tankers carrying less than 70,000 metric tons in weight or with a capacity less than 150,000 freight tons can go through the Canal. Since 1967 the world-wide tendency has been towards supertankers with a capacity for carrying over 100,000 tons in weight. In his recent article in the *National Defence Review* of October 1976, Admiral Labrousse estimated that there were 665 of these ships, fifty of them French, sailing between the Gulf and Europe, while between the reopening of Suez and December 1975 only three French tankers (and sixty-eight cargo boats) went through Suez. Each year without fail France imports 120-130 million metric tons of oil, and in 1975 three-quarters of this came from Persian Gulf countries.

The sea routes which run through the Straits of Hormuz and round the Cape pass either through the Mozambique Channel or between Réunion and Madagascar. They are long; the latter, the "reserve route" (*route de rechange*), is 4,800 nautical miles. The need, however, is not to protect a sea route but the ships which travel along it, and, when they sail in convoy, maritime air defences can be concentrated around them. In times of unrest this necessitates well-organised naval control bases so that escort boats and maritime patrol aircraft can operate. In the event of a more widespread war France could probably guarantee this protection only by means of cooperation with her Atlantic Alliance partners, who would have the same interests as France, or with countries concerned that sea communications should be unrestricted, such as Iran.

In a military alliance the only weight which a party carries is that of its contribution to the common cause. France's maritime power is limited, and that which she exercises in the Indian Ocean will never be very marked. The most important aspects of this power are the facilities which she can provide: ports, support bases, and aerodromes, these last now being essential with the development of maritime air patrols. However, potential local troublemakers who might harass French ships must be borne in mind. Support bases, which may be no more than a stretch of water where reinforcement ships can be stationed, are likely to be extremely valuable. Given that the scale was different, this was the atoll strategy used by the Americans in the Pacific during the Second World War; a strategy they seem to be using again with Diego Garcia. This is the opposite tactic to that of large bases constructed by empire-builders to last for centuries, such as those built by the British in Singapore. The French version of this tactic is the network of bases in the Indian Ocean for which Diego Suarez was the model.

The port of Djibouti is a special case. When Suez was reopened Djibouti once more became relatively important as a stage on the way to Réunion and as a port of call for boats heading towards the Indian Ocean; but it will never have the prominence which it had when it was first occupied. The territory is well positioned for observation of the Horn of Africa, and is near the Arab countries. It occupies one side of the Bab al Mandab Strait, opposite Perim Island.

However, a more delicate problem is that of the stabilising role which Djibouti plays between two of the neighbouring countries: Ethiopia, whose main interest there is the railway, and Somalia, which claims that Djibouti belongs to her, as also the Ethiopian province of Ogaden and a small part of Kenya. Certain sections of French opinion hold that evacuation will help to remove the final traces of "colonialism", which will facilitate her relations with the Third World. However, this will not necessarily produce the desired effect; the old proverb says that if you want to kill the dog you say it is mad, and there will always be accusations of "neo-colonialism" levelled when politically necessary.

France still has some commercial interests in the area. These gained in importance when the Suez Canal was reopened and when the Persian Gulf countries began to have funds at their disposal. One of the major clients is Iran, to which heavy goods can only be transported by sea and through the port of Abadan, despite the congestion there. France is well placed from the point of view of engineering and nuclear power stations.

A difficult and controversial aspect is that of arms sales, which are essential if France is to remain independent in the field of arms manufacture. A complete range of arms, some constructed under licence, have been sold to a large number of countries of very different political colours. In the *Military Balance* for 1976–77 it can be seen that French arms were bought by the Arab countries, particularly Saudi Arabia, which has 300 AMX 30 tanks, and has ordered 100 more. Iran has bought some SS11 and SS12 ENTAC anti-tank missiles, and has ordered the EXOCET sea missile and has sixteen Superfrelon helicopters. Helicopters, of various types like Alouette II and III, Gazelle, Puma, and Superfrelon, are one of the most commonly found French products in the countries round the Indian Ocean, including Malaysia, Singapore and Bangladesh. Pakistan has three Daphne submarines and a number of aircraft, including Mirage IIIs and three Breguet Atlantic sea patrol craft. India has a quantity of aircraft of French make.

As for South Africa, the French President has, both in 1975 and 1977, touched on the exclusion of land and air weapons from French cargoes delivered to South Africa, although this would not affect contracts already signed. South Africa already has three Daphne submarines. The figures given by the Stockholm International Peace Research Institute in the *SIPRI Year Book 1975* help us to see the French arms trade in its correct proportions. In 1974 France came fourth as an exporter of arms to the Third World with a value of 343 million dollars, behind the Soviet Union (1,467 million), the United States (940 million) and the United Kingdom (481 million).

The proclamation of the new Independent Republic of Djibouti on 26th June 1977 marked the end of 117 years of French rule in the Red Sea. The French have left a large force in Djibouti on a training mission to the Republic's defence force, thus maintaining their traditional role in the Southern Oceans. The equilibrium of the situation is precarious – a tribal feud or foreign intervention could upset Djibouti at any time. The prospect is for a sharpening of suspicious and hostilities all round.

THE IRANIAN CONTRIBUTION

Rear-Admiral Shoa Majidi

Rear-Admiral Shoa Majidi graduated from the Italian Naval Academy in 1956 and began his naval career as navigator of *Iis Palang*. In 1958 he attended the Italian anti-submarine specialisation course and then held various posts in the Imperial Iranian Fleet including Commanding Officer of several ships. In 1962 he was assigned to *Iis Karkas*, a coastal minesweeper, and was involved in its transit from the East Coast of the United States to the Persian Gulf. In 1963 he attended the Italian Hydrographic Institute for two years, where he received the degree of Master of Naval Science. Returning to Iran in 1965, Captain Majidi served at Imperial Iranian Navy Headquarters as Aide to the Commander-in-Chief of the Imperial Iranian Navy and as Naval Operations Planning and Reorganisation Project Officer. In 1968 he was transferred to the United Kingdom for duty as Executive Officer in connection with the transfer of *HMS Artemis*, the first Iranian destroyer. While in Britain he attended various courses, including Naval Tactics at the Royal Naval College, Greenwich. Captain Majidi graduated from the United States Naval War College in 1971 and, in 1972, from the Imperial Iranian National Defence University. In September 1972 he was assigned as Commander, Imperial Iranian Destroyer Division One, and Commanding Officer of *Iis Palang*. In March 1975, he was assigned as Director of Planning for the entire Imperial Iranian Navy and Chairman of the IIN Reorganisation Committee. Since November 1976 he has served as Acting Deputy for Personnel to Commander-in-Chief, IIN, and as Vice-chairman of the IIN Review.

The Strategic Importance of the Persian Gulf

THE CONCERN of Great Powers about the Middle East, especially the Persian Gulf, has been motivated by considerations extraneous to the area and its people – matters of geography, communications, raw materials, the global balance of power and so on. Since the time of Peter the Great, it has been Russia's policy to gain access to the Persian Gulf. Napoleon's invasion of Egypt in 1798 and Germany's lightning drive to the east in the Second World War had similar motives. In competing for the Middle East, the Great Powers often contrived to produce instability in the Persian Gulf area. They helped to inspire local rivalries so as to improve their own positions.

Petroleum has given the area an added strategic significance, for 70 per cent of the world's supply of oil is located in the Middle East, mostly around the Persian Gulf. Middle East oil is not only the most plentiful, but the most economical, in the world; the cost of extracting one barrel of oil in the Persian Gulf is about one-ninth of the cost of extracting a barrel in the United States. Western Europe relies on this oil for three-quarters of its supply; Japan is 90 per cent and Australia 69 per cent dependent on it. The continuous flow of Persian Gulf oil to the Free World, especially Western Europe and Japan, is vital for the global balance of power.

Stability in the Persian Gulf is a prime objective of the littoral states. Hence, Iran recognised Bahrain's independence, ending a century and a half of dispute. Some outside powers may want to discourage the creation and extension of any regional defence organisation in the Persian Gulf, in order to extend their own power. In short, they would like to divide and rule.

The Strategic Importance of the Indian Ocean

The Indian Ocean area has assumed global importance for the following reasons:

1 The increasing need for oil.
2 The Soviet Union (along with the other Communist *bloc* countries) has decided to increase its influence in the Red Sea and other parts of the Indian Ocean.
3 India's policy of resisting China with the support of the Soviet Union.
4 China's continuing attempts to increase its influence in the Indian Ocean.

5 China and India have succeeded in producing nuclear power.
6 The Free World countries' lifeline would collapse if the Indian Ocean highway were lost, because this would effectively deny them the use of the Suez Canal, Cape of Good Hope and Malaysian Straits trade and oil routes.

The reopening of the Suez Canal forced the Free World to consider the amount of ship traffic in the Indian Ocean. There has been a significant increase in the number of supertankers which cannot pass through the Suez Canal. At the present time, 50 per cent of the ocean tankers cannot pass through the Canal and it is estimated that this number will increase to 65 per cent by 1980, whereas it was only 1 per cent in 1966. Although the Canal is losing its importance for the oilers, it will continue to be commercially important. Some 140 million tons of commercial goods will be carried through the Canal by 1980, compared with only 65 million tons during the first year after the Canal was reopened. By the end of 1975, 3 per cent of the world's cargo was carried through the Suez Canal. By 1980 this will increase to 4 per cent.

The Indian Ocean is now crossed by one-third of the world's oilers. Out of 1,600 oilers, more than 80 per cent belong to the United States, Britain, France, Italy, Norway, Spain, Finland, Portugal, Belgium and West Germany; 43 per cent of these oilers belong to NATO countries.

The Soviets have significantly expanded the number of their ships in the Indian Ocean. By observing the decisions made by the Soviets, one can deduce the objectives they wish to obtain by deploying their ships, both naval and commercial, in the Indian Ocean. These are as follows:

1 To observe the naval activities of the Free World fleet, and to establish their own communications.
2 To protect their power and influence over littoral countries of the Indian Ocean.
3 To obtain new naval bases, while weakening and expelling the Free World countries from their traditional bases, and to increase Soviet political influence and decrease the influence of the Free World.
4 To provide attack forces with an expanded offensive capability (in coordination with the overall plans of the Soviet *bloc*).
5 To cut the links between CENTO nations and to suffocate NATO by choking off the flow of petroleum.
6 To influence more and more countries of eastern Africa.

7 To force certain countries to create regional conflicts for political purposes, to isolate NATO countries and to upset the economic and political union of NATO and the rest of the Free World.

In recent decades the Soviet Union has achieved certain inroads in the Middle East, which have smoothed the way for spreading its influence in the Indian Ocean. It has, for example, obtained a large market for selling its armaments, and established the dependency of Arabian countries on the Soviet Union; obtained access to a very important region with great oil reserves; established military bases in strategic locations of the region; expanded pro-Socialist régimes in the area; and shifted power and influence at the international level for its own advantage.

A presence in the Indian Ocean is an old Soviet aim. Certain littoral states of this region have opened their doors to the Soviets. The first appearance of the Soviet Navy in the Indian Ocean took place in 1968. It began with a cruiser, a destroyer and a frigate calling on Mogadishu, Umm Qasr, Bandar Abbas, Karachi and Colombo. During the 1960s, a mere fourteen Soviet warships visited the Indian Ocean. Today's display of naval forces, equipped with sophisticated weapons, in the Indian Ocean, and its missile armoury in Somalia, are part of the USSR's geopolitical strategy.

The Communists put paramount importance on political considerations in every move they make. It is natural that in such a case, if the political cost of influence is too high, they will accept something less than complete success for the time being. Simultaneously they will develop an alternative plan for the attainment of their goals, i.e. to exploit the weaknesses of the Free World in political, economic, military and international affairs.

Most specialists knowledgeable about Communist *bloc* resources believe that the Soviet Union will itself encounter a shortage of oil during the next two decades. These same experts also believe that the increased consumption of oil inside the Soviet Union, together with the exporting of oil to the Eastern European Communist *bloc*, will soon decrease the Soviet reserve oil wells at Tyumen. In addition, exploration of oil reserves in Siberia will be very costly, as it will create the difficult problem of long transportation and supply lines for relatively low-quality oil. The Soviets could more feasibly provide the oil needed by Eastern Europe from the Middle East. The USSR has made many attempts to gain influence in this region for the sole purpose of dipping its hands into the plentiful oil reserves that exist there.

When the Suez Canal was closed, it was, to a great extent, to the disadvantage of the Soviet Union. Now that the Canal has been reopened, the Russians are able to reach more easily into the Indian Ocean, thereby extending their sphere of military influence, with a much shorter route to naval bases there. For they are bound to seek a better working relationship with Egypt, closer ties in the Red Sea, use of ports at Hodeidah and Aden, and control of the People's Democratic Republic of Yemen (Aden) and of the Bab al Mandab Strait.

Meanwhile the Soviet Union established smooth working relations with India under Mrs Gandhi, Mr Shastri and Mr Nehru. This relationship was founded upon long-term Soviet loans and technical assistance. In return the Soviet Union has hoped to obtain bases or, at the minimum, docking and support privileges. Links with India may not be as close under the Government elected in 1977, but Soviet influence cannot be ignored.

In Africa, the USSR has expanded its position in the eastern part, and clearly hopes to acquire new bases in southern Africa by gaining influence over Mauritius, the Republic of Malagasy and other islands.

The Imperial Iranian Navy is a vital part of the defence system. Defence decisions are part and parcel of political, economic and technological considerations. Although the concept of seapower has not entirely escaped change, its foundation, the sea, has remained the same as ever and its significance has varied little. The sea remains the most effective transportation highway on this planet. It covers almost three-quarters of the earth's surface, and with few exceptions it is everywhere navigable; by means of rivers and channels it reaches deeply into the adjacent countries.

Although the airway spans equal distances and is able to reach land-locked areas, the cost of air transportation is incomparably higher than that of any other means of transportation. This fact can be simply demonstrated: one horse power (1hp) moves approximately 7 to 8 kilogrammes of payload by air, approximately 40 to 90 kilogrammes by road, 500 to 700 kilogrammes of payload by rail and 1,000 to 4,000 by sea.

These figures obviously do not take into consideration the speed of transportation. In comparison with road and rail, the seaway has the advantage of being indestructible since it requires no repair and can be used almost throughout its entire expanse.

Congestion will therefore not occur and even the largest transports can be re-routed at immediate notice.

There is another aspect of national dependence on freedom of the seas. Those who buy abroad must sell abroad. Any serious interruption of access to overseas markets can be catastrophic to producers, in a world where production is as highly specialised as it is in today's world. Unemployment can mount rapidly and the cutting off of sources of foreign income can mean a reduction in supplies of essential foreign exchange and a deficit in a country's balance of payments that can quickly drain away monetary reserves and undermine the national money.

The seas are, moreover, an essential source of food and raw materials. Every day world population increases by 100,000. It is estimated that a billion and a half people alive today have never had an adequate supply of protein in their diet. Fish is an excellent source of protein, and one scholar estimates that there is enough protein in the sea to supply adequate food for 300 billion people, if the full resources of the sea, as well as fish, are efficiently harvested. The sea is also a tremendous storehouse of at least fifty minerals, and 50 per cent of the world's available oil resources lie under the water.

The observation of Themistocles that "He who controls the sea has command of everything" holds good today. Some nations develop seapower as a result of natural or spontaneous economic or social movements, and other nations, not dependent on trade or overseas territory, desire seapower for conquering or enforcing their will upon others and so gain more wealth, strength and influence.

Seapower, like a three-legged stool, rests upon these supports: a merchant marine, cooperation of friendly nations such as may provide overseas bases, and a fighting force – a navy. Seapower itself is founded on economic power.

The Imperial Iranian Navy is not established upon territorial ambitions, but – as H.I.M. the Shahanshah Aryamehr has stressed – the need for cooperation among the Persian Gulf littoral states to ensure the region's peace and stability and Iran's determination "to become strong enough to guard this region alone if the need arises. The Persian Gulf and the Straits of Hormuz in truth constitute Iran's lifeline if this area were in any way threatened, our very life would be in danger." H.I.M. the Shahanshah has repeatedly affirmed that any guarantee of security and stability in the areas of the Persian Gulf, Gulf of

Oman and Indian Ocean by resisting Great Power intervention can only be possible when the countries of these regions are strong enough.

In this context must be placed H.I.M. the Shahanshah's recommendation of an economic common market in the region, including all Indian Ocean littoral states. A country like Iran cannot be indifferent to what is happening around her or to her lifelines. Hence H.I.M. the Shahanshah's emphasis on cooperation. Iran "has shown that it responds to a request for help from others without hesitation. If we had not moved into Oman, Dhofar might have become another Angola; and, who knows, we may have seen Cuban soldiers there. That is why I stress that the countries in this region must strengthen themselves until world disarmament can be enforced." Iran is looking to extinguish any Communist brush fire in this area as soon as it starts. Because when the expanse of fire has become too big, it can only be put out by the intervention of nuclear powers. A Persian proverb runs: "When the fire is big enough, it burns dry objects and wet alike."

Iran plans to become one of the strongest countries in the world. Such strength requires seapower. Authority at sea, coupled with air superiority, produce a general reputation of power, which in turn allows an effective voice in international affairs. It protects an extensive world-wide sea trade, vital to the national economy. It guarantees defence. It deters hostile powers – a function expressed by Tirpitz's famous "Risk Theory", that if a navy could not be made strong enough for victory against every opponent, yet it should be made so strong that its destruction would cost even the greatest power such enormous losses that the risk alone would act as a deterrent against attack.

For Iran specifically, adequate seapower should ensure the protection of the Persian Gulf, Gulf of Oman and Indian Ocean, in cooperation with friendly nations, and deny Iran and its resources in the Persian Gulf and Gulf of Oman to any hostile power. It allows the fulfilment of political or military commitments to friendly forces in the area.

Conclusions
A THE CHALLENGE
1 The oil supply routes to the Free World countries are long and vulnerable and open to attack by Communist *bloc* countries.
2 The Communist Super-powers will not get involved in regional crises directly. Unless the end result is assured both from the

military and the political point of view, the Communist Super-powers will involve themselves in local crises only by using third party countries as they used the Cubans in Angola.

3 Increasing Communist *bloc* activities are conspicuous in the Indian Ocean area to project power and influence and establish more satellite countries as part of their overall global strategy to extend their sphere of influence world-wide.

4 The Communist *bloc* is trying to influence the developing nations of the world by displays of naval superiority and by expert use of modern communications and mass media techniques.

5 Communist forces focus attention of the NATO countries on the NATO frontiers, while they exploit, almost unhindered, weaker areas of the world.

6 The Communist powers try to widen the gap between poor and rich countries.

7 The Communist Powers take political and psychological advantage of internal problems such as those in southern Africa.

8 Communist *bloc* strategy encompasses many factors: economic, political, psychological and ideological as well as military; none stands alone.

B THE REQUIRED RESPONSE

1 Partnership is the key to Free World defence strategy, not only militarily but commercially.

2 Free World defence strategy, based on the resources of the most powerful countries, must ensure the participation of all
. Free World countries. It must be comprehensive and global, and look to the twenty-first century.

3 The rich and industrialised countries of the Free World, including NATO countries, have to accept greater responsibility for global defence strategy by proper political, economic and military assistance to the weaker Free World countries – without, however, sending any manpower which could create political crises.

4 Regional Free World defence alliances, demonstrating strong resolve against Communist aggression, must be maintained.

5 The problems of those areas of the Free World must be resolved so as to forestall exploitation by Communist countries.

176

AUSTRALIA
AND THE
INDIAN OCEAN

Robert O'Neill

Dr Robert O'Neill graduated from the Royal Military College, Duntroon, in 1958 and from the University of Melbourne, with first-class honours in engineering, in 1961. He studied at Oxford University 1961–1965 as a Rhodes Scholar, first reading for a BA in Politics, Philosophy and Economics, and then writing a thesis on "The German Army and the Nazi Party", for which he was awarded a Doctorate of Philosophy. After returning to Australia he served in Vietnam with the 5th Battalion, Royal Australian Regiment, 1966–1967. He was mentioned in despatches for his work as Battalion Intelligence Officer. After leaving the Army in 1968 he became a Senior Lecturer in History at the Royal Military College, Duntroon. He joined the Department of International Relations, Research School of Pacific Studies, Australian National University, as a Senior Fellow in 1969. Since 1971 he has been Head of the Strategic and Defence Studies Centre, Australian National University. He is the author of several books, including *The German Army and the Nazi Party*, *Vietnam Task* and *General Giap: Politician and Strategist*. He is the Armed Services Editor of the Australian Dictionary of Biography and is currently writing the official history of Australia's role in the Korean War. In recent years he has also been heavily engaged in the development of new ideas for Australian defence policy and is the author of many articles on that subject.

IN 1971, the Joint Foreign Affairs and Defence Committee of the Australian Parliament produced a major report on the strategic significance of the Indian Ocean and force deployments in and around it. This report, while not alarmist, suggested that Australia should be very alert to changes in the balance of power in the Indian Ocean. Much of importance has happened since then. Here I am concerned to examine events which have taken place since 1971 in two spheres. The first comprises international developments which have influenced strategic interactions in the Indian Ocean area generally. The second comprises significant changes which have occurred in Australia's strategic situation during this period.

The events of late 1973 demonstrated dramatically the importance of oil from the Middle East for the whole of the Western World. In situations in which the interests of the Arab nations and Western Europe collide, the Arabs are in an extremely strong position to exert pressure through the solidarity of OPEC. Of course there are many forms of counter-pressure which Western nations can employ, but, short of the use of physical force, none can rival the short-term crippling effect of denial of oil. The transfer of great wealth from Western countries to the major oil-exporting nations reinforces the growing significance in diplomatic, economic and strategic terms of the latter group for the former. New diplomatic initiatives have been launched throughout the Middle East by the West, sales of Western exports have been promoted energetically in the Middle East, and enormous increases are taking place in the size of the armed forces of some of the oil exporters. The strategic importance of the north-western part of the Indian Ocean has therefore grown rapidly in the past five years.

Coupled with this rise in influence of the oil-exporting nations through OPEC has been a world-wide tendency to follow suit by exporters of other commodities. No other cartels or attempts at forming cartels have been as successful as OPEC, but the increasing apprehension felt by industrial countries for their future access to vital raw materials, and the energetic striving by raw materials exporters for what they regard as a more just world economic order, have together greatly strengthened the economic dimension of international conflict. One result has been the emergence of "resources diplomacy", and another has been the repeated emphasis given in contingency studies of the strategic future to the "resources scenario", i.e. a type of conflict in which

178

one or more of the importing countries uses military force against an exporter to guarantee supply on favourable terms.

It is much too early to say how far this trend will go. Careful analysis of costs versus gains in such situations may dissuade national leaders from pressing conflicts to the point of military force. However, misunderstandings, aggressiveness or plain irrationality on the part of one side or the other in such a dispute could lead to the use of force. While one may remain basically optimistic that resource-oriented warfare will not break out in the Indian Ocean area, it seems fair to note that the chances of avoiding such a clash have decreased somewhat by comparison with the situation in 1971.

In the past five years the world has seen a revolution in conventional weapons technology. A little of this new weaponry was displayed in the 1973 Arab-Israeli war, such as terminally guided missiles for use against tanks, aircraft and ships; electronic counter-measures against warning, command and guidance systems; night-vision apparatus for ground forces; and satellite surveillance of both battlefield and rear areas. Many other new technologies are under development, and there has been considerable progress in all these fields since 1973.

The availability of this new weaponry, together with all of the existing motives for international conflict in the Middle East, Africa and South Asia, suggest that the capacity of many nations to fight wars will be enhanced in the near future. This enhancement will not necessarily maintain the existing balances of force. Rather the wealthier nations will be able to increase their leverage over the poorer, and the latter will become more dependent upon Super-power allies for countervailing weaponry or forces. Inevitably this situation will lead to the growth of new tensions in already troubled areas. The Super-powers, as the chief but not the sole sources of this new weaponry, will become more closely linked to regional conflicts. This closer linkage also confers on the Super-powers a greater capacity to exercise control once such conflicts break out, but they cannot bank on being able to prevent initial use of these new weapons by opposing states. Rather they may have to wait until the re-supply stage before their influence becomes effective, and even then they may find that stubborn client states can be very difficult to bring into line with Super-power desires.

Thus there are new incentives for hostile neighbours to launch attacks, both pre-emptive and otherwise, if they see a favourable opportunity. There are, of course, contrary pressures, such as the sheer cost and destructiveness of these forms of warfare, but again it seems fair to note that new weapon developments add to the uncertainties which bedevil predictions of future events. On the one hand moderation and humanity may prevail, but on the other we may see much more serious conflicts around the Indian Ocean littoral than have ever taken place before.

This potential for eruption gives the Super-powers greater incentives for direct influence throughout this area so that regional conflicts do not harm their own perceived interests, both individual and shared. Should nuclear proliferation occur in the Indian Ocean region, in addition to the new conventional weaponry, then many local conflicts will have much greater potential for drawing in the Super-powers.

Whereas South-East Asia was the dominant area of protracted conflict in the 1960s and early 1970s, southern Africa is taking its place in the mid- and late-1970s. Both Super-powers have been involved to some degree in supporting opposing régimes in Angola. If this tendency persists with respect to Rhodesia and South Africa, then a very bloody future lies ahead of the people who inhabit the southern African countries. The relative strength of the current South African and even the Rhodesian Governments vis-à-vis their opponents, together with the domestic implications in the US and Western Europe of support for White supremacy, suggest that Western involvement in such conflicts will be indirect. Nonetheless the importance of the mineral wealth and the strategic position of South Africa provide a major incentive for the West to work for change in such a way that the eventual outcome will not be a Soviet-controlled southern Africa.

Similarly, conflict between Eritrean insurgents and the Ethiopian Government has heightened tensions in the Horn of Africa and increased the significance of Ethiopian access to the port of Djibouti. The Soviet naval facility at Berbera probably has some relationship to these tensions: in return for the use of Berbera the Soviets have strengthened the position of the Somali Government in dealing with its neighbours, particularly the Republic of Djibouti (formerly TFAI). A Somali thrust for Djibouti could trigger a major conflict between the clients of the two Super-powers, with implications for control of access to the Red Sea and the Suez Canal. The Berbera facility is also of use to the Soviets in developing their capacity to support naval forces in the north-western sector of the Indian Ocean. The collapse of the

Soviet position in Egypt has created further incentives for the Soviets to seek shore facilities on the African east coast.

Thus, generally, Africa presents more dangers of armed conflict, both local and regional, in the next five years than in the previous five. In such conflicts the Super-powers will have strong incentives for involvement.

Since 1971 the Soviet naval presence in the Indian Ocean has risen, albeit moderately. It is possible to explain this presence in terms both of defence against American ballistic missile submarines firing on central parts of the USSR, and of preservation of Soviet interests in Africa and the Middle East generally. But it certainly gives the Soviet Union a powerful capacity for taking advantage of new situations as they arise.

Perhaps the most important dimension of the Soviet naval presence in the Indian Ocean for the present and short-term future is the psychological. Whereas in the light of failure in Vietnam, the Watergate scandal, lack of activity in Angola and problems within the NATO Alliance, the Western position appears weak, that of the Soviet Union seems to be gathering strength in both military and diplomatic terms. Although such a comparison may be deceptive because of other factors which are omitted from consideration, it is important because many people in different countries believe that is the way things are.

Soviet influence in the Third World has been strengthened through ideological sympathies and the supply of weapons, and there is a general propensity to view the USSR as tougher than the West. The greatest danger of this perception is that the Soviets may come to believe in it themselves, if they do not already, thereby diminishing their caution in approaching situations where American interests are involved. Until the United States can demonstrate greater success in countering Soviet inroads on her diplomatic position, the danger will exist that many countries, particularly Indian Ocean littoral states, will tend to overrate Soviet strength and underrate that of the United States.

From an Australian viewpoint the rate of increase of the Soviet naval presence in the Indian Ocean is not so rapid as to justify fears for Australia's own security in the short term, but, regarding the longer-term situation, vigilant observation of Soviet activities is called for.

Just as the Soviet naval presence in the Indian Ocean has risen in the past five years, so also has that of the United States. While American spokesmen point to Soviet activities as the cause of increased visits by units of the Seventh Fleet, it is apparent that the US Navy is not leaving the Soviet Navy in a position of uncontested supremacy in the Indian Ocean. The current low levels of the Indian Ocean strengths of both navies are scant indication of their respective high-level capacities in the case of an emergency. Much here would depend upon the situation in other parts of the world, whether the northern Soviet bases were ice-bound, whether the Soviets had free use of the narrow waters out of the Black Sea and the Sea of Japan, and the degree to which the Suez and Panama Canals were open.

Hence all that can be said with certainty about the naval activities of the Super-powers in the Indian Ocean is that both are increasing gradually and that neither dominates the area by its level of force. Clearly in this situation each will watch the other and a degree of mutually induced escalation may take place in a self-sustaining and potentially unstable manner.

However this propensity has to be viewed against the general background of Soviet-US détente, which acts to moderate such mutual escalation. While the avoidance of direct conflict between themselves has any practical significance as a shared policy goal of the two Super-powers, the Indian Ocean confrontation will tend to remain at a low level on both sides. Should either side wish to depart from the general objective of reduction of tension, then the power complexion in the Indian Ocean could become trans-formed rapidly.

Obviously, therefore, Australia has a strong and direct interest in the degree to which both Super-powers strive for reduction of tension. This is not to say that Australia's best diplomatic course is to steer mid-way between the two, because, in the event of a clash, Australia has a vested interest in America's success. None-theless, sensible advocacy of and support for détente should be an important principle guiding Australian attitudes towards the activities of the Super-powers in the Indian Ocean. Diego Garcia may be accepted as a *quid pro quo* for Berbera, but there support for US escalation can rest unless the Soviets acquire new facilities elsewhere or increase their influence in the Indian Ocean.

The continuing round of conferences regarding the Law of the Sea has revealed a growth in the strength of those states who wish to place increasing controls on the use of the sea and the sea-bed by others. While the detailed outcome of these conferences cannot be foreseen with any confidence, it does look as if the 200-mile economic zone concept will come into general acceptance and that some additional controls may be placed on passage of narrow waters by their littoral states. Such tendencies would enhance the strategic position of countries on either side of the main entrance points to the Indian Ocean – the Straits of Bab al Mandab, Hormuz, Malacca and those of the Indonesian Archipelago. Should those countries create difficulties for the Super-powers in terms of passage of either merchant or war ships, then they may be subject to some direct pressure.

If use of the narrow entrances becomes more difficult, use of the broader passages around the Cape of Good Hope and south of Australia would increase, especially by warships, and therefore the strategic significance of South Africa and Australia could rise. Both countries will be able to exercise comprehensive surveillance above and below the surface, if they equip themselves suitably. If they develop their strength further, or if they act as a host for the weapons systems of others, they could have a long-range capacity to interdict shipping movements into and out of the Indian Ocean. Australia, through her naval forces, including naval air power, already has a moderate interdiction capacity. The development of the cruise missile offers both countries greater strength in this regard.

Because the Soviet Union is more dependent than America upon the Suez Canal and the Malacca Straits for access to the Indian Ocean, any restriction on use of the narrow entrances by warships would disadvantage the Soviets more than the Americans. While South Africa and Australia remain basically pro-American, the Soviet Navy will not be in a favourable position to control the broad entrances. Therefore while Soviet diplomacy may focus more strongly on the states which control the narrow entrances to offset this inferiority, it is evident that in a situation of major conflict the Soviet strategic position in the Indian Ocean is weaker than that of the United States.

Apart from a resumption of warfare between Israel and her Arab neighbours, there are two other areas where serious hostilities could add to tensions within the Indian Ocean area generally: the Arabian Peninsula and the Indian sub-continent. Currently Indo-Pakistani relations are not as bad as in 1971, but the problems faced by all governments in the sub-continent are so great that resort to arms at some future stage cannot be ruled out. The 1971 clash between India and Pakistan revealed how rapidly the area could become polarised as the interests of both Super-powers were involved. Any renewal of such extreme tensions between India and Pakistan would be likely to draw the Super-powers more deeply into commitments which could have consequences for the Indian Ocean at large. Conflict between Pakistan and Afghanistan is another possibility which could draw in the Super-powers.

Bangladesh remains particularly troubled internally, and her relations with India have not been uniformly smooth. India must therefore be very concerned that her populous and impoverished eastern neighbour does not slide back into complete chaos. Consequently Indo-Bangladeshi relations may be worth close study in the next few years.

From this brief review of salient developments, it will be evident that, in the past five years, the strategic significance of the Indian Ocean has increased markedly – for littoral powers, for the Super-powers and for all who are dependent upon Persian Gulf oil. This rise in strategic significance has led to greater uncertainty in predicting the future course of international relations in the area. The range of issues on which conflicts can take place has widened. The means of violence are being enhanced at a spec-tacular rate. The Super-powers are continually being drawn towards a regional arms race. However, growing sophistication and experience on the part of the leaders of littoral states in dealing with problems of diplomacy and strategy have helped the development of a moderating influence, and the Super-powers have shown through their own bilateral diplomacy their recog-nition of the periods of increasing tension. Thus, while problems for peace and security magnify and proliferate, the future prospect for the Indian Ocean region is not without hope. Pro-vided that all interested states keep each other informed of their own points of view, avoid blatant aggression and, by their own weakness, do not invite attack, then rapid deterioration of regional relations should be avoidable in the short term at least. However, while the leaders of littoral nations may seek to avoid conflict, they may nonetheless be propelled towards it by growing internal pressures. Consequently the continuing potential of the Indian Ocean region for serious international conflict must be borne in mind in determining Australia's future foreign and defence policies.

Changes in Australia's Strategic Situation
Whether one likes it or not, the era of a forward defence posture has now passed – not so much as a result of any Australian action

but because the United States and Britain have withdrawn their forces from the Asian mainland. Consequently it becomes much more important for Australia to be able, through Australian-based efforts, to carry out surveillance over, and to respond to threats in, her western and north-western approaches. The most forward element of Australia's defences which will be sustainable in future is that which can be supported from her own western and north-western coast.

Quite apart from the added strategic significance conferred by the passing of forward defence, the importance of western and northern Australia has been increased greatly by the growing prominence of the minerals industry. The areas of greatest richness – the south-west of Western Australia, the Pilbara and the North-West Shelf – are all dependent for their security upon Australian control of the adjoining waters of the Indian Ocean. Their output is becoming increasingly important in contributing to Australia's income and in providing vital raw materials to other countries, particularly Japan. So there is an equally increased need to protect them from outside interference.

All Australian governments in the 1970s have experienced difficulty in dealing with a basic dilemma presented to our diplomacy by conflicting interests in the Indian Ocean. On the one hand, Australia desires friendly relations with other littoral states, amongst which there is a significant consensus of opinion that the Super-powers should not have base facilities in the Indian Ocean. On the other hand, Australia has a formal alliance with the United States, which all major Australian political parties uphold as the basis of Australia's security. Accordingly Australia has permitted the Americans to build the North-West Cape communications station, has offered the US Navy base facilities at Cockburn Sound and has supported the extension of the American base on Diego Garcia.

There can be no avoiding this dilemma for any responsible Australian government. It would be foolish to attempt to adopt entirely either awkward alternative. Therefore in this situation Australia's interests would best be served by taking a low posture on both the Zone of Peace, Freedom and Neutrality Proposal and on the US extension of the Diego Garcia facilities. As soon as Australia becomes declamatory in favour of either, painful but necessary contradictions in our diplomatic stance are highlighted for all to see. Most states have to live with elements of contradiction in their diplomacy and it is a sign of maturity to accept this situation quietly, in the short term, seeking the understanding of friends on both sides of the question and avoiding the unnecessary provocation of others. For the long term Australia should exert her influence so that a Super-power arms race in the Indian Ocean is not stimulated by any events within her control. Hence it is in Australia's interests to strive to do more for her own defence in the Indian Ocean, so that the need for a US presence there is decreased.

I have argued that the range of issues from which conflicts could grow in the Indian Ocean has widened in recent years. As the strategic and economic significance of the area grows and the sophistication of weaponry available to warring parties rises, so it becomes increasingly difficult to forecast the future course of international relations in and around the Indian Ocean.

Therefore greater importance attaches to the gathering of information on future events and to the study of the various ways in which threats could be presented to Australia. Essentially such threats fall into three categories: non-violent infringements of Australia's sovereignty over her island territories, coastal waters, mainland coast and airspace; low-level attacks on Australian territory, shipping, aircraft and offshore installations; and major attacks aimed at population centres, the defence forces and economic targets.

To meet the first kind of threat Australia needs a constant peace-time surveillance capacity over the coastal areas and island territories. The second kind requires a ready-reaction force to be kept permanently available for rapid deployment. The third requires that Australia maintain a core force of sufficient size to be expanded to match the threat within the warning time likely to be available.

Because of the uncertainty of the future in the Indian Ocean, it is difficult to assign probabilities to these particular threat levels. Therefore it is important to have all three of these capacities within Australia's force structure.

Some Conclusions Regarding Australian Defence Policy

The maintenance of sovereignty in time of peace calls for significant naval and maritime air deployments to cover Australia's western and north-western approaches. The RAN facility on Cockburn Sound, HMAS *Stirling*, is particularly important in this regard but more patrol boats are badly needed. When they are available an additional patrol boat facility will be required between Fremantle and Darwin to avoid long journeys to and from patrol areas for short-range craft. Somewhere in the Port Hedland–Broome region would be a good central spot in relation to the facilities currently available at Darwin and Fremantle. The RAN's present Attack-class patrol boats are nearing the end of their operational life. Not only must they be replaced, but the existing meagre capacity must also be expanded both in numbers and in individual capabilities.

Maritime patrol aircraft are in short supply for Australia's needs. The Minister for Defence has estimated that, if the 200-mile economic zone concept comes into general use, Australia will acquire a new surveillance responsibility covering 2.5 million square miles; that is, an area almost as big as the Australian continent itself. Two squadrons of long-range maritime patrol aircraft cannot hope to meet this requirement. Furthermore, because one of these squadrons is stationed at Edinburgh, near Adelaide, its aircraft face a major transit flight of over 1,000 miles before they cross the western or north-western coastlines. If it is accepted that there is a standing requirement for LRMP aircraft coverage of the eastern waters of the Indian Ocean, then one squadron should be stationed close to the west coast.

The other main means of surveillance such as a coast-watcher system, naval aircraft, radars, satellites, remotely piloted vehicles, sonobuoys and towed arrays of underwater listening devices must not be neglected. The coast-watcher system needs refurbishing. The Tracker aircraft and Sea King helicopters of the RAN have a major role to play in Indian Ocean surveillance and therefore should be available regularly in that area. Over-the-horizon radars, satellites and remotely piloted vehicles are all important for the future, and therefore we should commence making provision for acquiring some of these new-technology products as soon as possible. The Jindalee project for the development of an over-the-horizon radar is a step in the right direction but others are also necessary. Australia has a notable record in the field of anti-submarine warfare devices and this should be nurtured.

Some threats, such as sub-national guerrilla attacks, offer little or no warning time. It is conceivable that such groups operating from Europe, Africa or the Middle East could approach Australia via the Indian Ocean and then attack economic installations or people in the vicinity of the west coast, either in the course of operating against third parties or to coerce Australia directly into making them some concession. Armed criminals may offer violence. Difficulties in relations with Indonesia could lead to a type of maritime confrontation. Other nations wishing to use Australia's maritime economic zone may ignore her wishes unless she can mount some force to exert her rights.

To meet these situations, small forces must be readily deployable to threatened areas. Therefore all three services should have the capacity to react quickly in the west and north-west. The RAN should have one or two destroyers and several well-armed patrol craft available in the west. The Army should be able to move a few hundred troops to counter low-level violence on land within hours of the threat's appearing. The RAAF should be able to deploy units, particularly ground attack and maritime strike and transport aircraft, to the west and north-west, again within a few hours.

While it is not anticipated that major threats could materialise out of the Indian Ocean without some warning, it would be wise to move now to shorten the response lead-time, particularly in terms of the infrastructure which the Australian services would require – base and operational facilities, including hardening and dispersal, supply dumps and transport links. In addition the resources and knowledge of the local population should be utilised by involving them voluntarily in reserve or territorial defence organisations. A more adequate core force, backed by substantial reserves, must be developed to reduce from six to eight years to three to four years the time currently required to create a nation-wide defence capacity against a major threat.

The joint service nature of modern defence operations suggests that the three services should be linked into a tri-service functional command structure. This structure could be subdivided to facilitate the development of expertise in particular functions of common application throughout Australia and her maritime environment, e.g. a Maritime Defence Command, a Continental Defence Command and supporting commands in the logistics and training areas. These functional elements could then be subdivided geographically to reduce the span of coverage of subordinate formations, e.g. the Maritime Defence Command could be divided into an Eastern (Pacific Ocean) and a Western (Indian Ocean) Region; the Continental Defence Command could be divided into four Regions – North-east, South-east, South-west and North-west. Thus the Western Maritime Defence Region would cover the approaches to the North-western and South-western Continental Defence Regions.

Some additional funding would be required for such a command structure, but, as it would be a *sine qua non* for the conduct of any major operations in defence of Australia, the finance should be made available as a matter of urgency. Otherwise the lead-time which Australia faces in shaping appropriate responses to various kinds of threat will be unnecessarily long, and the Defence Force components will not have been able to develop the systematic expertise in meeting the differing operational problems of Australia's major geographic regions which such a structure would encourage.

These four conclusions should not be thought of as being relevant only to defence against threats from the Indian Ocean. They apply in general terms to the defence of all parts of Australia. Before it is possible to plan for the defence of the west of Australia in any detail, we must have some notion of the defence requirements of the other major areas. Therefore priority must be given to the development of national planning to cover strategic and tactical doctrines, force structure, equipment policy and the relationship between military defence, economic defence and diplomacy. Defence of the whole must be considered before defence of a single part. If a greater awareness of Australia's defence needs as a mature independent nation can be fostered, it will contribute significantly to the achievement of a vital goal.

SOVIET
AMBITIONS IN
LATIN AMERICA

Robert Moss

Robert Moss is Editor of *Foreign Report, The Economist's* confidential weekly, and Director of the National Association for Freedom. He is a former Lecturer in History at the Australian National University. He is a regular contributor to many British and American publications, including the *Daily Telegraph*, the *New York Times Magazine, Commentary, Harper's* and *National Review*, and lectures at many universities and defence academies, including the NATO Defence College. His books include *The Collapse of Democracy, Urban Guerrillas*, and *Chile's Marxist Experiment.*

LATIN AMERICA is the only continent (apart from Australia) which has not moved leftward over the past decade. Military rule is the standard form of government; indeed, there are only three significant countries left in mainland South America – Mexico, Venezuela and Colombia – that do not have military régimes. The local Communist parties are weak and faction-ridden, although Soviet commentators claim that they muster some 500,000 members in the continent as a whole. While Latin America has served as a laboratory for the entire range of Marxist revolutionary techniques – from rural guerrilla warfare through terrorism to revolution through the ballot-box and the attempt to suborn nationalist-minded military régimes – successive experiments have failed.

But the Russians have not been chastened by the experience. The published statements of Soviet policy-makers and academic experts suggest that Latin America is viewed, more than ever, as an area of critical strategic importance. There are two key reasons. First, the Russians have succeeded, through the Sovietisation of Cuba, in manufacturing a reliable Latin American proxy whose forces were used in the successful bid to seize Angola and are now being deployed in the widening African conflict as well as in more shadowy efforts to promote international terrorism and expand Communist influence in Puerto Rico and the Caribbean. Second, the Russians hope to practise the same *strategy of denial* that has inspired their bid for hegemony in central and southern Africa and in Latin America, which is perceived as the "strategic rear" of the United States. This involves the effort to destabilise anti-Communist governments that are aligned with the West and to encourage economic nationalism in the hope of blocking access for the United States to vital raw materials and sea-lanes, and to create new threats to its southern flank by stirring up trouble in the Caribbean.

It is worth recalling that Russia's boldest attempt to expand its influence into the Western Hemisphere took place fifteen years ago, when strategic missiles were transported to Cuba. In the ensuing crisis, Khruschev was forced to make a tactical withdrawal; it is estimated that, if a nuclear war had resulted at that stage, *ten times* as many Russians as Americans would have been killed. Today, according to some analysts (notably General George Keegan, the former deputy chief of US air force intelligence and Admiral Elmo Zumwalt, former chief of US naval operations) the ratio has been approximately reversed. The outcome of a re-run of the Cuban missile crisis in the late 1970s is uncertain, and the present confusion of American policy towards Latin America – which has succeeded in arousing the hostility and suspicion of pro-Western military régimes – could create the ideal conditions (in the Russians' eyes) for a new Soviet attempt to test US reflexes in the Caribbean.

Attacking America's "Strategic Rear"

It is widely appreciated that the Russians are pursuing a *strategy of denial* in Africa – hoping to isolate the West from vital sources of raw materials. The Russians' own statements disclose that the same strategy is being applied in Latin America. Soviet analysts stress that US dependence on imports of raw materials from Latin America has major strategic implications. According to a full-length study published in Moscow in 1972, the US will face "sharp problems" in connection with the demand for new types of raw materials used in missile, communications and atomic industries and in electronics which Latin America is able to supply.[1] The upsurge of economic nationalism is interpreted as a trend that will make Latin America "one of the most vulnerable sectors of US imperialism's rear".[2]

The emphasis of a symposium sponsored by the Prague-based publication *World Marxist Review* in Havana early in 1977 was on the expulsion of foreign corporations from Latin America. The Venezuelan Communist delegate, Jeronimo Carrera, offered nationalisation as the panacea, and his own country's takeover of the oil industry as a shining example. "The policy of protecting non-renewable national resources", he insisted, "calls constantly for prompt action to put an end to their reckless exploitation."[3]

Soviet ambitions in Latin America reached their peak after the election of Salvador Allende as the "Popular Unity" candidate in Chile in September 1970. A year later, the master Soviet sub-verter, Boris Ponomarev (chief of the international department of the central committee of the CPSU), wrote that :

> Today the attention of Marxist scientists is focused more and more on the recent experience of the revolutionaries on the Latin American continent. The victory of the national unity block in Chile, the progressive changes in Peru and the major successes of the revolutionary struggle in Uruguay and several other countries lead us to believe that the revolutionary process there is continuing to develop at a faster pace than in other parts of the non-socialist world. This is truly a "continent in upheaval".[4]

But the Latin American revolutionaries have suffered a long series of major setbacks since the Cuba revolution of 1959.

The rural guerrillas of the 1960s were defeated by sophisticated counter-insurgency techniques; urban guerrillas suffered the same fate in Uruguay and Brazil in the face of ruthless military repression, although the terrorist problem has not yet been solved in Argentina; election via the ballot-box came to a bloody end in Chile in September 1973, with the coup against Allende, and proved a fiasco at the polls when Marxist coalitions ran for office in Uruguay in November 1971 and in Venezuela in December 1973.

The Russians have not despaired of bringing Communism to mainland Latin America. But they display considerable opportunism in their short-term tactics, hoping to exploit anti-US emotions and economic nationalism in democracies like Venezuela (or Argentina under Perón) and military dictatorships like Peru and Panama and to impress the armed forces (which form the present régimes throughout two-thirds of Latin America) with the military exploits of their Cuban protégé and the sophisticated hardware which they have given it.

To forward their negative goal of weakening the United States by creating trouble at its back door, the Russians have been ready to cooperate with military dictators, democratic parties and New Left revolutionaries in Latin America. They have supported most variants of economic nationalism, and most Latin American governments caught up in disputes with the United States — whether over fishing rights, the lifting of OAS sanctions against Cuba, or sovereignty in the Panama Canal Zone.[5]

Lessons of Chile

The Russians have always publicly supported the concept of "armed struggle" in Latin America, but the emphasis has frequently shifted in favour of other tactics, including the creation of "popular fronts" or the effort to work with the "national bourgeoisie" or the armed forces in opposition to US interests. Chile has a distinct, and continuing, importance in Soviet theory since it was there, between 1970 and 1973, that the prospects for revolution via the ballot-box were tested for the first time — an experiment with even greater significance for countries like France and Italy than for neighbouring Latin American states. Soviet analysts and Moscow-line Chilean Communists continue their post-mortems into the causes of Allende's failure and their discussion of the new tactics to be adopted in Chile and in Chilean-style situations that could arise elsewhere.

A series of important articles on the lessons of the Chile coup was published by three members of the political commission of the Chilean Communist Party, Volodia Teitelboim, Orlando Millas and Rodrigo Millas (all of whom now live in exile) in *World Marxist Review* in the first three months of 1977. Teitelboim concluded that Allende's government had erred in Chile by refusing to accept alternatives to "peaceful struggle" through constitutional means. Communists, in his view, should refuse to allow themselves to become "Gullivers bound hand and foot by legality". He also took up the theme of Boris Ponomarev (in the first major Soviet appraisal of the coup[6]) that in Chile-type situations, the Marxist Left must set out to neutralise the armed forces through agitprop in the barracks to undermine the soldiers' "false conception of public duty" and to encourage potential revolutionary sympathisers. Significantly, the Chilean Communists today do not indulge in the facile rhetoric of left-wingers in Western countries against the "Fascist" military who rule the country, since they still hope to win support inside the barracks.

A Soviet commentator, A. Viktorov, followed up with an article in *Pravda* on 1st March, 1977 in which he cited Chile as a recent example of how it is impossible to achieve socialism "within the framework of a bourgeois state or a bourgeois democracy". He coined a pleasant euphemism, "peaceful violence", to describe the process by which the political rights of the "exploiting class" would be removed as a prerequisite for the transition to socialism.

Since the Chilean Communists have taken to issuing statements of this kind, supported by their Soviet backers, it is perhaps understandable that – despite the outright banning of political parties in Chile in the spring of 1977 – they have had little success in forming the much-advertised "anti-Fascist front" with the Chilean Christian Democrats.

On the other hand, Soviet and Communist-backed efforts to isolate and destabilise the Pinochet régime through an ambitious propaganda campaign did not slacken in the first three years after the coup. Chile Solidarity Committees in the major Western countries brought together Social Democrats, Communists and Trotskyites. In Britain, the anti-Chile campaign received the support of major trade unions. In the United States, Orlando Letelier, a former Allende minister and ambassador to Washington, orchestrated a major campaign to win the support of American liberals – notably in Congress, the media, and groups sponsored by the Church – for the exile cause. After he was murdered under mysterious circumstances in Washington in September 1976, the papers found in his briefcase disclosed that Letelier had been operating as a paid Cuban agent – receiving $1,000 a month from Havana – and had maintained intimate contacts with Cuban and Soviet *bloc* intelligence officers, including Julián Rizo, a key operative of the Cuban intelligence service, the DGI, working under cover as a member of Castro's delegation to the United Nations in New York.

Similar tactics began to be applied to the government of President Videla in Argentina after Perón's widow, "Isabelita", was toppled by a coup in March, 1976. Although "Isabelita" – as the head of a notoriously corrupt and inefficient government – was a less attractive martyr-figure than Allende, the anti-Argentina campaign snowballed. In Britain, Argentina's claim to the Falkland Islands was used as a peg for pseudo-nationalistic attacks on Videla's régime, rather as Spain's claim to Gibraltar was used in Franco's day. In a leading article on 2nd May, 1977 *The Times* actually quoted a supporter of the Montoneros guerrilla group as a reputable journalist – shortly before the Montoneros ambushed and seriously wounded the Argentine foreign minister, Admiral Guzzetti.

Moscow's Cuban Proxies

Cuba is the vital instrument of Soviet ambitions in Latin America and beyond. The Cubans provide an all-purpose expeditionary force for the Russians. It was the presence of some 15,000 Cuban troops – and the abdication of the Western powers[7] – that brought about the victory of the pro-Soviet MPLA in Angola's civil war. In the first half of 1977, the Cuban presence in Somalia and South Yemen was increased; Cuban military advisers were despatched to Ethiopia under a joint arrangement with Russia and Libya; some 200 Cuban instructors in Iraq provided training courses for Palestinian and other transitional terrorists; and the Cubans maintained huge military missions as far afield as Laos (an estimated 1,000 Cubans) and Vietnam (1,500).

The Cuban intelligence service, the Dirección General de Inteligencia (DGI), which is under the direct supervision of KGB General Vassiliy Petrovich Semenov and his staff in Havana, was deployed at the Russians' behest in Western as well as Third

World countries. A DGI defector, Gerardo Peraza, has reported that the KGB succeeded in 1970 in compelling Raúl Castro (Fidel Castro's brother) to purge all suspected anti-Soviet officials from the service.

The long-awaited first congress of the Cuban Communist Party took place between 17th and 22nd December, 1975, as the airlift of Cuban troops to Angola accelerated. It celebrated the conversion of the Castro régime to Moscow-line orthodoxy. The draft constitution that was approved at the Congress was evidently modelled on the Soviet Charter of 1936. The Cuban Communist Party was awarded the status of "the highest leading force of the society and the state".[8] In his concluding speech, Castro delivered fulsome praise for the Soviet Union.

Cuba's full economic integration into the Soviet *bloc* had already been accomplished three years earlier, when it was admitted to Comecon as a full member. By that stage, Cuba's economic dependence on Russia – the basis for total Soviet satellisation of the country – was complete. Cuba's debt to Russia had already risen to nearly $4 billion. In early 1974, the deputy prime minister, Carlos Rafael Rodriguez, admitted that the Cuban and Soviet five-year plans for the 1976-80 period were being fully coordinated by their state planning organisations, Juceplan and Gosplan. Some 3,000 Soviet advisers (out of more than 6,000 stationed in Cuba) had been assigned posts in state-run firms and economic ministries and planning agencies in Havana.

There is continuing doubt among Western military analysts as to whether the Russians have genuinely abandoned the naval base at Cienfuegos in Cuba. The presence of a Soviet submarine tender in Cuban waters, and of an ocean-going tug (to make repairs on the high seas), suggests that Cienfuegos still provides naval support facilities for the Soviet fleet. More intriguing is the communications complex that the Russians have built, at a cost of $1.7 million as part of Havana's "fishing port". This is believed to be functioning as a communications centre for Soviet merchant and naval vessels in the Caribbean.

Support for Terrorism
The Cubans play a decisive role in supporting the emerging international terrorism in Latin America – notably the groups that converged in the Junta de Coordinación Revolucionaria (JCR), which was founded in February 1974, to concert the operations of

guerrilla movements in Chile, Argentina, Uruguay and Bolivia. Since all these countries are now governed by military régimes that are pursuing determined counter-terrorist programmes, the JCR has moved its main operational base to Paris, where it enjoys the covert support of the Cuban embassy. Some aspects of the Cuban involvement with Latin American terrorists in exile in Paris surfaced in press exposés of the activities of the young Venezuelan terrorist, "Carlos" (real name: Ilich Ramírez Sanchez). But the background deserves closer attention.

The original meeting at which the JCR was formed took place in Mendoza in Argentina and the groups represented included the Movement of the Revolutionary Left (MIR) from Chile, the People's Revolutionary Army (ERP) from Argentina, the National Liberation Army (ELN) from Bolivia, and the Tupamaros from Uruguay. A French connection was apparent even at this stage. Alain Krivine, the leader of the Ligue Communiste (the French section of the Trotskyist Fourth International), turned up at the Mendoza meeting. Subsequently, the JCR set up its Latin American headquarters in Buenos Aires and formed a "general command" whose founder-members were Mario Roberto Santucho (ERP), Patricio Antonio Biedma (MIR), Ruben Sanchez Valdivia (ELN) and Andres Felix Cultelli Chiribao (Tupamaros). Santucho was later killed by the Argentine security forces, and Cultelli was jailed.

The reverses that the revolutionary Left suffered throughout the "southern cone" of Latin America forced the leaders of the JCR into exile. The guerrilla school (complete with an underground rifle range), the secret arms factory (which would produce a simple machine-pistol, code-named JCR-1) and the documentation centre (where false passports and identity papers were mass-produced) which the JCR had set up in Buenos Aires in 1975 were all closed down by the security forces. But the ERP's elaborately organised system of safe houses continued to function.

JCR leaders were forced to rely more heavily on supporters and cover organisations farther north, such as the Casa del Pueblo Argentino in Mexico, the Latin American Press Agency (APAL) in Caracas – which helps to produce the JCR's bulletin, *Che Guevara* – and the Movement against Imperialism and for Socialism in Argentina (MASA) with offices in Miami, Los Angeles and San Francisco. MASA described itself as "an independent political organisation founded and directed in the

United States by Argentinians". It published a magazine, *Denuncia*, which claimed that the guerrilla groups in Argentina constitute a "regular army" in the sense in which the term is used in the Geneva convention. This claim became the focus for a major debate in Western media and the UN.

The Argentine ERP was the driving force in the JCR – largely for the obvious reason that Buenos Aires used to provide a safe haven for guerrillas from neighbouring countries and that the ERP, as a result of its lucrative kidnappings, had plenty of money to put into the kitty. It was on the direct initiative of the ERP (which was founded as the military wing of the Trotskyist Revolutionary Workers' party, or PRT) that its Bolivian sister-group set up a political support group, also entitled the PRT and organised along identical lines. It worked in close coordination with Colombian guerrilla groups, and broadened its membership to embrace a Paraguayan guerrilla group, Frepalina.

Guerrilla training courses for the JCR are provided by Cuba and a number of Middle Eastern countries, including Iraq and Libya. After visits by JCR envoys to Luanda (reportedly including Roberto Guevara, brother of the famous guerrilla leader killed in Bolivia), there was speculation that the Angolan Government would also offer training facilities. Negotiations between the JCR and Colonel Qaddafi's Government in Libya were conducted on the initiative of the Chilean MIR leader, Manuel Cabieses, by Eder Simão Sader. Although a Brazilian, Sader sat on the "external directorate" of the MIR. He visited Tripoli late in 1976.

The Cubans train JCR recruits on a 1,800 hectare estate near Guanabo which comes under the authority of the Interior Ministry. The minimum length of training is three months. Courses on urban terrorism in 1976 made use of translations of American Special Forces manuals and included lectures on the composition and deployment of the Chilean armed forces. Cuban officers are known by their nicknames: one of the tactics instructors at this camp, for example, is a lieutenant known as "Bolchevique" or "Bolche".

The day begins at 5.30 am, with an hour and a half of physical exercises, followed by breakfast and cleaning duties. Lectures are held between 8 and 12 am, followed by lunch and three hours of practical training in explosives, weaponry and tactics. The lights are turned off at 9 pm.

Training courses in rural guerrilla warfare are conducted in the province of Piñar del Rio, in the Sierra de los Organos, in an army school about twelve kilometres from Bahia Onda. The emphasis here is on survival in rugged mountainous terrain and operations against regular forces – whose role in manoeuvres is played by Cuban army conscripts, who simultaneously gain experience in counter-guerrilla tactics. The tactics instructor on these courses is a lieutenant known as "Abigail" who formerly belonged to the personal bodyguard of Raul Castro, the Minister of Defence. Guerrilla trainees at this camp are also given rudimentary instruction in tank warfare.

But the training courses go beyond routine military instruction; they cover the manufacture and use of false passports and identity papers, secret communications, and other tools of the terrorist trade.

The movements of one of the Argentine leaders of the JCR, Espinoza Barahoma, offer some insight into how the network operates. The Cubans equipped him with a false Costa Rican passport in the name of Guillermo Arce Roldán, together with books, maps and tape-recordings to familiarise him with the accent, history and geography of Costa Rica. After a fortnight's study, his Cuban controller subjected him to an oral examination to establish whether he was sufficiently plausible under his new cover. He was then sent on a mission to Argentina, following the round-about route of Havana-Moscow-Prague-Zurich-Paris-Buenos Aires. Supplied with clothing of American, Mexican and Peruvian manufacture, Barahoma used a Cuban passport for his trip to Moscow, where he was met at the airport on 16th December, 1975, by two DGI men based at the Cuban Embassy. The following day – assisted through controls by the two Cubans – he boarded a Cabana de Aviacion flight to Prague, where he was met by another Cuban official.

From Prague, he took a Czech airways flight to Zurich, where he used his Costa Rican passport. At the airport, he paid cash for a ticket to Paris on a flight leaving two hours later. The reason for using Zurich as a transit point was simple: he had been assured that immigration officials would not stamp his passport and that he would thus be able to disguise his movement out of the Soviet *bloc*. He completed his journey on an Air France flight to Buenos Aires, where he eluded arrest – although his Costa Rican passport was picked up by the police in an abandoned "safe house" in June 1976.

The JCR operates an impressive network of front organisations and support groups in western Europe, and maintains contact with bodies like the Chile Solidarity Committee, the Bertrand Russell Tribunal and human rights organisations. In West Germany its organisers maintain close links with the Latin American Student Association which has offices in Berlin, Munich, Hamburg, Aachen, Cologne and Frankfurt. Portugal became a major centre of activity after March 1975, when the JCR set up an office in Lisbon. A second office was subsequently established in the northern town of Oporto.

The JCR maintains a secret documentation centre in Paris which produces fake passports and identity papers. The JCR's most important front organisation in Paris – now active in conducting an international propaganda campaign against General Videla's régime – is the Argentina Solidarity and Information Centre (CAIS). It was set up with the backing of both of Argentina's major guerrilla movements, the (Trotskyite) ERP and the (revolutionary Peronist) Montoneros.

CAIS is controlled by a general secretariat and six committees, responsible for liaison with other groups – finance, culture, aid for refugees, propaganda, and foreign relations. Its chiefs are Rodolfo Mattarolo, an ERP leader who is also the senior JCR representative in Paris, and Luis Benito Berrutti Costa, a Montonero leader who has the title of secretary-general of CAIS.

A sample of CAIS's propaganda activities is provided by a report sent by Rodolfo Mattarolo to the PRT last December on efforts to influence film producers and to produce a propaganda film for the guerrillas of the JCR. "In the field of distribution", he noted, "we can now count on a number of instruments to ensure that material will be distributed throughout Europe and Latin America. As a first step, we will bring together all our comrades scattered throughout Italy in order to reorganise the equipment. . . . We will make the JCR film on the basis of the four reports that were filmed more than a year ago. This task was in the hands of our MIR comrades, but they told us recently that they are unable to complete it. We can count on the support of collaborators and friends in the media who will solve our technical problems and will do laboratory work for us for nothing."

Mattarolo expressed the hope that the Italian Government might be persuaded to put up cash for this and similar projects, and that further aid might come from African countries "that are extremely interested in the distribution of their own films in Europe and with which we have already discussed possible collaboration." He singled out Angola as the African country most likely to help.

Cuban and Uruguayan Communist Party (PCU) connections with Uruguay's terrorist movement, the Tupamaros, deserve a special note in the light of fresh evidence that has recently become available. During the violent troubles in Montevideo in the late 1960s and early 1970s, the PCU posed as a party of order, opposed to revolutionary terrorism. However, there is now documentation[9] to prove that, as early as 1967, the PCU took the decision to infiltrate the Tupamaros and exploit their dramatic success. The job was assigned to a certain Mauricio Rosencoff, who made regular trips to Havana, where he received cash from Fidel Castro – and instructions from the DGI. After the Tupamaros leader, Raul Sendic, was arrested in 1970 (possibly as the result of betrayal by the PCU or KGB agents in Montevideo, who included an intriguing middle-aged blonde called Dumnova) Rosencoff assumed operational control of the Tupamaros. He brought about a close tactical alliance between the PCU and the Tupamaros that only broke down in 1972, when the Bordaberry Government had at last begun to smash up the guerrilla "columns".

Target: Panama

Control of the Panama Canal and the withdrawal of American forces from the major installations in the Canal Zone is a primary Soviet objective in Latin America. The Panama Canal is one of the two routes by which ships can make the passage from the Atlantic to the Pacific Ocean. The other route is via the Cape Horn area, where the only secure waterways – the Beagle Channel and the Straits of Magellan – lie within Chilean territorial waters.

The Panama Canal has been aptly desibed as "the jugular vein of the Americas". It is used each year by some 15,000 ships from more than fifty countries; 70 per cent of the traffic originates or terminates in the United States, representing 17 per cent of overall American trade.

At the time of writing, the United States still enjoyed both sovereignty and legal title to the territory of the Canal Zone under the treaty of 1903 (concluded after the secession of Panama from Colombia)[10]. The treaty gave the United States "all the rights, power and authority within the Zone . . . to the entire exclusion of the exercise by the Republic of Panama of any such sovereign rights". Since 1904, the cost of the Canal to the United States –

for construction, maintenance, purchase of land, military investment, and annuities (*not* rent, since the Zone is sovereign US territory) to the Panamanian government – has been about $7 billion. But Dr Kissinger foreshadowed the termination of US sovereignty in the Zone when he initialled a Statement of Principles to govern negotiations with the Panamanian government in Panama City on 7th February, 1974. After the election of President Carter, it seemed likely that the US would eventually agree to forfeit its sovereignty in response to demands from Panama's left-leaning military dictator, General Omar Torrijos, for the "liberation" of the Zone.

The debate over the future of the Canal Zone presented the Russians and their Cuban satellites with a notable opportunity. The expansion of Soviet naval power has made control of the narrower waterways of the world – the Straits of Gibraltar, the Cape of Good Hope, the Suez Canal and the Panama Canal – one of the central strategic issues.

If the Principles to which Dr Kissinger set his initials in Panama City in 1974 are put into effect, the United States will be left as the owner of a canal company subject to the sovereignty of a tiny country with a record of internal instability (fifty-nine governments in less than eighty years) and an obvious vulnerability to outside pressure – notably from Cuba but also, potentially, from Michael Manley's increasingly radical government in Jamaica, since Panama has a sizeable Jamaican minority population. The effects of an effort to disrupt the Panama traffic would obviously be less severe than another closure of the Suez Canal or a threat to the Cape Route. But such a move would jeopardise important food shipments and plans to modernise the Canal in order to allow for medium-sized tankers carrying oil from Alaska.

Significantly, a Marxist government in Panama that exercised sovereignty over the Canal Zone could hope to apply pressure to some of the Latin American countries that rely on the Canal to a greater extent than the United States. Although the absolute figures are unimpressive, the relative percentages are striking. Thus more than a third of Chile's trade passes through the Panama Canal. For Colombia, the figure is 32.5 per cent; for Ecuador, 51.4 per cent; for Peru, 41.3 per cent; for Nicaragua, 76.8 per cent.

Cuba is the propaganda base for the international campaign to "liberate" the Panama Canal. The Cubans are the moving force in an organisation called the Latin American Economic System (SELA), which was set up in 1976 with interim headquarters in Panama City. Amongst other activities, SELA distributes films – including one entitled *The Fifth Frontier*, which purports to show American troops slaughtering Panamanian civilians.

Target: Caribbean

Against the backdrop of increased Soviet naval forays into the Caribbean, the Cubans are actively seeking to intervene in local politics throughout the area, looking back to the early 1960s, when Castro supported guerrillas throughout Central America. Cuban influence may have helped to ensure Michael Manley's success in the Jamaican elections in 1977; serious allegations of DGI involvement were made by opposition politicians.

There had been increasing contracts between the Cubans and the Jamaican Government throughout 1976. One of the more innocuous was the arrival of fourteen Cuban doctors in September – although it aroused local resentments. The *Kingston Daily Gleaner* quoted complaints from Jamaican doctors that their Cuban colleagues were unqualified, and nothing more than "medical orderlies".

Senior Jamaican police officers visited Cuba in January 1976, during the visit of Canada's Prime Minister, Pierre Trudeau, to study Cuban security techniques. Jamaica's Minister of Housing, Anthony Spalding, followed suit in March, supposedly to look at the work of the Jamaican construction brigades which were sent to Cuba under an exchange scheme that brought Cubans to Jamaica to help construct a secondary school and a sports stadium. At the same time, there were increased contacts between the Cuban Communist Party and the ruling People's National Party in Jamaica. The PNP's Secretary-General, Donald Duncan, spent two weeks in Cuba in June 1976, and a Cuban delegation headed by Jesus Montané Oropesa (a member of the central committee of the Cuban Communist Party) turned up for the PNP's congress in mid-September.

The government-run Cuban media gave effusive support to the PNP, and have played up attacks by Michael Manley on alleged CIA activities in the Caribbean. Manley invited the CIA defector Philip Agee to Jamaica to provide further material on this theme. Havana Radio justified Jamaica's state of emergency, in a broadcast in October 1976, on the grounds that it helped to bring about "the consolidation of progressive and revolutionary processes" in the Caribbean region, in the face of "anti-popular" plots by the Americans and the opposition Jamaican Labour Party. The official Jamaican view of the relationship was summed up by the Foreign Minister, Dudley Thompson, in an interview with the Jamaican magazine *Bohemia* late in 1976, in which he said that "nothing and nobody could break the bonds of friendship between our two countries".

Another Caribbean country where the Cubans have been gaining ground is Guyana. The Guyanese government denied reports that Cuban troops were stationed there in strength. But some observers remained unconvinced. While expanding their links with the Prime Minister, Forbes Burnham, and the ruling People's National Congress, the Cubans conserved their older ties with Cheddi Jagan's opposition People's Progressive Party. The Cuban Communist Party sent a delegation to the PPP's congress in July 1976.

A delegation of Guyanese Communists visited Havana late in 1975 for detailed discussions with Major Manuel Pineiro, chief of the DGI. In the summer of 1976, Pineiro led a Cuban delegation that visited Georgetown to attend Guyana's celebration of the anniversary of independence.

The rewards for Soviet and Cuban involvement in the Caribbean were apparent when the Prime Minister of Barbados, Errol Barrow, turned a blind eye to the use of the local airport as a transit point for Cuban troop-planes *en route* to Angola late in 1975. American pressure finally compelled him to issue a *pro forma* protest to Cuba and a public denial that he had known what was going on.

Conclusions

The area of immediate danger for Western interests in Latin America is the Caribbean and, in particular, the Panama Canal Zone. In the continent as a whole, the West can count on some important, and staunchly anti-Soviet allies, which could be destined to play a more significant international role than at present. Brazil (whose armed forces total more than 250,000 men) and Argentina (with 133,000 and the three other countries of the *cono sur*, with like-minded governments, behind it) could, for example, be key partners in a future defence pact to safeguard the South Atlantic region – one of the many regions that NATO, under its restricting charter, has been compelled to neglect. However, the Russians stand to gain from the fact that Western governments are visibly embarrassed by such allies, and are increasingly given to criticising their internal policies without thought for the possible consequences.

The attitude that President Carter struck during the early phase of his human rights crusade provoked the Argentinians into rebuffing all military aid from the United States; other military régimes quickly followed suit. It should not be forgotten that in Latin America – as in any country – nationalism is not a monopoly of the Left, and that if Washington's policy is to be conducted by men like Andrew Young, there is a serious possibility that a new brand of anti-Americanism will become the order of the day throughout much of the continent. The success of the Russians in selling advanced military equipment to Peru (and inserting a huge military mission in the guise of instructors) may have been diminished by the palace revolution in 1976; but it is a pattern that could be followed elsewhere.

At the very least, it deserves to be recognised (a) that the Western democracies and anti-Communist régimes in Latin America are part of a common "target area" for the Russians and (b) that while the defence of human rights is a universal cause, it is folly to presume that the government of a country torn apart by terrorism and economic chaos, and in which there may well be no tradition of constitutional government, will be able to conduct its business according to Queensberry rules. This is not offered as a blank cheque to endorse the real excesses that have been committed under military régimes in Latin America, but as a reminder that while it is easy enough to choose your enemies, your friends normally choose *you*. The West has lost a lot of real estate in recent years. It would be unfortunate if Western governments – in pursuit of a possibly noble, but also naive and uncalibrated, set of moral absolutes – proceeded to reject or even destabilise the one region of the Third World where anti-Communist governments are still in the majority.

Notes

[1] K.S. Sharazov, *S.Sh.A. i. Latinskaia Amerika* (Moscow: Polizdat, 1972).

[2] V. Vasilyev, "The United States' New Approach to Latin America". *International Affairs* (Moscow) No. 6, June 1971. For further examples of Soviet thinking along these lines, see Leon Gouré and Morris Rothenberg, *Soviet Penetration of Latin America* (University of Miami, 1975).

[3] *World Marxist Review,* Vol. 20, No.4, April 1977.

[4] Boris Ponomarev, "Topical Problems in the Theory of the Revolutionary Process" in *Kommunist* No.15, October 1971.

[5] James Theberge, *The Soviet Presence in Latin America* (Crane, Russak, New York, 1974) supplies useful background. See also Stephen Chissold, *Soviet Relations with Latin America* (Oxford, 1970) and J. Gregory Oswald and Anthony J. Strover (eds) *The Soviet Union and Latin America* (Pall Mall, 1971).

[6] See *World Marxist Review*, No.6, June 1974.

[7] See my articles in the *Sunday Telegraph*, 30th January, 6th, 13th and 20th February, 1977.

[8] *Granma* (20th April, 1975) contains the full text of the draft constitution, which was finally approved by referendum in February 1976. For a more detailed account of the party congress, see Edward Gonzalez, "Castro and Cuba's New Orthodoxy" in *Problems of Communism*, January-February 1976.

[9] Some of it has been published by the Uruguayan Government in *Documentos III*, 4th April, 1976. See also Peter Kemp's article in the *Spectator* on 9th and 16th April, 1977.

[10] For a full description of the legal position, see James P. Lucier, "Panama Canal: Focus of Power Politics" in *Strategic Review* (Spring 1974) and L. Francis Borchey (ed), *Report of Official Proceedings. Inter-American Conference on Freedom and Security* (Heritage Foundation, Washington 1976).

ARGENTINA AND THE SEA

Rear-Admiral Mario Lanzarini

Rear-Admiral Mario S. T. Lanzarini entered the Argentine Navy in 1934 and retired thirty years later with the rank of Rear Admiral. During his years in the Navy he held important posts, such as Destroyer Force Commander, Chief of Staff of the Sea Fleet, Chief of Operations of the Naval General Staff, President of the Naval War College and President of the National Defence College. Once retired, he devoted his efforts to maritime studies and to the teaching of strategy. For the last ten years he has been teaching an officers' training course at the Naval War College, and has been a member of the Centre of Strategic Studies Council since its foundation in 1970.

ARGENTINA'S INTEREST in the South Atlantic derives from various factors, all of which are directly related to the welfare and safety of the country.

The first, and most important, component is the maintenance of every political institution under national control, thus precluding their use for the benefit of groups or organisations acting ideologically or economically on behalf of interests other than those of the Argentine people.

The second is the maintenance of territorial integrity, including both the continental and insular territories and the Antarctic sector, as well as their corresponding territorial seas, exclusive economic regions and continental shelves and the air spaces enclosing them.

The third is the need to provide for the maintenance of the freedom necessary for foreign trade, thus improving our own situation and that of countries having commercial exchange with ours. This will help to secure and broaden our export and import markets, as well as maintaining undisturbed the resulting shipping flow.

Argentine has two security organisations responsible for guarding the borders: the Gendarmeria (land) and the Prefectura Naval (coasts). Compared with a population of 25,000,000, the Armed Forces are composed of around 140,000 men, 80,000 of whom belong to the Army, 35,000 to the Navy and 25,000 to the Air Force. The Gendarmeria's strength is around 11,000 and that of the Prefectura Naval around 9,000. The Defence budget is normally allocated a figure ranging from 1.5 per cent to 1.9 per cent of the Gross National Product.

The Army is organised into four Districts and has over 400 armoured vehicles, artillery, missiles and helicopters. It has rapidly and adequately adapted its structures and capabilities to counter-insurgency operations.

The nucleus of the Navy is an attack force with an anti-submarine capability consisting of 1 aircraft-carrier, 1 cruiser, 8 destroyers and 4 submarines. Two T-42 missile destroyers will shortly become operational and, in the medium term, 6 Y-21 frigates will also be incorporated. Mine-hunting and tracking ships as well as patrol, transport and landing craft are other elements of a navy capable of facing all the different aspects of war at sea, and of transporting, landing and supporting the Marine Corps, which is organised as a brigade, with a total strength of 6,000 men. It also has its own and well-balanced naval air arm.

The Air Force, with over 130 fighters and helicopters, is divided into bombing, hunting, attack, tactical support, transport, logistics support and training squadrons.

We shall now analyse the world situation in terms of the interactions of different countries, and the groups which can be formed from them on the basis of similarities, needs or differences. We can first identify a system composed of two great powers, the USSR and China, with consolidated Communist régimes, and a group of countries which are under their complete political control. Their declared aim is that this group should encompass the whole world, which explains their persistent expansive action aimed at placing the biggest possible continental mass under a single political control. We shall therefore call this group the Continental World.

Within the Continental World four different kinds of actions can be illustrated – the actions by the USSR directed towards maintaining complete political control over its satellite countries, if necessary involving military intervention such as took place in Hungary and Czechoslovakia; China's similar actions; the confrontation between China and the USSR, in their struggle for control over the Continental World; and, finally, actions arising from bilateral or regional issues among satellite countries.

Secondly, we identify a Maritime World, which is not integrated into a rigid system like the Continental World, but is made up of a *de facto* association between countries sharing common aims and similar ways of life. Since their components are not "Continental" countries, they can neither remain isolated nor be self-sufficient; which compels them to maintain a certain degree of inter-dependence with other nations in order to obtain what they lack or cannot produce.

We refer to nations which are sufficiently educated and homogeneous to solve their own problems, and which, not fearing inter-dependence, have reached the level of secondary powers with high *per capita* incomes. Their wealth has been achieved primarily through increasing participation in the international division of work, based on their own capabilities within the context of free competition. They contribute a significant percentage of their production to the world market. High quality and low cost – essential elements for successful international trade – have been obtained through the variety of the markets they supply or through the specialisation they have acquired.

This pattern generates world trade, which, in turn, requires transportation and therefore a shipping flow which is vital to the countries of this Maritime World. Indeed we call it "Maritime" the freedom of the seas is essential to it. We shall refer to the secondary powers of this Maritime World as maritime countries.

The United States of America is the third great world-power of our time. In its early days, it devoted itself to the development of an active continentalism, which ended with the conquest of its present territory. Then it became, to a certain degree, isolationist. Afterwards it played an active role in international trade by importing part of the raw materials needed for its industries and exporting the products of a highly sophisticated technology.

The United States exerts some political control over various countries, especially those in the Caribbean area, in order to satisfy its own commercial and defence requirements.

At present, its total imports account for only 5 per cent of its national product, against 20 or 25 per cent in the maritime countries; but even this 5 per cent puts America's volume of trade among the highest in the world. This fact might lead us to believe that, in addition to being a great world power, it must also be a maritime country and a member of the Maritime World. However, there is an important difference between the United States and a maritime country. Should the United States cease being a maritime country, it could still survive in isolation, since its population and "continental" territorial area would permit a high degree of self-sufficiency. On the other hand, should a maritime country lose its overseas trade, it would also lose its present economic status, dropping into impoverishment and even falling within some other nation's continental orbit. It follows that the essence of the Maritime World lies in the maritime countries, and that the United States may participate or not, according to its own interests. The United States does, in fact, participate in the Maritime World today, or rather both support each other, entering into defensive alliances, while each party maintains its own individuality. It may be assumed that, within this combination, the following actions are carried out:

Actions between the Maritime World and the United States, aimed at the consolidation of the whole and at the coordination of their respective actions in relation to the Continental World.

Actions among maritime countries, including the United States, arising from bilateral or regional issues and from efforts to obtain new markets.

Those countries included neither in the Continental nor in the Maritime World can be grouped under the general heading of "the Rest of the World", covering a number of heterogeneous, underdeveloped, in-various-stages-of-development, rich, poor, non-aligned countries, as well as the so-called Third World countries. They do not share common ways of life or political goals, except on a temporary basis depending on contingencies. They are apt also to clash with each other on local issues.

Among these four groups, that is, the Continental World, the Maritime World, the United States and the Rest of the World, the following actions take place:

Actions of the Continental World towards the Rest of the World, tending to incorporate country after country into its own system. The method consists of taking advantage of existing conflicts, or of those artificially created, in order to infiltrate itself, thus being able to control one of the parties in the conflict, which then receives all necessary help for taking over political power. The Continental World gains complete political control over the country concerned, determining from abroad the direction to be taken. Every possible method is employed, from the most subtle to the most inhuman.

Actions of the Continental World towards the Maritime World, in order to hamper its consolidation and organisation, interfering with every attempt to establish new associations and trying by every available means to destroy those which already exist.

Actions between the Continental World and the United States, with the former trying to neutralise the latter. The United States, in turn, reacts against the Continental World, exploiting internal tensions and the Sino-Soviet dispute, restricting as far as possible the action of both Communist powers towards the Rest of the World.

Actions of the Maritime World (including in this case the United States) towards the Rest of the World, aimed at acquiring more markets for its production. The past history of the United States and of some of the maritime countries, deftly exploited by the Continental World, has led the countries of the Rest of the World — especially the less developed ones — to consider such actions as some sort of an exploitation or economic imperialism. Since the Maritime World's real aim is to obtain

211

new members for the maritime community, the success of this effort depends mainly on the ability of these countries – over which the action is exerted – to reach an adequate level of development and to maintain their own political identity. The Maritime World should benefit from helping the countries of the Rest of the World towards reaching these two goals, thus naturally joining this Maritime World.

Actions by the Maritime World towards the Continental World, aimed at acquiring new markets. As in the previous instance, the achievement of this goal will depend on the degree of political independence which those markets have retained.

Some of these actions have provoked conflicts, the importance of which varies according to the parties concerned and with the circumstances in which they develop.

In our opinion, the significant conflicts affecting the world at present are the following:

Confrontation between Russia and the United States. On account of their enormous strength these two Super-powers could, by themselves, drag the world into a nuclear slaughter. However, the absurdity of such a holocaust greatly restricts the likelihood of this type of conflict in the near future.

Confrontation between Russia and China. The struggle for the leadership of the Communist World gives great significance to this conflict. The existence of a lengthy common border between the two countries increases the possibility of local military engagements.

Confrontation between Russia and the Maritime World. The successes achieved by Russia during the last few years in the contest for obtaining pre-eminence on the seas and in the expansion of its political influence over maritime countries contain intrinsic and obvious conflictive elements with the expansion of the Maritime World (including the United States).

Confrontation between Russia and the Rest of the World. This is the most common origin of the present conflicts, due to constant Soviet efforts to obtain political control over countries belonging to this group.

Confrontations among countries of the Rest of the World. The variety of local or regional situations in which these engagements develop generates conflicts that may become starting points for the more significant conflicts mentioned above.

The Situation in Africa

Africa contains various young countries which, having only recently become independent, are concentrating on the tasks of internal organisation. This fact, added to their economic difficulties, racial differences and tribal dissensions, generates a highly unstable situation which can be easily exploited by an agitator.

The USSR and China are attempting to gain political control over these countries. This, in turn, causes a reaction from the United States and concern among the maritime countries, which may be adversely affected in their hope of obtaining new markets. At the same time, the African countries themselves become aware that the actions of Russia and China may threaten their access to vital supplies.

The Cuban action in Africa – coordinated with the policies of the Soviet Union – started some time ago. Since the first Tricontinental Conference held in Havana in January 1966, Cuba has intensified its subversive presence in Africa through the creation of a liberation committee and by providing logistic, economic and military support to the national liberation movements.

After some disagreement about the support which should be given to those movements, both the USSR and Cuba started a joint action in Africa on the basis of some sort of division of tasks.

Since the Soviets wished to give an innocent appearance to their penetration in Africa, and considering the simultaneous Chinese action, they decided that direct responsibility for their subversive actions should be assumed by another country: but it was the Soviets themselves who, directly or indirectly, provided – and still provide – the necessary means for carrying out the plan, concealing the revolutionary activity of their agents under cover of financial aid.

In the early 1960s Cuba financed subversion in different countries of West Africa, trained several leaders of the revolution in Zanzibar, and maintained a long-term association with Cameroon's guerrillas. It also trained the militias of Congo (Brazzaville), Guinea and Guinea-Bissau.

Although it is impossible to provide accurate figures, the Cuban presence in Africa is not confined to the Angolan conflict. It also includes Congo, Guinea, Somaliland, Sierra Leone, and

213

others. But the large-scale war-support provided by the Soviets and the 14,000-man Cuban force contributed conclusively to the rapid success of the movement led by Agostinho Neto in Angola.

The Cuban Premier, Fidel Castro, told the press: "For ten years now we have been giving our support to the liberation movements of Guinea-Bissau, Angola and Mozambique, but from the moment the Angolan Government required our support, we multiplied our efforts, and I do not intend to deny that some units of our Army are fighting together with the men of Agostinho Neto."

Either through Cuba or directly, the Soviet Union exerts influence and has political, economic and military participation in all these African countries. It is intensifying its penetration in Somaliland, where it has been given access to the naval base at Berbera, and is trying to gain more influence in Mozambique and Tanzania; a fact which is detrimental to China. What happened in Angola proved that the Soviet's real aim is to gain political control over the greatest possible number of countries. The Angolan events show that the Soviet Union may be expected to take advantage of every opportunity for aggressive policies, especially in those countries where the Soviet-North American interest-ratio has not yet been clearly defined.

It is apparent that this action of Russia and Cuba will continue, and, having started in Angola, will expand eastwards and southwards. In March 1976, this issue was discussed in Conakry, capital city of the Guinean Republic, by Fidel Castro and his colleagues from Guinea, Angola and Guinea-Bissau. The Soviets, meanwhile, take advantage of every opportunity to justify their intervention in countries "fighting for liberation", and pretend that this is not incompatible with a policy of détente.

On 17th May, 1976, in an address to an African delegation, the Soviet President, Nikolai Podgorny, said that the policy of détente actually offered new opportunities for accelerating the processes of national liberation. In proposing a toast to the President of Mozambique, Samora Machel, he specifically denied that armed struggle for liberation was inconsistent with a policy of relaxing tensions.

China has always tried to support all the African liberation movements. Some time ago, it could be inferred that Peking was concentrating on the organisations operating in Portuguese colonial territories, and which might soon spread to Rhodesia and southern Africa, where they will, of course, meet the active competition of Moscow. To that purpose, China sponsored the creation of new movements which fractured the existing pro-Soviet groups. The meagre results obtained through this procedure, and the weakness of the response, have encouraged the Chinese lately to give their support to both pro-Chinese and pro-Soviet movements. At the same time, China carries on with its infiltration, propaganda dissemination and, particularly, financial assistance programmes. At present China maintains diplomatic relations with twenty-three African countries. It exerts a decisive influence over Tanzania – their diplomatic relations dating as far back as December 1960 – having supplied that country with a great deal of aid, including several loans and the construction of the railway linking Tanzania to Zambia and Zanzibar (where China is said to have installed missile launching platforms). It also exerts a significant influence over Mozambique – in opposition to Russia: but Mozambique, like many other African countries, accepts and refuses help as though trying, to a certain extent, to pursue an independent foreign policy.

China strongly disapproves of the Soviet activity in Africa, and press reports received from Peking contain severe charges against Russia, saying that, under the pretence of giving support to the liberation movements, its actual goal is the attainment of world hegemony in competition with the United States.

The official Chinese government newspaper, *People's Daily*, published a lengthy article attacking the USSR, in which it said: "Soviet revisionists are now trying to grasp Angola, not only because of its abundant mineral resources, but also for reasons of global counter-revolutionary strategy, in order to compete for world hegemony. They intend to take over Luanda, Lobito and other naval and air bases in Angola with a view to threatening America's and Western Europe's oil shipping from the east and south, and to controlling the South Atlantic; furthermore, they intend using Angola as a springboard for expansion in central and southern Africa. They are also trying to sabotage the liberation movements in all southern Africa. Their intrusion is an important step towards gaining complete control over strategic areas and strengthening their own strategic deployment in the struggle against the United States for world hegemony."

Meanwhile the actions of the United States rest on three principles – the increase of its own military power and that of its allies; military non-intervention in Africa; and development of joint economic action with the maritime countries.

215

The first point is implemented through strengthening NATO, which has approved a rearmament plan and discussed the situation in the South Atlantic as a result of the Soviet expansion in Africa. All planning concerning the Indian and South Atlantic Oceans became SACLANT's responsibility after November 1972.

At the same time, in the United States there is a constantly increasing demand for a strengthening of American military power, which, in conventional terms at least, has already been surpassed by the Soviets.

The second point – military non-intervention in Africa – is based on the implementation of a strategy which is more political and economic than military.

As for the third point – joint economic action with the maritime countries – the United States invited Great Britain, France, West Germany, Japan, Italy and Canada to a conference in Puerto Rico. There they decided to study mutual aid plans for financial crises and to cooperate more closely in their dealings with poorer nations.

The Threat and its Effects
Should the Russians fail in their future activities in Africa and limit themselves to the consolidation of what they have achieved, they would already have at their disposal enough bases to use against the Argentine Republic; that is, the threat has already materialised. The objectives of this threat include a struggle for political control, violation of territorial integrity and neutralisation of relations with foreign countries.

The "struggle for political control" refers to actions based on guerrilla groups, activists, infiltrators, the artificial creation of social and economic difficulties and the magnification of existing problems. At present this mode of action is confronted with increasing difficulties, owing to lack of support among the population and the determination of the Government. It is also impossible, or at least very unlikely, for this action to receive help from across the frontiers of neighbouring countries, which, after having undergone a similar process, are now ruled by military governments or by governments with strong military support, such as Bolivia, Brazil, Chile, Paraguay and Uruguay, all of which are determined to retain political control in national hands. The only remaining possibility would be to send an expeditionary force from Africa, landing at some point on our lengthy coastline, occupying a portion of our territory, declaring it "liberated" and initiating a "liberation movement", using that area as an operational base. At the moment, however, this possibility seems very remote.

For the Argentine Republic, territorial integrity implies protecting its continental area in South America, the Malvinas, Georgias and Sandwich del Sur islands, the Argentine Antarctic sector and the territorial seas, the maritime economic areas and their respective continental shelves. The territorial sea covers an area of twelve nautical miles adjacent to its coastline. In this area, as the only limitation to sovereignty, men-of-war of foreign countries are admitted under the right of innocent passage, but subject to regulations set forth by the Government. The maritime economic area covers the adjoining sea up to 200 miles from the coastline and the whole continental shelf, within which free sea and air navigation rights are fully maintained.

Throughout the territorial sea, the maritime economic area and the continental shelf, all living resources are considered to be the state's property and, generally speaking, cannot be exploited by foreign ships. Research, scientific and technical activities, other than those provided for in special bilateral agreements, are also forbidden.

But the USSR and many other countries refuse to accept that there is an exclusive right of property over the resources of the maritime economic area.

Russia claims that the right of "innocent passage" across the territorial sea should be the same for warships as for merchant ships, in accordance with International Law, i.e. without previous communication or special requirements. It denies the coastal state the right of jurisdiction over scientific and technical activities carried out in waters under national sovereignty.

The discovery in the early days of the present decade that the Antarctic sector claimed by Argentina was full of renewable (krill) and non-renewable (hydrocarbons and minerals) natural resources, the exploitation of which is technically feasible in the near future, spurred the appetite of the signatory countries to the Antarctic Treaty (made in Washington in 1959), as well as that of some non-signing nations with different degrees of pretension but equally powerful and dangerous ambitions.

The signatory parties to the Treaty oppose the non-signatory countries — especially India and Sri Lanka and the Afro-Asian *bloc* which demand the internationalisation of Antarctica.

The Soviet threat could therefore materialise through an intensification of the fishery and research activities carried out in the Argentine maritime economic zone by the countries of the Continental World.

The possibility also exists – although there is no sign of it so far – that some Afro-Asian country might begin, or announce an intention to begin survey activities in the Argentine Antarctic sector and be supported by the Soviet Union.

As regards the third aspect – Argentina's relationship with foreign countries – we think that since Argentina expects to become a member of the Maritime World, satisfactory relations can be achieved only if foreign markets are obtained and maintained, and if Argentina can provide for the safety of its shipping. In other words, if as a continental country the USSR wished to neutralise Argentina's outward efforts, the possession of bases in Africa and their political influence over several countries in that continent would place the Russians in a very favourable position for doing so.

In response to an Argentine proposal during the Conference on the Defence of the South Atlantic held in Buenos Aires in 1957, Argentina, Brazil, Paraguay and Uruguay discussed, for the first time, ways to defend their shipping. In 1966 a first meeting took place between the Commanders-in-Chief of the navies of those countries. The creation of a joint naval coordinating organisation was agreed, which, since 1967, has been in charge of shipping control and defence exercises, which are sometimes carried out jointly with the US Navy.

Because of its position in Africa, the USSR is well placed for an attempt at interfering with this shipping either through sabotage or port incidents, or by the provoking or threatening presence of naval units.

The USSR is also in a favourable position for interfering with the Cape Route, a most important waterway for the supply of oil to the countries of the North Atlantic.

Argentina's situation is less vulnerable than might be expected, since our import needs are moderate.

Our imports arrive from Bolivia, Venezuela, the Persian Gulf and Ecuador; those from Ecuador will increase if the exploration work now being carried out by YPF (the Argentine State Oil Company) achieves concrete results. A proper energy policy should also allow for a significant, though limited, reduction of crude imports from non-American countries.

YEAR	PRODUCTION*	IMPORTS*
1970	22.8	1.7
1971	24.6	2.5
1972	25.2	1.7
1973	24.4	3.4
1974	24.0	3.4
1975	22.9	2.5

million (cu. metres)

During the five-year period 1969–73 the total volume of Argentina's foreign trade, including oil, amounted to the following average values:

EXPORTS: 13.5 million tons; $2066.5 million
IMPORTS: 11.0 million tons; $1855.6 million.

On the basis of these figures and for the same five-year period, the percentages of trade with Africa and Asia, were as follows:

Africa: TOTAL EXPORTS	1.16% ton	$1.34%
Southern Africa: EXPORTS	0.22% ton	$0.35%
Africa: TOTAL IMPORTS	0.83% ton	$0.66%
Southern Africa: IMPORTS	0.35% ton	$0.35%
Asia: TOTAL EXPORTS	14.45% ton	$9.70%
Southern Asia: EXPORTS	12.79% ton	$2.19%
Asia: TOTAL IMPORTS	16.62% ton	$11.15%*
Southern Asia: IMPORTS	10.68% ton	$3.25%

excluding the USSR

These figures show that shipping with Africa – especially with southern Africa – is scarcely significant. Asian shipping is more important, but is mostly directed or could be directed through the Pacific Ocean.

As a country in the process of becoming a member of the Maritime World, Argentina is interested in all the markets of the world, including, of course, those of Africa. But such trade may become increasingly difficult as the USSR's political influence over African countries increases.

Soviet naval deployment in the Indian and the South Atlantic Oceans, and the bases and support points it has obtained along their coastlines (both gradually increasing), show that the

Russians have attained a comparatively favourable level of power in an area which, since it encloses the basic oil route for Europe and the United States, would be considered as a potential area of conflict. Russian supremacy in this area will permit the projection of Soviet influence into those parts of the continent where they can exert political control, discouraging by their mere presence any hostile actions, and encouraging actions in their own interest. Thus the interdependent life of the Maritime World will grow increasingly difficult, with a tendency to deteriorate further as the same situation is repeated in other seas of the world.

It is essential, therefore, that the Maritime World should understand the need to be strongly organised for defence, subordinating minor considerations to the major requirement. Consequently, the application of these concepts to the particular case of Argentina demands that the issues presently affecting its vital interests should be settled within a spirit of cooperation which would be a milestone in relationships between the countries of the Maritime World.

The Argentine Republic, because of its geographical position and its dependence on the sea waterways by which over 90 per cent of its foreign trade moves, must attribute vital importance to the South Atlantic Ocean and is deeply concerned about the increasing Soviet naval presence there, supported by bases in western Africa.

In these new circumstances, the Maritime World, jointly with the United States, must pursue a policy of cooperation aimed at the economic development of the South Atlantic countries, this being the best way to neutralise Communist penetration, by accelerating the incorporation of the greatest possible number of these countries into the Maritime World.

At the same time there is an urgent need for a naval force to counter-balance the Soviet presence in the South Atlantic, but the individual navies of the Latin American countries will not be strong enough without the help of other nations sharing similar interests in this ocean. So there must be closer relations between the navies, with combined training exercises at sea and an improvement in naval communications and in the regular exchange of information.

This would be the most effective way of preventing the danger that Soviet penetration, such as has already occurred in Africa, might spread into the southern region of the American continent.

CONCLUSIONS

This book has concentrated on a specific (though very wide) geographical area – an area south of the equator, in which, from various aspects, the Cape of Good Hope is the focal point. Many of the contributors themselves live in, or are particularly interested in, countries within or at least on the periphery of this area. How to defend the sea routes traversing the area and linking these countries to each other has been one of the main themes of the book.

But the strategic implications extend far beyond this southern area. The sea routes are lifelines, and at least one of the countries concerned – South Africa – is a source of raw materials, on which the heartlands of the Western World depend. This area of the Southern Oceans is the vital and vulnerable flank of Western Europe and the United States. So the subject of this book is essentially part of a larger subject: the defence of the West against militant Communism, particularly in the form of the Soviet Union's imperial ambitions and growing strength.

The problem has to be seen, therefore, within the context of the general military and politico-economic balance, or imbalance, now existing between the NATO countries on the one hand and the Soviet Union and her allies and satellites on the other.

The current state of this balance is not reassuring. The conventional forces of NATO in central and northern Europe are outnumbered two to one, in some cases three to one, by the Warsaw Pact forces opposite them. Until recently, the advantage which the Communists enjoyed in conventional forces was offset by America's substantial lead in the size and accuracy of her nuclear missile system. This lead has been diminishing fast. Overall it probably still exists, although the Russians now have more intercontinental ballistic missiles and more submarine-launched ballistic missiles than the Americans. But what sort of balance will emerge from the SALT II negotiations and other developments now pending is at best doubtful.

At sea, too, the Soviet Union has been rapidly catching up the United States. The already large Russian submarine fleet is being expanded at an alarming rate, and Russian aircraft carriers are coming into service for the first time. (Meanwhile, Britain's Socialist governments, in the interests of economy, have been depriving the Royal Navy of its aircraft carriers, commando carriers and most of its helicopters. In the RAF the number of maritime reconnaissance and transport aircraft has been drastically cut.)

Simultaneously, the political situation in Europe and around the Mediterranean has been "destabilised" to a considerable degree. Norway, which is close to the Russian fleet's main base in the Kola peninsula, Iceland, which commands the channels between the Arctic and the Atlantic, and Denmark, which controls the Baltic, have all been subject to Soviet political pressure. Iceland's "Cod War" with Britain and pacifist tendencies in Denmark have helped to weaken NATO's solidarity on the northern flank.

The Atlantic approaches to Western Europe and the Mediterranean are dependent on the security of the Iberian peninsula. Portugal very nearly fell into Communist hands in 1974 and can hardly be considered safe yet. The future of Spain, in the post-Franco era, is scarcely more certain, though there is hope that she may join NATO in due course.

At the other end of the Mediterranean, Greece and Turkey are at loggerheads. Seized with anti-Americanism, Greece has actually withdrawn from direct military participation in NATO, and Turkey has recently threatened to leave.

In Italy the Communist Party, which already has great power, may soon enter the government. In France a "popular front" government, including the Communists, was only just avoided in 1974 and seems quite likely to win the next election. What will happen in Yugoslavia when Marshal Tito goes, and how the West would react to a crisis there, remain ominously open questions.

The Middle East is still one of the most explosive areas in the world. The Russians have suffered a considerable reverse in Egypt, but appear firmly based in Syria, Iraq, Libya and possibly Algeria. Mr Mintoff plans to neutralise Malta by 1978, and has expressed his alignment with "the Third World" and with Communist China.

The Soviet fleet in the Mediterranean has been continually expanded since it first appeared in 1964, varying in size from some 30 surface ships and auxiliaries to twice that number, and now including the first of the new *Kiev* class aircraft carriers, which passed through the Dardanelles from the Black Sea in flagrant disregard of the Montreux Convention, prohibiting the passage of any warships larger than a cruiser.

The US Sixth Fleet continues to balance the Soviet Mediterranean Fleet, but, in successive defence cuts made by Britain's Labour Government, the Royal Navy and the RAF have been almost withdrawn from the Mediterranean area.

This is the background against which the Soviet thrust into Africa must be seen. Its ultimate strategic purpose is clear enough – to cut through NATO's southern flank and dominate the sea routes along which a great deal of Western Europe's oil must travel, and to deprive the West of the immense mineral resources of southern Africa. The importance of these factors has been spelled out by contributors to this book.

Because the Russian method has been to play on the fashionable themes of "racialism", "anti-colonialism" and "majority rule", strategic considerations have been blurred amid a forest of liberal clichés and responses. The subversion and overthrow of the Portuguese régimes in Angola and Mozambique, and their replacement by Marxist régimes, was a huge success for the Communists and a shattering blow to the West: but the initial Western response inclined rather to approval than to alarm, let alone to any vigorous counter-measures. The presence of Cuban troops and Soviet military advisers in Angola did create a touch of unease, but before long the American Ambassador to the United Nations, Mr Andrew Young, was saying that he thought the Cubans were a stabilising force and that it wouldn't really matter if African countries went Marxist "for a little while".

The next Communist targets are Rhodesia and South-West Africa: and, after them, South Africa itself. Again, the Western powers seem more inclined to help the aspiring Marxist factions than the anti-Communist authorities which currently control those territories. In an act of suicidal self-denial, the strategic facilities of South Africa (notably the great naval base at Simonstown), from which alone the Cape Route can be secured or dominated, are deliberately not being used by NATO forces. As South Africa's Minister of the Interior, Dr Connie Mulder, said recently, the "flabby response" of the Western nations to the Marxist challenge in Africa is more perturbing than the Marxist challenge itself.

Since the challenge is political as well as military, there is, of course, a political as well as a military dimension to be considered. To increase and encourage such understanding has been the purpose of this book.

Each contributor has drawn his own conclusions as to the importance, from the point of view of his own country, of the growing Soviet threat in the Southern Oceans. It is interesting to note that many of these conclusions coincide with each other and can be summed up as follows:

1 All the countries concerned are dependent on maritime trade and therefore fear the growing maritime might of the USSR which now gives every appearance of moving from defensive to offensive capabilities.

2 Europe, and to a lesser but growing extent, the USA and Canada, are dependent on Middle Eastern oil supplies. A hostile USSR could threaten the source of these supplies but could, with greater ease and less risk, interrupt the supply route at busy areas such as the   Straits of Hormuz or the Madagascar Channel.

3 Industrial Europe, and again to a lesser but growing extent the USA, are dependent, in many cases almost totally, on key minerals of which 60 per cent to 90 per cent are obtained from South Africa, which also possesses some of the world's greatest mineral reserves. Should the USSR obtain control over the source of these minerals the West would be open to blackmail from the USSR that would make the Arab oil boycott look like a child's tea party.

4 The USSR, her allies and sycophants, are exploiting racialism and African nationalism to the detriment of the West. Angola and Mozambique are already under Soviet domination; Rhodesia is next on the list, to be followed by Namibia and then South Africa itself.

5 These aims are to be accomplished, if possible, without direct intervention which might attract US counter-action. Third forces, such as the Cubans, nationalist guerrilla movements, etc, are the chosen tools. Success appears to be much closer than the majority in the West now believe.

6 Western influence in the Third World is to be undermined and later eliminated. A good start has been made in South-East Asia and on the Indian sub-continent. Southern Africa is now the main target.

7 So far the West has shown no concerted response. One of the reasons for this is that NATO's boundaries now end at the Tropic of Cancer. These cannot be changed unless the Treaty is re-negotiated; which is not probable. However SACLANT has now received permission to plan beyond this limit.

8 The need is for joint maritime forces from Western and other friendly nations to counterbalance Soviet forces in the South Atlantic and Indian Oceans. The bulk of these forces could be supplied by the USA, Britain and France.

9 The difficulty of providing a Western naval force is largely

political and due to the West's dislike of what is termed "apartheid". This dislike has been fanned by years of Soviet-inspired propaganda.

10 The South African Government in its pursuit of a policy of détente has recognised the need for a change in its internal racial policies. The real question is now one of timing.

11 The Marxists say that change can only be achieved by force, supported by the USSR and her satellites. Thus another dictatorship would be introduced into the African continent.

12 The West requires a change of policy through evolution which would preserve stability and improve, rather than destroy, the wealth on which standards of living are built. This, however, takes time, leads to endless disputes over timing and depends on the goodwill of both majority and minority races.

13 How long can such goodwill continue to exist? Soviet-directed pressures are inflaming the discontent of the Black majority and attempting to create a revolutionary situation which alone could end Western influence in southern Africa and so achieve the objectives of the USSR.

14 If the Western Powers sit back and do nothing, as they did over Angola, a direct confrontation, with all its disastrous consequences, becomes inevitable.

What should the West do? Here I hesitate to commit my colleagues who have produced this book. I personally believe that the Western Alliance should make it clear that they will not tolerate a Soviet take-over of southern Africa, starting with Rhodesia and Namibia. Once this has been established a considerable degree of stability will have been restored and Western influence can then be directed to the economic and political development of the Black majority. As in the history of each one of our countries, it must be recognised that this will take time and need considerable economic assistance. This is, however, in my view, the only way to achieve evolution and to defeat revolution, and as such would, given a firm Western lead, carry with it the vast majority of all races in southern Africa. Time is short; have we the courage to take positive action or are we going to allow all that has been created and achieved in southern Africa to be destroyed within the next five to ten years?

APPENDICES

Appendix I
South African Reserves as a Percentage of World Reserves in 1975

Mineral	World Ranking	Percentage World	Non-Communist World
platinum	1	86	99
chrome ore	1	83	84
vanadium	1	64	96
gold	1	49	61
manganese ore	1	48	84
fluorspar	1	46	50
diamonds	2	8	92
nickel	3	10	12
uranium	4	17	30
zinc	4	9	9
phosphate rock	4	8	8
asbestos	5	10	14
antimony	5	4	10
lead	5	4	5
iron ore	6	4	6
coal	6	2	4
titanium	8	2	40

South African Mineral Production as a Percentage of World Production

Mineral	World Ranking	Percentage World	Non-Communist World
vanadium	1	46	58
gold	1	59	· 74
platinum	1	55	88
antimony	1	21	31
chrome ore	2	30	47
manganese	2	24	41
diamonds	3	17	22
uranium	3	13	13
asbestos	3	10	19
nickel	7	3	4
fluorspar	8	5	6
coal	9	2	5

Balance of Production and Consumption of all Mineral Commodities

	Production as % of world total	Consumption as % of world total	Production as % of consumption
Western world	42.2	64.5	65.4
Communist world	26.9	25.9	103.9
Third World	30.9	9.6	321.9

South Africa's Mineral Exports in 1975

Western Europe	20.4%	Canada	4.1%
Japan	19.6%	Central & S. America	1.0%
West Germany	18.2%	Far East Asia	0.9%
U.K.	16.6%	Australia & New Zealand	0.7%
USA	10.6%	Middle East	0.3%
Africa	7.4%	Eastern Europe & USSR	0.2%

Percentage of total imports of minerals in 1974 supplied by South Africa to her five main trading partners

SOURCE: *South Africa's Strategic Minerals*
by W. C. I. van Rensburg and D. A. Pretorius.

	UK	WEST GERMANY	FRANCE	USA	JAPAN
platinum group	37	—	22	19	38
antimony	95	50	14	43	15
copper	4	10	1	66	21
iron ore	—	—	—	—	2
nickel	—	11	14	—	21
vanadium	60	50	31	57	62
chrome ore	30	29	17	30	37
ferrochrome	15	43	20	85	87
manganese	43	52	40	8	43
ferromanganese	27	14	—	36	—
asbestos	—	—	—	36	—
fluorspar	—	—	—	23	—
vermicilite	100	14	100	100	100

Appendix II
Sources of Crude Oil for NATO Nations
(unit: 1,000 Metric Tons)

SOURCE: *OECD Oil Statistics* 1976

FROM: / TO:	OECD area	Latin America	USSR	West Africa	Other Africa	Algeria	Libya	Egypt
Belgium	525	367	21	1,474	221	880	615	95
Canada	1	13,556	—	1,105	—	18	291	—
Denmark	23	—	436	889	89	—	138	—
France	1,141	752	1,191	10,551	459	5,873	2,183	179
W. Germany	624	2,154	3,093	10,105	2,052	10,214	14,795	207
Greece	—	—	849	—	737	532	101	79
Iceland	—	—	—	—	—	—	—	—
Italy	94	574	3,350	2,003	—	3,785	12,967	1,183
Luxembourg	—	—	—	—	—	—	—	—
Netherlands	98	286	—	7,668	51	427	313	—
Norway	259	—	—	808	—	—	227	—
Portugal	—	—	656	—	—	—	—	—
Turkey	—	—	—	—	—	—	1,138	—
UK	3,304	3,357	704	6,100	227	1,427	2,638	3,812
USA	30,379	31,626	—	38,026	3,625	13,003	10,974	227

FROM: Saudi Arabia	Iran	Iraq	Kuwait	UAE	Qatar	Other Middle East	Indonesia	Other Far East	TO:
12,739	5,358	1,617	2,314	1,452	124	587	—	—	Belgium
9,384	9,345	1,640	1,454	1,737	78	2,454	—	—	Canada
1,672	3,045	166	624	126	136	528	—	—	Denmark
33,482	13,291	12,018	6,723	13,814	2,357	2,067	—	—	France
18,555	14,189	1,404	2,692	5,151	1,255	807	—	—	W. Germany
5,082	1,380	2,917	122	—	—	1,123	—	—	Greece
—	—	—	—	—	—	—	—	—	Iceland
26,203	12,859	18,688	3,735	2,361	1,281	4,356	—	—	Italy
—	—	—	—	—	—	—	—	—	Luxembourg
12,386	17,415	1,940	5,438	5,737	961	416	—	—	Netherlands
623	2,114	46	1	923	128	617	—	—	Norway
709	1,375	2,818	—	80	—	—	—	—	Portugal
—	113	7,611	—	—	—	—	—	—	Turkey
23,304	20,523	3,064	11,707	2,497	3,936	5,077	—	—	UK
34,516	13,693	95	195	5,807	897	—	18,639	263	USA

Appendix III
Some Ports and Airfields
relevant to the Protection of the Cape Route

The table gives a few details of the more important ports and airfields flanking the Cape Route from the time it leaves the Persian Gulf until it enters NATO waters. Those in the PDRY and Somalia have been included because, although they are more directly relevant to the passage of the Red Sea, they have until now provided the main support for Russia's Indian Ocean Squadron.

Although no African country should be regarded as permanently lost to the Russian sphere of influence, countries have been listed in three categories. Those that for the present afford Russia such facilities as she might require in the exercise of her maritime power, the Republic of South Africa, and the others. These last could perhaps be labelled by subtle shades of difference as leaning to the West, or to the East; few, if any, are genuinely uncommitted.

So far as ports are concerned, the Republic of South Africa is in a different category from any other part of the continent. Not only has she outstanding harbour and cargo-handling facilities but she has extensive capability for heavy ship repairs with an ample industrial back-up.

Airfield development in Africa has been rapid. There are now more than fifty International airports equipped to handle the latest jet air-liners and cargo aircraft, and over 200 regional and domestic air-terminals. In 1976 the Russians opened regular flights by Aeroflot to Bissau, Accra, Luanda, and Maputo.

Ports and Airfields where Russia has or can expect to enjoy Facilities.

PDRY

PORTS *Aden* Ex-Royal Navy facilities. Inner harbour 9 sq. miles. Little Aden refinery can produce 3.5 million tons of fuel oil a year for bunkering.

AIRFIELD *Aden* Ex-RAF station. Runways 2,554m, 1,368m.

Somalia
PORTS *Berbera* Recently enlarged by Russia. Provides 3 deep-water berths for cargo or war ships and 2 for tankers. A Russian forward base for her Indian Ocean squadron.
Kismayu Good harbour for smallish vessels.
Mogadishu Lighterage, good holding ground but exposed.

AIRFIELDS *Berbera* (near) Runways 1,450m, 1,280m being extended to over 4,000m.
Hargeisa Runways 2,280m, 1,340m.
Mogadishu (Mil) Runways 2,500m.

232

Mozambique

PORTS   *Beira* 10 berths for ocean-going ships up to 30ft draught at low water.

Maputo 12 berths for ocean-going ships. 74 cranes including one of 80 tons.

Porto Amelia Very fine natural harbour, under development.

Nacala One of the finest natural harbours on the East African coast. The largest vessels can use it. Under development. The old wharf can take 3 ocean-going vessels with draughts of 24–31ft. 2 others can berth vessels with draughts up to 49ft.

AIRFIELDS   *Maputo* Runways 2,700m, 1,700m.

Beira Runways 2,400m, 1,660m.

Nampula Runways 2.000m, 1,500m.

Angola

PORTS   *Lobito* Berths for 3–4 ocean-going ships. 100 ton floating crane.

Luanda One of the finest harbours on the west coast. Berths for 7 ocean-going and 8 coastal ships. 5 deep-water piers.

Cabinda Good port and protected bay. No deep-water piers.

AIRPORT   *Luanda* Runways 3,300m, 2,600m.

Congo (Brazzaville)

AIRPORTS   *Brazzaville* Runways 3,300m.

Dolise Runways 1,800m.

Guinea

PORT   *Conakry* Berthing for 20,000 ton ships, up to 32ft draught.

AIRFIELD   *Conakry* 2 runways of 3,300m.

Guinea-Bissau

PORT   *Bissau* Well sheltered and safe with sufficient water for largest vessels.

AIRPORT   *Bissau.*

Republic of South Africa

PORTS   *Durban* Largest port in Africa, 15th in the world. Includes 7-berth deep-water pier. New 5-berth pier for container ships. 7 tanker berths. Grain and bulk ore-handling machinery. Graving docks and floating dock. Heavy ship repair facilities.

Richards Bay Recently developed for tankers. Ships up to 150,000 tons and 60ft draught can enter. Being deepened to take 250,000 ton ships.

East London 2,000m of commercial berthing. Tanker terminals. Ship repair facilities. Graving dock.

Port Elizabeth Bulk ore-handling. Tanker terminals. Some ship repair.

Cape Town Being further developed. 24 berths fitted for oil bunkering. Three tanker terminals. Graving docks. Bulk cargo handling.
Walvis Bay (Namibia) Excellent harbour. Ships of any draught can enter. Tanker terminals. Wharfs 3,435m long. Bulk cargo-handling.
Simonstown Modern Naval base. Graving dock and means for carrying out major refits to warships.

AIRFIELDS *Durban* Runways 2,442m, 1,681m.
Cape Town Runways 3,200m, 1,290m.

Other Ports and Airfields

Kenya
PORT *Mombasa (Kilindi)* Good deep-water moorings. Oil tankers up to 65,000 tons. Berthing for 13 vessels with draught up to 32ft.

AIRPORTS *Mombasa* Runways being extended to 3,500m, 2,100m.
Nairobi Runways 3,344m.

Tanzania
PORT *Dar-es-Salaam* Main quay can berth 8 vessels but ocean-going ships anchor in stream and are unloaded by lighter. Dockyard for minor repairs.

AIRPORTS *Zanzibar* Runways 1,463m.
Dar-es-Salaam Runways 2,378m, 1,000m.

Malagasy
PORT *Diego Suarez* Ex-French naval base.

AIRFIELDS *Diego Suarez* Runways 1,485m.
Nossi-Be Runways 2,190m.
Tamatave Runways 2,200m.
Grand Comoro Is. Runways 1,355m, 737m.

Zaire
PORT *Matardi* 9 large vessels at high water, extensions planned.

AIRFIELD *Kinshasa* International Airport. 30 modern airports planned, but few would have any import in terms of maritime power.

Ghana
PORT *Takoradi* 8 deep-water berths.
AIRPORT *Accra* Runways 2,925m.

Senegal
PORT *Dakar* Port includes ex-French Navy dockyard. Includes dry dock, 5 slipways and repair facilities.

AIRFIELDS *St Louis* Runways 1,900m.
Dakar Runways 2,000m, 2,410m, 2,030m.
Ziquincher Runways 1,345m, 1,200m.

234

Appendix IV
Soviet Intelligence Presence in Africa
SOURCE: Institute for the Study of Conflict (London)

COUNTRY	TOTAL PRESENCE SEPT. '76	TOTAL PRESENCE NOV. '74	INTELLIGENCE OFFICERS SEPT. '76
Angola	3	—	2
Botswana	1	—	—
Benin	34	32	9
Burundi	4	5	2
Central African Republic	16	14	7
Cameroons	20	18	5
Chad	13	9	3
Congo (Brazzaville)	16	15	6
Equatorial Guinea	9	10	4
Ethiopia	46	36	22
Gabon	1	—	1
Guinea Bissau	13	2	5
Ghana	44	58	13
Guinea	19	10	4
Kenya	46	39	18
Lesotho	2	—	1
Liberia	3	6	2
Malagasy Republic	12	4	6
Mali	57	66	14
Mauritania	21	13	6
Mauritius	23	21	13
Mozambique	4	—	—
Nigeria	125	104	40
Republic of Niger	18	7	3
Rwanda	7	8	2
Sao Tome and Principe	1	—	—
Senegal	79	63	31
Sierra Leone	21	21	7
Somalia	29	28	10
Tanzania	64	53	19
Togo	27	21	5
Uganda	40	37	11
Upper Volta	13	8	3
Zaire	37	16	17
Zambia	50	42	27
Totals	**918**	**766**	**318**

Explanation: first figure is total Soviet official presence in each country, as verified in September 1976; second figure, where given, is corresponding number in November 1974; third figure is total of known intelligence officers—KGB and GRU (or military intelligence).

Appendix V
Population census: South-West Africa. 6th May 1970

POPULATION GROUP	NUMBER	PERCENTAGE OF TOTAL	ESTIMATE MAY 1975
Ovambo	342,000	45.9	397,000
Whites	91,000	12.1	107,000
Damara	65,000	8.6	75,000
Herero	55,000	7.4	61,000
Kavango	50,000	6.7	57,000
Nama	33,000	4.5	38,000
Coloured	28,000	3.8	33,000
East-Caprivi	25,000	3.4	29,000
Bushmen	22,000	3.0	25,000
Rehoboth-Basters	16,000	2.1	19,000
Tswana	4,000	0.5	4,000
Other	15,000	2.0	17,000
Total	**746,000**	**100.0**	**862,000**

Appendix VI
Distribution of Russian Navy by Fleets

The following tables show the normal distribution of the Russian Navy between the Northern Baltic, Black Sea (includes Caspian), and Pacific Fleets. Since adopting a forward policy the traditional coast defence role of the Russian Navy has been assumed by a large number of Fast Attack Craft.

TYPE	NORTH	BALTIC	BLACK SEA	PACIFIC	TOTAL
Submarines					
SSBN	47[1]	—	—	11	58
SSGN	28	—	—	12	40
SSN	26	—	—	6	32
SSB	15	—	—	8	23
SSG	16	2	1	9	28
SS	51	74	49	44	218
SSR	1	—	—	2	3
Total	184	76	50	98	402

TYPE	NORTH	BALTIC	BLACK SEA	PACIFIC	TOTAL
Surface Ships					
Aircraft carriers	—	—	1	—	1[2]
Helicopter carriers	—	—	2	—	2
Cruisers	10	6	9	6	31[3]
Destroyers	32	28	29	27	106[4]
Frigates	24	26	36	25	111
Corvettes	37	80	48	31	196
Intelligence ships	16	8	15	15	54
Fast Patrol					
Hydrofoil	—	16	21	—	37
Missile	25	41	34	35	135
Patrol	10	39	4	7	60
Torpedo	15	50	20	40	125
Total FPB	50	146	79	82	357
Amphibious Forces					
Landing ships	2	4	3	3	12
LC Tank	12	15	18	15	60
Landing craft	15	16	30	20	81

[1] Includes 15 of the new Delta class armed with nuclear ballistic missiles
having a 4,200 mile range.
SSBN nuclear propelled, nuclear armed, ballistic missiles
SSGN nuclear propelled, nuclear armed, glide missiles
SSN diesel propelled, nuclear armed, ballistic missiles
SSG diesel propelled, nuclear armed, glide missiles
SS diesel propelled, fleet and patrol submarines
SSR diesel propelled, radar pickets.
[2] This is the first of a class of three Kiril class aircraft carriers, a second is nearing completion.
[3] Almost two-thirds of the Cruisers have guided missiles as their main armament.
[4] Rather less than half the Destroyers have guided missiles as their main armament. Eight
Destroyers are specialised anti-aircraft ships equipped with SAM.

Naval Air Arm

The Russian Navy has its own Air Arm. This consists of over 700
combat aircraft mainly stationed to support the Northern and Black
Sea Fleets. The inventory includes 280 Tu-16 with anti-submarine
capability, 55 Tu-95 and 100 Be-12 reconnaissance aircraft, 55 Tu-22
strike and recce aircraft, 250 anti-submarine warfare helicopter, and
150 Tu-16s used for in air refuelling and recce.

Marines

Each Fleet has a Regiment of Naval Infantry, believed to number
about 17,000.

Appendix VII
Naval Strengths of Countries with Interests
in the Southern Oceans
SOURCE: *Janes Fighting Ships* 1976–1977

	ARGENTINA	AUSTRALIA	BRAZIL	CHINA	CUBA	EGYPT	FRANCE	INDIA
Aircraft carriers (L = light)	1(L)	1(L)	1(L)	—	—	—	2(L)(1)	1(L)
Cruisers and light cruisers	2	—	—	—	—	—	2	2
Destroyers	9(1)	5	12(6)	8(3)	—	5	20(4)	3
Frigates	(6)	6(2)	3	23(1)	3 Res	3	27(11)	25(2)
Corvettes	12	—	10	35(4)	19	12	22	(?)
Ballistic missile submarines (N = nuclear) (D = diesel)	—	—	—	1	—	—	4(N) 1(D) (2N)	
Cruise missile submarines (N = nuclear) (D = diesel)	—	—	—	1(D)	—	—	—	—
Fleet submarines	—	—	—	1(?)	—	—	(1)	—
Patrol submarines	4	4(2)	8(2)	60(6)	—	12	20(3)	8
FAC missile	(2)	—	—	120(20)	23	18	4(1)	8
FAC torpedo	2	—	—	240(10)	24	26	—	—
FAC gun	2	—	—	438 (20)	—	—	—	—
Patrol craft	5	12	14	39	29	?	6	8
Minelayers	—	—	—	—	—	—	—	—
Ocean minesweepers	—	—	—	16	—	10	11	—
Coastal minesweepers/ minehunters	4/2	3	8(2)	6	—	—	29/7	4
Inshore minesweepers	—	—	—	—	—	2	3	4

IRAN	IRAQ	JAPAN	SOUTH AFRICA	UNITED KINGDOM	UNITED STATES	USSR	VENEZUELA	
—	—	—	—	1+2(L)	14(2N) +7(2N)	1(2)	—	Aircraft carriers (L=light)
—	—	—	—	10(2)	27(4) (+8 res)	37(2)	—	Cruisers and light cruisers
3(4)	—	29(4)	2	3(5+1)	100(27)	108(2)	4	Destroyers
4	—	16(1)	7(6)	61(6)	65(10)	98	6	Frigates
4	3	20	—	—	—	207	—	Corvettes
—	—	—	—	4	41(N) (4N)	55 (16N) 23(D)	—	Ballistic missile submarines (N=nuclear) (D=diesel)
—	—	—	—	—	1 res(D)	42(N) 28(D)	—	Cruise missile submarines (N=nuclear) (D=diesel)
—	—	—	—	9(3+1)	65 (27+2)	38	—	Fleet submarines
(3)	—	16(2)	3(2)	19	12(3)	204	4(1)	Patrol submarines
(12)	10	—	(6)	—	1(5)	120	—	FAC missile
—	12	5(1)	—	—	—	125	3	FAC torpedo
—	4	—	—	—	—	65	3	FAC gun
10	26	10	5	14(7)	28	115 +90	—	Patrol craft
—	—	1	—	1	—	2	—	Minelayers
—	—	—	—	—	25 (12 res)	185	—	Ocean minesweepers
3	—	30(5)	10	21/16 (+2)	—	119	—	Coastal minesweepers/ minehunters
2	—	4	—	6	—	100	—	Inshore minesweepers

	ARGENTINA	AUSTRALIA	BRAZIL	CHINA	CUBA	EGYPT	FRANCE	INDIA
Minesweeping boats	—	—	—	—	—	—	—	—
Assault ships	—	—	—	—	—	—	2	—
Landing ships	4(1)	—	2	48(4)	—	—	5	1
Landing craft	20	6	—	465	—	17	29	6
Depot repair maintenance ships	—	—	2	1	—	—	9	3
Survey research ships (large and small)	7(2)	4(1)	17	13	7	—	11	3
Supply ships	—	2	—	16	—	—	6	1
Large tankers	1	—	1	—	—	—	5(1)	1
Small tankers	2	—	1	10	—	—	5	5
Hydrofoils and ACVs	—	—	—	70	—	(3)	—	—
Misc	18(1)	15	16	380+	7	6	164(2)	6

IRAN	IRAQ	JAPAN	SOUTH AFRICA	UNITED KINGDOM	UNITED STATES	USSR	VENEZUELA	
—	—	6	—	—	—	—	—	Minesweeping boats
—	—	—	—	2	10(4) (+4 res)	—	—	Assault ships
2(4)	—	4(2)	—	7	47* (+4 res)	18(1)	6	Landing ships
1	—	68	—	59(2)	100	60 +81	—	Landing craft
2	—	4	—	4	28 (24 res)	64	—	Depot repair maintenance ships
—	—	5(1)	1	4 + 9	40 (5 res)	128(3)	5	Survey research ships (large and small)
2	—	—	1	7(2)	78 (8+21 res)	5	—	Supply ships
(1)	—	—	—	17	49 (2+14 res)	26	—	Large tankers
1	—	1(1)	—	6	—	18	—	Small tankers
14	—	—	—	5	2	42+	—	Hydrofoils and ACVs
7	3	56(1)	9	251	200+	350+ 54 AGIs	12	Misc.

*Police

241

Appendix VIII
Revolt in Africa
Dates of Coups or Attempted Coups d'Etat
since Independence

Ethiopia Independent for many centuries except for short Italian occupation.

1847 **Liberia** became independent of USA.

1910 **South Africa** became independent of GB.

1922 **Egypt** became independent of GB.

Post-World War II

1951 **Libya** became an independent federal kingdom.

1952 **Egypt** General Neguib seized power. King Farouk exiled.

1954 **Egypt** Colonel Nasser seized power. Egypt became a republic.

1956 **Tunisia** became independent from France as a kingdom.

Sudan became independent from GB and Egypt.

Morocco became independent from France as a kingdom.

1957 **Tunisia** became a republic.

Ghana became independent from GB.

1958 **Sudan** Successful military coup under General Ibrahim Abboud who became President.

Guinea (Conakry) became independent from France.

1960 **Ethiopia** Military revolt put down.

Congo (Brazzaville) became independent from France.

Congo (Kinshasa) became independent from Belgium. Joseph Kasavubu became Head of State.

Cameroun became independent of France and GB.

Central African Republic became independent of France.

Chad became independent of France.

Dahomey became independent of France.

Gabon became independent of France.

Ivory Coast became independent of France.

Madagascar became independent of France.

Mali became independent of France.

Mauritania became independent of France.

Niger became independent of France.

Senegal became independent of France.

Somalia became independent of France.

Togo became independent of France.

Upper Volta became independent of France.

Nigeria became independent of GB.

1961 **Tanganyika** became independent of GB.
Congo (Kinshasa). Cyrille Adoula's government recognised. UN invasion of Katanga.
1962 **Algeria** became independent of France.
Burundi became independent of Belgium.
Rwanda became independent of Belgium.
Uganda became independent of GB.
1963 January **Togo** Assassination of President Olympio. Army NCOs made Niklas Grunitzky Head of State.
June **Zanzibar** became independent from GB as a Sultanate.
October **Dahomey** Army coup under Colonel Soglo overthrew President Maga.
December **Kenya** became independent of GB.
1964 January **Zanzibar** Revolution deposes Sultan. Sheikh Karume becomes Head of State.
February **Gabon** Attempted coup against President Miba put down with the assistance of French troops.
Kenya, Uganda and **Tanganyika** Revolts put down by British troops.
April **Sierra Leone** became independent of GB.
October **Malawi** became independent of GB.
Zambia became independent of GB.
Tanzania Tanganyika and Zanzibar unite as Tanzania.
1965 February **Gambia** became independent of GB.
June **Algeria** Colonel Boumédienne deposed President Ben Bella.
October **Burundi** Army officers launched unsuccessful coup: 100 killed, 50 executed.
November **Congo** General Mobutu deposed President Kasavabu.
November **Dahomey** General Soglo deposed President Apithy.
November **Rhodesia** declared unilateral independence.
1966 January **Central African Republic** Colonel Bokassa deposed President Dacke.
January **Upper Volta** The army deposed President Yameogo.
January **Nigeria** Prime Minister Sir Abubakar Tafawa Belawa and Regional Premiers killed in army takeover. General Ironsi becomes Head of State.
January **Nigeria** Officers' coup d'etat and murder of Sir Abubakar Belawa. Major General Ironsi suppressed the revolt and assumed power.
February **Ghana** Army seized power from President Nkrumah. General Ankrah became Head of State.
February **Uganda** Prime Minister Obote suspended the constitution and assumed presidential powers. President Mutesa, the Kabaka of Buganda, escaped to England.

1966 July   **Nigeria** General Gowon became Head of State after the assassination of General Ironsi.

July   **Burundi** King Mwambutsa IV deposed in favour of his son who became King Ntare V.

September   **Botswana** became independent from GB.

October   **Lesotho** became independent from GB as a kingdom.

November   **Burundi** King Ntare V deposed and a republic proclaimed by the Prime Minister Michael Micombero and a group of army officers.

November   **Togo** Abortive attempt to seize power by supporters of the late President Olympio. President Grunitzky assumed full powers.

1967 January   **Lesotho** The King placed under arrest by the Prime Minister and the leaders of two opposition parties arrested.

January   **Togo** President Grunitzky and the army take over the government.

March   **Sierra Leone** Governor-General and Prime Minister Sir Albert Margai arrested and the army take over the government under Lt. Col. Juxon Smith.

April   **Togo** Unsuccessful attempt to assassinate the President.

May   **Nigeria** The Eastern Region secedes as Biafra.

December   **Dahomey** President Soglo overthrown by the army and a revolutionary military government set up under Lt. Col. Alley.

1968   **Mauritius** became independent from GB.

Nigeria Civil war ending in the defeat of Biafra.

April   **Sierra Leone** Colonel Juxon Smith is replaced by a military junta.

August   **Congo (Brazzaville)** President Massamba-Debat was deposed by the army, took over again and was later banished and replaced by Captain Alfred Raoul.

August   **Chad** French troops called in to suppress rising in north and north-east.

September   **Swaziland** became independent from GB as a kingdom.

September   **Burundi** Attempted coup d'état defeated.

October   **Equatorial Guinea** became independent from Spain.

November   **Mali** President Keita deposed by the army. Liberation Committee formed under Lieutenant Mousa Traore.

1969   **Equatorial Guinea** Coups against the President failed, two leaders shot.

May   **Sudan** Army overthrow the government of Mohammed Mahgout and establish military rule.

September   **Burundi** Attempted coup d'état defeated.

1969 October **Kenya** Parliamentary opposition banned.

October **Somalia** President Rashed Shermarke assassinated, take-over by the army, the Prime Minister and acting President arrested and parliament dissolved.

December **Dahomey** Military take-over. The Prime Minister Dr Emile Zinzon arrested. Colonel Kouandete takes over.

December **Uganda** President Obote wounded in an assassination attempt.

1970 March **Congo (Brazzaville)** Attempt to overthrow President Ngouabi failed.

April **Sudan** The Mahdi murdered by government forces.

July **Libya** Plot to overthrow the military government discovered and plotters arrested.

August **Togo** The army foiled an attempt to overthrow President Eyadema.

August **Sierra Leone** Army officers arrested to forestall a "second attempted coup in one week".

August **Congo (Brazzaville)** President Ngouabi announced that an attempted coup had been crushed.

1971 January **Uganda** President Obote deposed by a military coup while on his way home from the CWPM's Conference at Singapore. General Amin takes over.

March **Sierra Leone** Attempted coup suppressed after President Stevens called in troops from Guinea.

July **Morocco** Attempted coups against the King failed.

July **Sudan** Coup and counter coup; suppression of the Communist Party.

August **Congo** General Oltenga and other army officers imprisoned for a plot to overthrow the government.

August **Chad** President Tomalbaye overcame a coup against his government.

October **Congo** Former ministers and governors arrested on charges of plotting to assassinate General Mobutu.

1972 January **Ghana** The army led by Colonel Acheampong took over in the absence abroad of the Prime Minister Dr Busia.

February **Congo (Brazzaville)** Attempted coup by some army units.

February **Dahomey** Attempted coup by part of the armed forces.

April **Tanzania** Sheikh Karume of Zanzibar, the first Vice President of Tanzania, assassinated.

April **Burundi** Abortive coup followed by long drawn out reprisals.

1972 May **Madagascar** Overthrow of President Tsiranana's government. General Ramanantsoa takes over.

July **Ghana** Colonel Acheampong's National Redemption Council announced defeat of plot to restore Dr Busia the former Prime Minister.

July **Sudan** General Numeiri announced the discovery of a plot against him.

August **Morocco** Abortive attempts to assassinate King Hassan.

October **Dahomey** Military coup led by Major Kerekou.

November **Tanzania** Reports that Oscar Kambona, former foreign minister, was plotting President Nyerere's overthrow from Mozambique.

1973 January **Sudan** General Numeiri announced the discovery of a plot against him.

February **Dahomey** Assassination plot discovered and army officers arrested.

February **Congo** (formerly Congo Brazzaville) President Ngouabi announced the defeat of a coup led by Lieutenant Diawara.

March **Liberia** Assistant Minister of Defence and two army officers convicted of planning a military coup and the assassination of the President.

March **Morocco** Minor armed risings against the government put down.

March **Uganda** General Amin announced that an attempt on his life had been foiled.

April **Swaziland** King Sobhuza carried out a palace coup seizing power and banning political parties and parliament.

April **Central African Republic** President Bokassa announced the arrest of his minister of state for plotting against him.

May **Uganda** Abortive army coup in the absence of President Amin at the OAU Conference in Addis Ababa.

June **Chad** C-in-C of armed forces placed under arrest, accused of plotting to assassinate President Tombalbaye.

June **Ivory Coast** Announcement of a conspiracy to stage a military coup d'état against President Houphouet-Boigny.

July **Guinea** Allegations by President Sekou Toure of plots against his government.

July **Ruanda** General Habyalimana overthrows President Kayibanda.

1974 January **Central African Republic** President Bokassa arrested trade union leaders on the suspicion of plotting against him.

January **Lesotho** Government announced discovery of a plot by the Basutoland Congress Party.

1974 February **Upper Volta** Army seized power and dissolved the National Assembly. General Namizana remained President.

March **Uganda** Abortive coups by Brigadier Charles Arube.

March **Ethiopia** Anti-Government plot by the army foiled.

April **Nigeria** President Hamoni overthrown in an army coup led by Lieutenant Colonel Kountche.

August **Tunisia** A leftist attempt to overthrow the government foiled.

September **Ethiopia** The Emperor, Haile Selassie, deposed by a left-wing army group under Lieutenant General Andom.

Guinea-Bissau became independent from Portugal

November **Ethiopia** General Andom executed and replaced by Major-General Benie.

November **Uganda** Uganda commanders foiled in an attempt to overthrow President Amin.

December **Central African Republic** Attempted coup by Gendarmerie officers.

1975 January **Dahomey** Failure of a coup by Captain Assogha.

February **Madagascar** Colonel Ratsimandrara took over power from General Ramanantsoa, was then assassinated and replaced by General Andrimahazo.

April **Chad** President Tombaldaye overthrown and killed. Replaced by General Malloum as head of Supreme Military Council.

May **Cape Verde** became independent from Portugal.

June **Mozambique** became independent from Portugal, under Marxist President Machel.

July **Nigeria** General Gowon deposed in his absence at the OAU conference and replaced by General Murtala Muhammed.

July **Sao Tomé** became independent from Portugal.

July **Comoroes** became independent from France.

August **Central African Republic** President Bokassa announced that a further attempt had been made to overthrow his government.

August **Nigeria** Arrest of the Vice-President for plotting to seize power.

August **Libya** Attempted coup by army officers against Colonel Gaddafy foiled.

September **Sudan** Further attempts of an army coup against President Numeiri failed.

September **Uganda** Report of a further attempted coup by army officers against President Amin.

September **Dahomey** (now called **Benin**) Plot to overthrow the military government to reinstate President Zinzou foiled.

November **Angola** became independent from Portugal.

247

1975 December **Ghana** Colonel Acheampong announced failure of a plot against him.

1976 February **Central African Republic** Attempted assassination of President Bokassa by members of the army.

February **Nigeria** Assassination of the Head of State, General Murtala Mohammed in an abortive coup led by Lieutenant Colonel Dinka.

February **Angola** President Agostinho Neto of MPLA recognised as leader of Angola, but civil war continued.

March **Nigeria** Attempted coup led by a former minister.

April **Comoroes** Discovery of a plot to assassinate the Head of State, Mr Ali Soilih.

June **Uganda** A further two attempts on the life of President Amin reported.

July **Sudan** Further attempts on the life of President Nimeiri.

July **Uganda** Reports of further attempts by army units to overthrow President Amin.

July **Seychelles** became independent from GB.

October **Transkei** became independent from South Africa.

November **Burundi** Army revolt deposes President Micombero and he is replaced by Lieutenant Colonel Jean-Baptiste Bagaza.

1977 January **Benin** An attempted coup by mercenaries against President Mathieu Kerekou.

February **Ethiopia** Death of seven officers of ruling military council and emergence of Lieutenant Colonel Mengistu Haile Mariam.

March **Congo** President Marien Ngouabi assassinated and succeeded by Colonel Joachim Yhombi-Opango.

April **Chad** An attempt on the life of President Felix Malloum failed.

May **Angola** Attempted coup against President Neto failed.

May **Ethiopia** Attempted coup suppressed. Cuban and Soviet advisers introduced.

June **Afars and Issas** became independent from France.

June **Comoroes** A group of young islanders occupied the airport in an attempt to overthrow the President.

June **Seychelles** Prime Minister Albert Rene overthrew President James Mancham in coup. Rene now President.

June **Uganda** Reports of attempted assassination of President Amin.

July **Sao Tomé** Reports of a plot to overthrow government.

248

INDEX

INDEX